Cormac McCarthy, Philosophy and the Physics of the Damned

Cormac McCarthy, Philosophy and the Physics of the Damned

Patrick O'Connor

EDINBURGH
University Press

Edinburgh University Press is one of the leading University Presses in the UK. We publish academic books and journals in our selected subject areas across the humanities and social sciences, combining cutting-edge scholarship with high editorial and production values to produce academic works of lasting importance. For more information visit our website: edinburghuniversitypress.com

Edinburgh University Press Ltd
The Tun – Holyrood Road, 12(2f) Jackson's Entry, Edinburgh EH8 8PJ

Typeset in 11/13 Adobe Sabon hv
IDSUK (DataConnection) Ltd

A CIP record for this book is available from the British Library

ISBN 978 1 4744 9726 8 (hardback)
ISBN 978 1 4744 9728 2 (webready PDF)
ISBN 978 1 4744 9729 9 (epub)

Contents

For Ruth

Acknowledgements

The archival work for this research was supported by two travel grants from the British Association for American Studies (Founders Research Travel Award) and the Wittliff Collections at Texas State University in San Marcos (International Award). My sincere thanks go to all concerned. I would especially like to express my deepest gratitude to the archival team at the Wittliff Collections, particularly Carol Alvarez, Katie Salzmann and Sherri Turner-Herrmann, who provided all you would need from an archival team: they were professional, detailed, methodical, kind and helpful in every way. They also warmly extended me some Texan hospitality which I will not forget.

Some of this work has been adapted from previously published material. All of it has been revised for this book. All other material in this work is hitherto unpublished. I would like to thank Stacey Peebles, editor of *The Cormac McCarthy Journal*, for permission to reprint 'Saving Sheriff Bell: McCarthy, Derrida and The Opening of Mercantile Ethics', 15, no. 2 (2017), 152–76; Marek Paryż, editor of the *European Journal of North American Studies*, for permission to reprint 'Anti-Matters: Mortal Ethics in Cormac McCarthy's *The Road*' [Online], 12, no. 3 (2017); and Taylor and Francis Group LLC (Books) US for permission to reprint 'Literature and Death: McCarthy, Blanchot and Suttree's Mortal Belonging', *Philosophical Approaches to McCarthy: Beyond Reckoning*, ed. Chris Eagle, London: Routledge (2017), 73–92.

I would like to thank the following Cormackians for their patience, generosity and willingness to listen to my philosophical fumbling concerning McCarthy's literature: Chris Eagle, Julius Greve, Katka Kovářová, Katja Laug, Chris Thornhill and Rick Wallach. Thanks are also due to Sonja Lawrenson, Ruth O'Connor, Lin Farrar and Pete Farrar, who were all more than a big help.

Finally, special thanks must go to James Daly who, many years ago, deep in the mountains of Kerry, kicked all this off by making me read *The Crossing*.

Introduction

The world does not speak. Only we do.

Richard Rorty[1]

Cormac McCarthy is the most interesting of literary writers. In straightforward terms, his writing has all the ingredients that make good books. His books are exciting, well-paced, violent, intense and visceral; his characters reveal the most acute suffering, loss and redemptive longing of the human condition. Stylistically, McCarthy's scriptural prose transports readers to monstrously enchanted reveries which are at once beautiful, sublime and terrifying in their vividness. It is not surprising, then, that McCarthy's literary status as one of the most significant authors of the twentieth and twenty-first centuries is secure as both a popular best-selling author and as an artist who has achieved distinct literary recognition. Notwithstanding the Nobel Prize for Literature, which still eludes him, McCarthy has received a host of major awards and prizes, including the Saul Bellow Award for Achievement in American Fiction (2008), the Pulitzer Prize for Fiction (2007), the McArthur Fellowship (1981) and a Guggenheim Fellowship for Creative Writing (1969).

If the importance of literature were only measured by its timelessness, McCarthy might come up short. This would be not at all due to a lack of perennial appeal or relevance in his works, but instead concerns the unique way his literature endures. McCarthy's work, his novels particularly, actively resist any ahistorical or literary classification. And this is precisely why McCarthy is endlessly fascinating: not simply because his writing appeals to classical enduring themes such as good and evil, love and mourning, redemption and fallenness, courage and tenacity, coming of age, revenge – although McCarthy is comfortable offering literary representation of these themes too – but because he is a profoundly historical writer. He writes with a sense of how through contemporary history, historical change itself is made manifest, whether in the guise of generational tension, technological change, economic displacement or class antagonism. McCarthy is thus significant because his work is visceral, philosophical and reflective concerning new ways in which the great metaphysical questions of life and death are continually renewed. In his 2007 *Rolling Stone* interview with David Kushner, McCarthy says as much: 'If it doesn't concern life and death [. . .] It's not interesting.'[2]

McCarthy judges the ultimate bar of significance in terms of questions of life and death, which begs the urgent question as to what philosophical resonance is present in his writing. That McCarthy has philosophical interests, or even is a philosophical novelist, engaging with issues which should be relevant to any philosopher, is obvious. If we assemble a cursory list of common themes in McCarthy's writing, we can clearly see that he is broadly concerned with the nature of things. For example, his work encompasses questions relating to justice and law, metaphysics and ontology, the nature of language, the ethical status of human beings and the consequences of political organisation, all posed with his own distinctive bodily and geographical aesthetics. However, to say all this is not enough, because it does not get to the crux of McCarthy's writing, nor more specifically to the philosophical concerns therein.

What it is necessary to come to terms with, if we are to get to grips with the body of thought, writing and reflections which McCarthy bestows upon us, is the distinct synthesis of literature and philosophy which animates McCarthy's work. Indeed, it will be my contention in this book that McCarthy offers a unique type of literary philosophy, one that transcends the conventional generic definitions of either 'literature' or 'philosophy' as distinct objects of study. However, to be clear at the outset, my approach will not preclude the study of McCarthy in literary or philosophical terms. For example, I do not flatly exclude any methods of critical analysis which examine assumptions, style or formal arrangements of a text, nor those which illuminate how McCarthy's characters offer cascades of insight for how to examine philosophical themes of ethical deliberation, cognitive salience, the question of evil, linguistic communication, or the status of law and order. I will engage with some of these questions. I am merely suggesting that there is something more, something deeper, occurring in McCarthy's work too. As a thinker, McCarthy is concerned with the health of the totality of phenomena in the cosmos. While admittedly the totality and status of all existing phenomena is a broad remit, it is nonetheless, in the end, the only destination, that which all aspects of philosophy return to: what is the point, and why do things matter?

If we are to ascribe to McCarthy the unusual appellation of 'literary philosopher', it is therefore clear that this needs explanation.

Some claim could be made on the suggestion that McCarthy is a philosophical novelist of equal stature with the great writers in the canon of philosophical novelists, such as Margaret Atwood, Albert Camus, Herman Hesse, Ursula Le Guin, Toni Morrison, Thomas Pynchon and Jean-Paul Sartre. However, to classify writers in this way would be to miss something essential. My point is rather that McCarthy, as a writer, transcends disciplinary boundaries. While McCarthy is an extraordinary master of literary style and form, this is simply not sufficient if we are to appreciate the historical destiny which McCarthy announces in his writing for humanity. The status of literature for McCarthy exceeds mechanical aesthetic considerations. This is to say, McCarthy's concerns with status and fate, life and death, clearly indicate that his work is not simply about subjective interpretations or examinations of the stature of works of literature. To the degree to which McCarthy dextrously adopts the mechanics of literary art such as style, form, character development and setting, this always simultaneously happens within a grander metaphysical style, pressing towards the status and nature of reality itself. Thus, McCarthy's individual literary works are not reducible merely to questions of textual meaning, genre and narrative. These issues may certainly be explored; however, to understand McCarthy fully, it is necessary to attempt to transcend such classificatory constraints. Thus the crucial significance of McCarthy's writing must, as McCarthy recommends himself, confront the most pressing and urgent questions of our age.

So to take McCarthy's cue, that literature is a question of life and death, must itself be bracketed. Ultimately, however curious we are, it matters little what McCarthy himself thinks or intends, nor what his biographical details reveal about his political views, interests and literary opinions. Nor, for that matter, does our own subjective reception and interpretation of his texts ultimately matter. Instead, the power of McCarthy's writing itself is marked by brutal intransigence and resistance. McCarthy's writing has a life of its own. His distinct accomplishment is to elevate his literature beyond bare formal considerations, letting language reveal both the long and short history of the fate of an unfolding humanity and the things which matter to it. Therefore, I will claim that McCarthy is a literary philosopher, rather than, say, solely a literary writer or a philosopher, as we might understand those terms in the conventional sense.

If McCarthy is a writer who impresses on his readers the fate of humanity, and the decisive stakes of humanity's past, present and future, then it is therefore necessary to fill out this picture. The argument of this study is thus that McCarthy holds a consistent philosophical orientation across the span of his literary output. My general aim is to explain how McCarthy's literature (novels, plays, screenplays, philosophical essays and unpublished archive material) offers a 'tragic ontology'. This tragic ontology refers to the titular 'physics of the damned' of this work. When using the term 'physics' I am not deploying it in its conventional usage, to describe a discipline of the material sciences. Instead, I am using the term in accordance with its roots in Ancient Greek philosophy, where *physis* is reality itself. Ordinarily this term is translated into English as 'nature', but it has a much richer resonance than we might associate with a normal understanding of nature as the domain of inquiry referring to the biological phenomena of the material world, or in the sense of phenomena which are designated as belonging to the elements of the natural world, such as trees, flowers, animals, rivers and mountains.

Physis in its Ancient Greek rendering is a term that is simultaneously philosophical, scientific and religious, and therefore is an apt expression for conveying what I am attributing to the literary-philosophical dimension of McCarthy's writing and thinking. I argue that McCarthy offers a distinct blend of the spiritual and the material. That such 'physics' is 'damned' also takes its instruction from Ancient Greek philosophy. To say, as we conventionally do, that nature is a specific phenomenon relating to material and biological processes, would be to draw a stringent demarcation between thought and reality. Reality is effectively all that is the case, governed as it is by immutable laws. However, attributing 'law' to 'nature' would not really make sense for the Ancient Greeks as this would require the imposition of human constructs on nature. Strictly speaking, there cannot be laws of nature, since laws refer to the organisation of human communities as related to issues of sovereignty and obedience. Nature itself has no laws, nor indeed any requirement to obey such laws. To be specific, the 'damned' refers to *physis* as a domain of lawlessness affecting the human community. It is strictly not a question of salvation and redemption. Rather, my claim is that McCarthy, through his literary philosophy, or his literature as a form of thinking, aims to reveal how that domain of lawlessness affects, conditions and contests human communities.

More practically, this study aims to elucidate how McCarthy articulates a consistent philosophical perspective pivoting on philosophical themes of mortality, the political, nihilism, materialism and language. Tracing these themes from the publication of his earliest novels to his most recent philosophical essays, it is my contention that McCarthy offers a unique synthesis of spiritual, political, ethical and materialist concerns, the understanding of which is essential for coming to terms with the stakes of his literature. Insofar as McCarthy may be labelled a master of the English-language novel generally, and American fiction more precisely, this always occurs with respect to broader philosophical questions which McCarthy himself raises.

In order to pursue this literary-philosophical line of inquiry further, I will draw on literary-minded philosophers – Plato, Friedrich Nietzsche, Jacques Derrida, Maurice Blanchot – to argue that McCarthy operates conceptually, stylistically and formally at the intersection of philosophy and literature. This will in turn allow me to argue as to how McCarthy blends the 'material' and the 'metaphysical' throughout his work. While in strict philosophical terms materialism and metaphysics are not normally held to be natural allies, this synthesis is precisely what I argue makes McCarthy's work compelling, and in turn what makes it a critical exemplar of literary philosophy. By offering a nuanced appreciation of this singular mixture of materialism and metaphysics, I will be able to describe how McCarthy's broader philosophical ontology plays out regarding questions of literary form, mortality, ethics, language and politics, arguing that it tackles the urgent and relevant questions of our age such as technology, the fate of politics, the environment, and the very possibility of language and community.

There has recently been a definitive burgeoning interest in the philosophical dimensions of McCarthy's work. While there are some books and journal articles which deal with how McCarthy deploys philosophy in his literature, these tend to remain isolated to specific issues and themes. Chris Eagle's edited collection *Philosophical Approaches to Cormac McCarthy: Beyond Reckoning* (2017) provides a variety of contributions which explore the role of philosophy in the works of McCarthy from a variety of perspectives. In the main, however, existing theoretical scholarship on McCarthy tends to focus on theological, juridical, naturalist and postmodern readings of his work, or otherwise focuses on specific philosophers. To this end, I argue in this book that what distinguishes McCarthy's work is a uniting of his novels and other outputs with key philosophical tropes from materialism, aesthetics, environmental ethics and existential philosophy. My aim is to show how McCarthy offers a specific 'physics of the damned', sowing consistent philosophical insights into the finite nature of human experience throughout his *oeuvre*. By examining his recent foray into the philosophy of language in *Nautilus* (2017), and through the incorporation of archival material, I aim to offer a distinctive account of how McCarthy views the intersection of language, metaphysics, materialism and science which is untheorised hitherto.

Though there are some extended scholarly works examining the role of philosophy in McCarthy's writing, there are currently none that articulate the centrality of materialism, language and ethics in McCarthy's work in the way I attend to here. Most significantly, Ty Hawkins, Petra Mundik and Julius Greve offer important, valuable and insightful elaborations of the philosophical and spiritual import of McCarthy's work. Ty Hawkins's short treatise *Cormac McCarthy's Philosophy* offers an attempt to render clear just exactly what McCarthy's philosophy is. Hawkins argues that McCarthy is an actual philosopher, asserting that his work holds insights for questions of metaphysics, ethics, epistemology and narrative.[3] While Hawkins's basic thesis is brilliantly audacious and his insights on ethical subjectivity will inform my own work, I would have respectfully to disagree with the guiding spirit of his overall position. The philosophical inflection of McCarthy's work does not equate with a systematic philosophy. McCarthy, in the novels which constitute the majority of his writing, does not write in a philosophical way; he does not construct and compose his prose in defence of arguments, nor is his work explicitly organised around the construction of systematic treatises concerning the different branches of philosophy such as metaphysics, ethics, metaethics, logic, aesthetics and politics. When he does write in a direct philosophical register, as he did in his essay 'The Kekulé Problem', as well as its rejoinder in *Nautilus* (2017), these are exceptional cases, and cannot be assumed to be representative of the entirety of McCarthy's corpus even if, as I will show in this book, the latter essay is singularly useful for understanding McCarthy's philosophical concerns. In addition, the prose of this essay is still infused with enough of an enigmatic and poetic quality to be able to situate it within a literary-philosophical tradition of philosophical writing, rather than as a purely analytic philosophical piece.

Of course, philosophy is not necessarily restricted to written communication; it has a longstanding tradition of oral and dialogical thinking. On this point, Hawkins's claim has much more purchase, especially when examining questions of narrative and dialogue. Still, in *Whales and Men*, where it should be noted McCarthy most extensively adopts philosophical dialogue, across the span of the various drafts, it is distinctly the case that philosophical dialogue is often removed between first and final drafts.[4] To say categorically that McCarthy is not a philosopher, though, does not mean that we ought not to attempt to investigate how he deploys both philosophy and literature in order to offer a unique contribution to literary philosophy.

The other most significant appraisals of McCarthy's philosophical writing come from Petra Mundik and Julius Greve. Mundik's *A Bloody and Barbarous God: The Metaphysics of Cormac McCarthy* (2016) explores theological themes in the work of McCarthy. Whereas much of Mundik's book foregrounds important connections between the mystical, esoteric and gnostic tropes in McCarthy's literature, my book will deviate from Mundik's overall conclusion, which argues for the importance of religion to McCarthy's work. Instead, I propose that while a spiritual reading of McCarthy is important – and Mundik provides a brilliant exposition of this line of enquiry – it is only one dimension of McCarthy's writing. For a full philosophical understanding of all McCarthy's literature, it is vital also to account for the ethical, materialist, linguistic, evolutionary and scientific elements when reading his *oeuvre*.

Greve, for his part, offers a very important, imaginative and innovative analysis of McCarthy's theory of nature. Greve's analysis is restricted to reading McCarthy through the philosophical tradition of German Idealism and its legacy. In his *Shreds of Matter: Cormac McCarthy and the Concept of Nature* (2018), Greve makes special reference to the work of Friedrich W. J. Schelling, Lorenz Oken and debates pertaining to contemporary speculative realism. Largely, I find little to disagree with in Greve's thesis concerning the status of nature, nor with his guiding intuition that there is a philosophical kernel, navigating a path between science and philosophy, in evidence in McCarthy's understanding of nature across the span of his work.[5] The conceptual focus of my work does, however, differ from Greve's interpretation in a number of respects. By focusing on McCarthy as a literary philosopher, I aim to consolidate Greve's analysis, especially by focusing on questions of ethics, language, nihilism, politics and evolutionary theory, and more generally by examining how McCarthy is more aligned with philosophers – Nietzsche, Derrida, Blanchot – who emerged in the twentieth century, in the wake of nineteenth-century German Idealism.

In terms of what I am attempting to accomplish in this book, I will argue that what distinguishes McCarthy's work is the uniting of his novels and other outputs with key philosophical tropes from materialism, aesthetics, ethics and existential philosophy. This involves showcasing how McCarthy, through the depictions of his characters and their physical, geographical and evolutionary setting, illuminates the finite and transient nature of human existence. I will demonstrate how McCarthy renders his characters at once archaic, mythic and contemporary in their efforts to transcend the predicament of existing in a physical universe. This is a necessary object of study because no philosophical novelist illuminates the tensions between humans as a frail sense-making animal and their participation in the long arc of the physical universe with such dramatic force as McCarthy. What underlines McCarthy's unique contribution to the philosophical novel generally, and to American literature particularly, are the ways in which he depicts how moral psychology emerges as a struggle against, and with, the reproduction of life in a material and physical universe. Thus, I will make the case that McCarthy is one of literature's 'great unifiers', uniting science and spiritualism, matter and spirit, nature and culture, as well as the ethical, literary and philosophical spheres.

To accomplish my goal, this book is organised into seven chapters. Therein I engage in an in-depth investigation of McCarthy's most philosophically pertinent texts, concentrating on key representative texts taken from his earlier, middle and later periods. Most extensively, I will be drawing on the following texts: *Suttree*, the unpublished screenplay *Whales and Men*, *Blood Meridian*, *The Road*, *The Sunset Limited*, *No Country for Old Men* and 'The Kekulé Problem'.' I will also draw on other significant texts to consolidate my argument such as *The Orchard Keeper*, *Outer Dark*, *Child of God*, *The Stonemason* and *The Border Trilogy*. I will also incorporate detailed archival research which I have carried out at the Wittliff Collections at Texas State University, where the 'Cormac McCarthy Papers' are housed. In this way, I aim to offer as complete a philosophical account of all of McCarthy's work as possible.

In Chapter 1, 'Older than Language: Cormac McCarthy on Language and Evolution in *Whales and Men* and "The Kekulé Problem"', I begin by showing how McCarthy brings different disciplines into dialogue with each other. Specifically, the chapter develops McCarthy's philosophical enquiries into the relationship between language, evolution, science and the unconscious. The importance of this chapter rests on the fact that there has not until now been a thoroughgoing analysis in this vein. This, therefore, will be the first piece of research to articulate McCarthy's philosophical approach to language. Building on McCarthy's archival materials, specifically the screenplay *Whales and Men*, his recent essay in the popular science magazine *Nautilus* and its rejoinder, as well as the literary works themselves, I argue that McCarthy conceives of language, evolution and the unconscious philosophically. This chapter is necessary to offer a distinct account of how McCarthy deploys philosophy. Particularly, regarding language, I assert that McCarthy attempts to subvert any easy distinction between thought and reality by showing how language acts as a mediator between the short and long history of human communication.

Chapter 2, 'Literature and Death: *Suttree*, McCarthy and Blanchot', will build on the analysis in the preceding chapter on language to begin to explore how McCarthy understands language as literature. This chapter also uses Maurice Blanchot's theory of literature as an interpretive tool to excavate how McCarthy's work operates in both philosophical and literary registers. Blanchot explains that literary meaning emerges from a resistance to generic classification. I expand upon Blanchot's position to offer an account of the ways in which McCarthy adopts a similar strategy. Pinpointing *Suttree* as the culmination of McCarthy's early Appalachian period, I argue that McCarthy's writing to this point, and *Suttree* especially, makes apparent the structure of his ontology and ethics through the novel's execution of both form and content. Indeed, here I will show that McCarthy's literature performs a metaphysical evacuation of form and content to broach questions of philosophical significance. We will thus begin to see how McCarthy, in his writings, is a thinker who consistently reveals the significance of philosophy for the practice of literature, illuminating in turn what literature unveils for philosophy.

Chapter 3, 'Spirits in Cinderland: *Blood Meridian*'s Nietzsche', will argue that to understand the philosophical vision of McCarthy further, it is imperative to examine his most violent work, *Blood Meridian*. If McCarthy's literature can be said to have an ethical perspective then it is necessary to tackle his literature precisely where it appears to be most nihilistic and cynical. This chapter shows that *Blood Meridian* can be understood as offering a cogent representation of Nietzsche's accounts of active and passive nihilism. This analysis further enables me to outline how McCarthy conceives of the relationship between metaphysics, the natural world and ethics. If nihilism implies a repudiation of philosophy, metaphysics, knowledge and ethics, then I argue that we can detect clear evidence of how McCarthy offers a glimpse of how we can extricate ourselves from the predicament that *Blood Meridian*'s depiction of metaphysical collapse and amorality stages. The upshot of this reading is that it will provide a direct and nuanced response to Vereen Bell's far-reaching insight on the ambiguous nihilism of McCarthy in Bell's landmark studies 'The Ambiguous Nihilism of Cormac McCarthy' (1983) and *The Achievement of Cormac McCarthy* (1988).[6]

In Chapter 4, 'In the Shadow of the Forms: *The Sunset Limited* as Educational Encounter', I will turn my attention to McCarthy's dramatic work *The Sunset Limited*. This is essential to my overall thesis as the play provides a nominally polar opposition between two distinct philosophical traditions. *The Sunset Limited* is therefore important for understanding the philosophical dimension of McCarthy's *oeuvre*, since the play demonstrates his distinctive literary strategy of viewing humans as placed between spiritualism and materialism, matter and meaning, despair and hope. The play's two central protagonists (Black and White) represent opposing forces of the theological and religious, the rational and materialist. This chapter argues that the apparent educational asymmetry of the two characters in fact reveals a more profound solidarity, albeit a solidarity tragically forsaken in the work itself. Furthermore, I scrutinise the ways in which *The Sunset Limited* adopts Platonic themes. While I argue that McCarthy falls short of a full-throated Platonism, I do find evidence in the text of how both characters educate each other beyond competing and antagonistic opinions.

Chapter 5, 'Anti-Matters: Mortal Ethics in *The Road*', consolidates the analysis of the preceding chapter by showing how McCarthy's synthesis of scientific and metaphysical themes has direct philosophical consequences for his understanding of the ethical relations between humans. My argument in this chapter is that there is an unambiguous material ethics on display in *The Road*. While McCarthy is not offering a naïve materialist reductionism, there is a sense that human endeavour is caught up in the wider material processes of the world. In a direct reversal of a theological cosmos, the characters of the novel participate in the broader material dissolution of the universe. The consequences of this weird metaphysics allow us to grasp more clearly the philosophical, ethical and political imaginary of *The Road*. This is particularly evident in relation to questions of structure, memory and a suspicion of community. The chapter concludes by explaining how *The Road* depicts a radical difference between those entrenched in cults and communities and those who are refugees, those without borders, those without walls.

Having established McCarthy's distinct mortal ethics, it is necessary to expand on this insight to offer a fuller account of his understanding of ethical deliberation, by examining *No Country for Old Men*. In Chapter 6, 'Saving Sheriff Bell: Derrida, McCarthy and the Opening of Mercantile Ethics in *No Country for Old Men*', I argue that rather than adopting the common strategy of viewing McCarthy's novel as a paean to a lost conservatism, there is a subtler philosophical reading available. Utilising Derrida's account of ethics and responsibility, I argue that McCarthy offers a very rich account of ethical deliberation. On the surface the novel presents a putative conservative ethics, where Sheriff Bell laments the current state of social laws and yearns for the simplicity of natural justice. However, I contend that the moral fulcrum of the novel dwells in the deepening wisdom of Bell in the face of Chigurh's mechanisation and naturalisation of ethics.

In Chapter 7, 'A Maelstrom of Doing and Undoing: McCarthy's Political Imaginary', I will extend my analysis of the ethical sphere to examine the political inflection of McCarthy's writing. This chapter provides a summative account of themes developed throughout this book. I will begin by responding to the work of David Holloway and Dianne C. Luce, alongside a discussion of McCarthy's *The Orchard Keeper* and *The Stonemason*. Concentrating on political philosophy, I argue that the best way to understand the political implications of McCarthy's literature is by situating his work as a response to Alexis de Tocqueville's *Democracy in America*. If McCarthy is one of literature's 'great unifiers', uniting science and spiritualism, matter and spirit, nature and culture, then I argue that this tendency is replicated in the political sphere. The political dimension of McCarthy's work can be understood as an effort to unite order and chaos, civility and anarchy, character and fate, and thus also the strained relations between the ruler, the ruled and the misruled. As mentioned, the realm of nature and reality itself is lawless in and of itself. It will therefore be important to understand how such lawlessness inflects McCarthy's political aesthetic. Thus, I will conclude this work by illuminating the anarchic dimension of McCarthy's *oeuvre*. While I do not think that McCarthy offers a philosophical or political theory about a feasible and workable anarchism, I will suggest that to understand the political imaginary of McCarthy's writing it is crucial to comprehend the vibrant anarchistic spirit animating his work, which has hitherto been critically unacknowledged.

One of McCarthy's most incisive interpreters, Steven Frye, in his introductory essay to *The Cambridge Companion to Cormac McCarthy*, situates McCarthy somewhere between Nietzsche and Plato. Frye follows Luce's suggestion in *Reading the World: Cormac McCarthy's Tennessee Period* that the presence of philosophy in McCarthy is drawn directly from the various myths found in Plato's dialogues.[7] Frye also suggests that a necessary supplement to Luce's reading is Nietzsche's suspicion of philosophies that venerate a transcendent idealism. I think this is broadly right. McCarthy, as a writer, takes seriously Nietzsche's dictum 'God is dead'. As with Nietzsche,

McCarthy, as thinker, writer, philosopher, is not making some spurious or simplistic atheistic claim about the existence or non-existence of God. He is merely asking, where can we go from here?

Notes

1. Richard Rorty, 'The Contingency of Language', *London Review of Books*, 17 April 1986, <https://bit.ly/3nG9b8i>
2. David Kushner, 'Cormac McCarthy's Apocalypse', *Rolling Stone*, 27 December 2007, <http://www.davidkushner.com/article/cormac-mccarthys-apocalypse>
3. Ty Hawkins, *Cormac McCarthy's Philosophy* (Gewerbestrasse: Palgrave Macmillan, 2017), 2.
4. Cormac McCarthy, *Cormac McCarthy Papers (1964–2007)*. The Wittliff Collections. Alkek Library, Texas State University in San Marcos, Box 97: Folders 1–9.
5. Julius Greve, *Shreds of Matter: McCarthy's Concept of Nature* (Hanover, NH: Dartmouth College Press, 2018), 20.
6. Vereen Bell, 'The Ambiguous Nihilism of Cormac McCarthy', *The Southern Literary Journal* 15, no.2 (Spring 1983): 31–41.
7. Steven Frye, 'Histories, Novels, Ideas: Cormac McCarthy and the Art of Philosophy', in *The Cambridge Companion to Cormac McCarthy*, 6–7.

Chapter 1

Older than Language: Cormac McCarthy on Language and Evolution in *Whales and Men* and 'The Kekulé Problem'

Cormac McCarthy's popular science article 'The Kekulé Problem' provides a critical summary of the novelist and playwright's long-standing interest in language, philosophy and evolutionary theory. [1] Therefore, I will begin by presenting an extended analysis of McCarthy's philosophical theorisation of language, evolution and the unconscious. Beginning with McCarthy's most explicit philosophical engagements will enable me to sharply clarify the philosophical register of his work. If McCarthy's writing attempts to draw different disciplines together, this impetus is clearest in his understanding of language, where we see him writing in a philosophical, literary and scientific manner. Working through McCarthy's unpublished screenplay *Whales and Men*, his novels, and 'The Kekulé Problem' itself, I will argue that a longstanding concern of McCarthy's is his effort to reconcile scientific, philosophical and literary discourse. More specifically, this chapter argues that McCarthy conceives of humans as retaining unconscious evolutionary forms alongside an explicit sense-making capacity. This position further enables McCarthy to develop a unique literary-philosophical discourse within his fiction and non-fiction.

While McCarthy is widely renowned for his novels, screenplays and dramas, his work is of enduring interest to philosophers. As mentioned in my Introduction, there has been a variety of interpretations of his fiction ranging across existentialism, post-structuralism, theology, ecocriticism and psychoanalysis. [2] However, there is no extended analysis of McCarthy's philosophical observations on the relation between language, evolutionary science and the unconscious. This, therefore, is the first piece of research to articulate McCarthy's philo-sophical approach to language. Building on McCarthy's archive mate-rials, specifically the screenplay *Whales and Men*, and his recent essay in the popular science magazine *Nautilus* and its rejoinder, as well as the literary works themselves, I examine herein how McCarthy con-ceives of language, evolution and the unconscious philosophically.[3] Broadly, this research provides a novel method for integrating scien-tific insights with literary themes as a form of literary philosophy. By 'literary philosophy' I mean the way McCarthy writes in a distinctive register, stylistically and formally incorporating insights from evo-lutionary biology, metaphysics, philosophy and literature. Literary Darwinism, as advocated by Joseph Carroll and Dennis Dutton, might be considered an obvious precursor here.[4] The argument that art and literature may solely be understood as an evolutionary phenomenon is a truism; evolution produced the human species, which in turn pro-duced literature. However, this approach is too general for my pur-poses, serving only to level differences between science, linguistics and literary convention. I will use McCarthy's example to demonstrate how an author can deploy philosophy in order to negotiate discourse that emerges from scientific knowledge, psychology, ethics and liter-ary conventions without eliminating the respective differences of each discipline. McCarthy's longstanding interest in science, evolutionary theory and linguistic acquisition provides a template to articulate a unique synthesis of literary and philosophical tropes. I will focus here on one example of McCarthy's effort to unite literature and science, regarding the intersection of language and evolutionary theory. More specifically, this chapter demonstrates the philosophical significance of McCarthy's reflections on language and science, making explicit his theorisation of humans as a nexus of both unconscious evolutionary forms and a distinctive sense-making capacity. This position enables McCarthy to develop a unique literary-philosophical discourse for illuminating his fiction as well as non-fiction. This analysis will there-fore provide critical insights for unlocking the overall philosophical vision which informs McCarthy's literary work, as well as permitting me to argue that he offers a distinctive philosophical register for con-joining literature and science.

Whales and Men and language beyond thought

One of McCarthy's most sustained engagements with language, evolution and science is found in the unpublished and unproduced screenplay *Whales and Men*. This is a ponderous screenplay set in Florida, the West of Ireland, Sri Lanka and the United Kingdom. The chief protagonists are marine biologist Guy Schuler, the Irish aristocrat and adventurer Peter Gregory, a wealthy former medical student called John Western and his soon-to-be ex-girlfriend Kelly McAmon. A minor character called Eric also features in the drafts. The action follows scientists and environmental activists aboard the *Farfetched* and the *Albion* who study and explore the life of whales. Beginning with Guy euthanising seventeen beached whales, the plot proceeds with a short trip on which the characters swim with and observe whales, then proceeds to a longer research voyage where they witness a massacre of a pod of whales, apart from a baby whale which Schuler is also forced to euthanise. Kelly develops a spiritual and emotional bond with this baby whale. The narrative concludes with a maiden speech by Peter addressed to the House of Lords, exhorting fellow politicians to save the whales. Throughout the piece, characters engage in long philosophical ruminations on scientific and metaphysical questions.

Stylistically, the text is closer to a philosophical dialogue than a conventional screenplay. Platonic dialogues are the obvious comparison, although with its long discussions of purpose, cause and design, David Hume's *Dialogues Concerning Natural Religion* is perhaps a more obvious philosophical forerunner of *Whales and Men*. As with all dialogue-driven narratives, characters' opinions and perspectives do not necessarily coincide with the author's viewpoint. However, the characters' collective concerns indicate McCarthy's views of the philosophical problems he was working through at this point of his career. Generally, characters are motivated by the physical and metaphysical wellbeing of whales. Their discussions refer to two key themes pertinent to this analysis. Firstly, the characters offer critical observations on the metaphysical consequences of humans acquiring language. Secondly, they discuss the limitations and benefits of scientific knowledge and evolutionary biology.

Regarding language, there is an overt prelapsarianism in evidence in *Whales and Men*. Language, description and scientific explanation are secondary phenomena aberrating from an original reality. At one point, in an earlier draft, Peter evokes *Genesis*, suggesting that the human acquisition of knowledge is inherently corrupting: 'There was no evil in the world until man sought knowledge.'[5] In a pencilled marginal comment, McCarthy has Peter suggesting that humans are the evil serpent from the Biblical story: 'We were the serpent. The bible is right. Evil is a man-made creation like argyle socks and hydroelectric dams.'[6] A direct equivalence is thus drawn between the world as it is and the derivative nature of language:

> Nomenclature is the very soul of secondhandedness. Everything that is named is set at one remove from itself. We endow all of creation with names and then carry the names away. We carry them off and file them away and stand watch over them. We experience nothing. Just names. The vicarious in possession of ersatz.[7]

Similar sentiments echo across McCarthy's fictional work. In *Suttree*, when Suttree and his friends realise they are playing cards on a gravestone, they find the names of the deceased worn away, marking a difference between our powers of ascription and the world itself. *The Road* presents a world 'shorn of its referents'.[8] In *The Border Trilogy*, Quijada informs Billy Parham: 'The world has no name. The names of the cerros and the sierras and the deserts exist only on maps. We name them [so] that we do not lose our way.'[9] In *The Border Trilogy*'s epilogue, Billy meets a traveller who distinguishes between language as narrative and a deeper form of knowing where there are: 'no idioms but only the act of knowing and it is this we share in dreams and out'.[10] The consequence of having an advanced vocabulary is that humans exist in a fallen state. We use language as a tool for making sense of the world, but such sense-making abilities alienate us from the very reality we attempt to describe.

Indeed, the very act of naming objects entails a form of ontological mutilation. Assigning names to particular objects implies a segmentation of reality. Kelly, the most theologically inclined character in *Whales and Men*, suggests that it would be pointless for God to name himself: 'Why would he name himself anyway? To distinguish himself from what?'[11] If God is another name for 'oneness', then oneness cannot be circumscribed by particular names, since particularity by definition indicates demarcation.

According to McCarthy, language has further malign consequences. If language entails classifying, demarcating or fragmenting, then by necessity we are preordained to undermine the unity of reality. In other words, our urge to attach words to objects means we are inherently destructive. Such existential pessimism is essential to the moral force of the screenplay. The characters come to comprehend that since language is inherently destructive, the impending ecological catastrophe the characters worry over is inevitable. The mutilation of the reality language performs also extends to other communicative modes. For example, we are 'enslaved by the history we write, not freed by it'.[12] Our desire to write, archive and record our expression divorces us even further from the world: 'We live in our own archives. Not even among bones but among measurements of bones. A few sketches. Comments. Speculations.' Elsewhere, 'Then life is an illusion. Articulation masks the facts of the inner mechanism.'[13] Even our use of symbolism does not escape the pernicious consequences of having language. Peter sees all modes of communication as the primary factors alienating us from the world. Language literally imprisons us, obstructing our way to deeper understanding: 'I began to see all symbolic enterprise as alienation. Every monument a false idol. Language has conditioned us to substitute our own creations for those of the world. To replace the genuine with the ersatz. The living with the dead.' For the jaded aristocrat Peter, effectively we turn the Garden of Eden into a 'detention center'.[14]

There are three obvious points to draw from *Whales and Men* regarding how McCarthy philosophically conceives of language. Firstly, language is a human invention. It is a tool we use for making sense of the world, a tool peculiar to humans.[15] This is a claim McCarthy repeats later in 'The Kekulé Problem'. Secondly, language works as a system of signs. Signs imply reference to an object; however, the signs we use become so successful at substituting for the things themselves that we fail to notice they are an abstraction. We take the sign for the thing:

> What gradually became apparent to me was that language was a thing corrupted by its own success. What had begun as a system for identifying and organizing the phenomena that make up the world had become a system for replacing those phenomena. Language was like the evil aliens in the horror movie that take on the forms of things and gradually replace them altogether. They look like the thing but they are not the thing. Language usurps things.[16]

Thirdly, a tragic by-product of our use of language is the impetus it provides for hubris and domination. For Peter, language is a way of: 'containing the world. Everything named becomes that named thing. It can never be something else.'[17] The misanthropic Peter sees such hubristic desire as self-defeating: 'We always knew that our desire to be God would finish us off.'[18] We are dual creatures, beings alienated from the primordial unity of reality but complete with the desire to use our sense-making faculties to control and dominate that reality. Our desire to name the world obscures the very thing we are describing, because: 'the name is not the thing'.[19] John goes so far as to suggest that only a complete negation of expression will restrict humans' destructive tendencies: 'nothing will stop us only silence itself'.[20] The general misanthropy of Peter does not go unchallenged, however.

Most obviously, Kelly offers a bulwark against the more cynical Peter's reflections on language. Kelly's character represents a purported oneness of reality. She is the screenplay's avatar of a unified cosmos. Her attention to the nature of 'creation' and the future – she wants children, and has them by the end of the plot; she saves a lion cub from auction to send it to a nature reserve – offers an ethical alternative to Peter's cynicism. By endorsing the existence of a unified underlying reality, she also gives voice to the fundamental connection between different species which exists prior to the veil language draws over the world:

> I see your and I see my hand. (She reaches out and puts their hands outstretched alongside each other) and I see that the similarities are so much greater than the differences that I know there is a connection there that no separation in time or space can invalidate or void. I know that you are at least my brother and at another level which is harder to reach but no less real I know that you are me. Not figuratively. Not a metaphor. For real. In the flesh. It's an understanding that has nothing to do with problem solving. It's an act of pure cognition. It's an event. I guess what I think is that Yes I believe in God but I dont know how he is. I dont know what his name is.[21]

Kelly's act of pure cognition, or intuition, is superior to the problem-solving nature of linguistic cognition. Julius Greve also confirms McCarthy's strategy of adopting intuitions from a non- or pre-linguistic realm outside of language as central to his poetics.[22] We see direct evidence of this poetics in *Whales and Men*'s Kelly. For Kelly, we are owned by something other than us. Kelly represents a pantheistic stance in which reality is identical to divinity. The pantheistic cannot be located, since reality is ubiquitous and precludes location to a single point.[23] Even if Kelly prophetically glimpses a more fundamental reality, this does not exclude her scepticism of language. Kelly offers her own sceptical take on language. Language individuates humans, deluding us with a sense of ownership and possession. A non-distinguished world is therefore also a moral good for Kelly, since it manifests the fundamental commonality we share with the world and other species.

An absolute environmental cataclysm is presaged throughout *Whales and Men*. McCarthy will return to the aftermath of such an event in the more pessimistic text *The Road*. The screenplay, however, offers clearer alternatives for how humans might respond to looming catastrophe. Despite the impending ecological collapse, *Whales and Men* offers concrete meaningful alternatives to the inexorable deterioration sparked by human impact on nature. McCarthy uses Kelly's tentative mysticism to mitigate the dominant negativity of Peter's nihilistic and gloomy musings, an opposition more decisively articulated in McCarthy's drama *The Sunset Limited*. We also find a softening of outright pessimism in other characters. By the end of the screenplay the different characters adopt different approaches to achieving meaning and coherence, to combat the metaphysical and cosmological nihilism precipitated by the wanton slaughter of the whaling industry. If nihilism is essentially destructive, then the characters engage in creative tasks to combat the cosmological emptiness that resides at the heart of the screenplay. All the central characters engage in projects of renewal thanks to their encounter with the whales. Schuler continues to seek meaning through working with whales and through his activism. Kelly ends up marrying Peter, symbolically uniting their philosophical perspectives of life and death, creation and destruction. As Stacey Peebles notes: 'Kelly's visceral understanding of one-as-another is made material by the end of the story, when she is pregnant with her and Peter's second child.'[24] John ends up working in a hospital in a developing country near a war zone. He enters a caring profession and is last witnessed caring for the future by providing medical aid to a young girl. At one point, McCarthy has John writing to Kelly informing her of his redemptive longing which, even if dwarfed by the reality of evil, demonstrates his belief in the human capacity for renewal: 'I know that we are lost but I no longer believe that we are doomed. That which we are lost to still exists and if there is a way out then there is a way back . . . I take back what I said about destiny.'[25] Even the relentlessly cynical Peter turns to parliamentary politics to make a positive political intervention on behalf of the whales.

The evidence for the more redeeming side of Cormac McCarthy's work is on display in *Whales and Men*. This is also evident regarding questions of language and meaning. While language is largely considered a malevolent force, it is also the device through which characters gain an enlightened perspective on the deeper web of connections which bind humans with the physical and biological spheres. As mentioned, *Whales and Men* is closer to a philosophical dialogue than a workable screenplay, and it is dialogue which helps an ersatz community of interlocuters gain an obscure glimpse of humans' deeper kinship with metaphysical and scientific conceptions of reality. This is what Peebles calls the 'ties that bind humans and ecological systems together'.[26] Writing in another context, Greve describes McCarthy's binding impetus as the 'entanglement of *bios* and *logos*'.[27] In McCarthy's screenplay we also find a unique meld of the Platonic and the scientific, of the metaphysical and the discourse of knowledge. Language is at a remove from reality, its function is instrumental, used for copying, mechanising, archiving and replicating. However, to suggest McCarthy endorses an outright Platonism would be to miss the point. The screenplay does not come down on the side of either Platonic ideas or the empirical world. Instead, McCarthy articulates a synthesis of both modes. This is especially evident in how McCarthy approaches scientific language in *Whales and Men*.

On the surface, logical and objective disciplines are not exempt from McCarthy's suspicion of the negative consequences enabled by language use. Mathematics is taken as just another form of linguistic symbolism. Eric echoes physicist Richard Feynman's depiction of pure mathematics as an abstraction from the real world.[28] He suggests: 'I just think that things like mathematical equations only really exist in people's heads. I don't think the world knows anything about mathematics.'[29] Equally, scientific discourse itself is taken as an elaborate form of language. There is a disjunct between our scientific description of the world and the world itself: 'Eric is right. These laws we attribute to everything are our ideas. The way the world works *is* the way it works. It's not a law.'[30] Scientific nomenclature is limited to ostension only. What scientific discourse refers to can only ever approximate reality, rather than be reality itself. There is a further doubtful note struck on the limitations of scientific discourse: 'I think science has a real problem in recognising its own shortcomings. No discipline has ever explained the world. To imagine that one can is the greatest superstition of all.[31] The critique that science and religion are closer than either proposes is extended to evolutionary biology:

> Darwinism explains the mechanism of an elaborate system . . . It is a belief system, ultimately. Its adherents tend to militancy. They brook no contradiction. Their theory is unprovable in principle. You cant rewind the universe and run it over again. Scientific proofs are reproducible proofs, that's what make them science isnt it? Darwinism dismisses the captain and puts the stoker at the helm. The conjugations of chance that it demands to fill in its schedule beggar belief. In the end it explains nothing but itself.[32]

Thus, McCarthy sees the scientific discipline of evolutionary biology as engendering the differentiating function of language.

Evolution works through a specialisation of species, providing competitive advantage within different environments. The more complex and specialised our species become, the more difficult it becomes to discern commonality among ourselves and the world. Guy suggests:

> If you look at the history of species there seems to be no selective advantage to intelligence. Maybe for individuals, but not for the species. It's the microbes who have largely ignored selection for three and a half billion years that remain with us and probably will remain when we are gone. They seem almost immortal. The process of evolution seems to be about specialization and adaptation and yet these are the very things that seem to mitigate against survival itself.[33]

While intelligence and, as we have seen, language, have an evolutionary function at an individual problem-solving level, this is not necessarily the case at a collective species level. Hence the comparison with microbes. Microbes have less intelligence but are more resilient in adapting for survival. Microbial life is unburdened of the specialisation and differentiation which language has implanted in humans. The tragedy of human existence resides in our inability to bring together unity and division. The one and the many is one of the oldest philosophical oppositions in the Western philosophical canon, and McCarthy in *Whales and Men* sees the enduring value of this most primordial of paradoxes. When John asks the empirically minded Schuler about whether he believes in God, he says: 'No. Larger questions again. I dont think that the world is made up of things. I dont think it's that simple.'[34] The trouble resides in our inability to reconcile the whole and the part.[35] Humans are tragically trapped between oppositional traits: our ability to differentiate, demarcate and categorise and our desire to apprehend the unified, the common and the whole.

It should be noted that McCarthy is not devaluing scientific activity.[36] Evolution itself is not rejected. While the characters do question the potential of scientific exploration becoming hubristic, notwithstanding Peter, the characters of *Whales and Men* are resigned to the reality of the evolutionary status of human development. However, our desire to classify biological processes through evolutionary theory, rather than evolution *per se*, occludes our capacity to see the world in a coherent way. The specific by-products of evolutionary development, such as language and intelligence, dim our ability to discern our common heritage with other species. At one point,

Schuler recalls the debunked scientific theory that ontogeny recapitulates phylogeny, which suggests evolutionary stages are repeated in the gestation of foetuses. It is clearly not the case that McCarthy is endorsing a pseudo-theory – this is immediately pointed out in the script – but instead it is clear he is evoking how our current linguistic capacities and intelligence hold a muted kinship with the ancient evolutionary processes that continue to inform our current identity:

> And that was what I saw. A blue whale fetus. Curled up in a glass vial. Holding its hands out. I had an uncanny sense that we were somehow included in the whale's history. That we were what the whale could have been.[37]

McCarthy holds an essentially tragic view of the universe and our place in it; the human is flawed due to the inevitable oscillation between the one and the many, the whole and the part, species and individual and system and component.

For McCarthy, the tragedy of our existential status is that we lose sight of the common:

> The world <that> we possess and cherish is not the world of possibility but the world accomplished. Because it is the sum of our memories we believe it to be communal in nature. Yet there is nothing more particular. Commonality is precisely what is lost. The past on the other hand does not exist at large.[38]

Similarly: 'The future on the other hand because it is problematic and unexpressed is generic and impartial. The future is an equal opportunity employer. It is the same for all.'[39] The point of McCarthy's observations is to show how the human's individual sense-making capacity, particularly as manifested in evolutionary explanation, does not make us exceptional creatures. Conventionally, human dexterity with language implies our intelligence and superiority over other species. McCarthy rejects this view in *Whales and Men*. Language is precisely the very thing which makes us less intelligent, confining us to a determined past which we in turn take to be all that there is, unable to glimpse beyond the world we name. It is language which predetermines us with the lesser and more self-destructive traits of our evolutionary nature.

As argued above, there is a redeeming dimension to *Whales and Men*. Their encounters with whales prompt the characters to revitalise their activities, and the screenplay ends with them reaffirming

a pact with the future. Whales are taken as exemplars of a superior type of vocalisation and communication, one not individual but
informed by a more generic communal longing. John reflects: 'But
the pain of one whale is the pain of all. A thousand miles across the
sea the outraged blood and nerve and muscle convey their agony
unchecked. And that is the meaning of their community.'[40] A yearning of the personal and idiosyncratic for the common and whole
underpins the literary-philosophical concerns of *Whales and Men*.
Furthermore, biology and meaning exist in mutually complicated
ways. The status of our evolutionary heritage engenders us with a
drive for survival and destruction, caught between past and future,
creation and dissolution. The traces of memory, language, history
and our long past particularise us. They are written, so to speak. The
future on the other hand is open, contingent and where we might
potentially find a common destiny with the world and its species.
The eponymous whales of the screenplay provide us with hints of
how we can be otherwise. Peter suggests other places we may find
similar counsel: 'It seemed reasonable that <perhaps> there might
still be hints of such a dialogue in dreams or in clairvoyance or ESP
and that was why we dismissed such things. Even simple moments
of peace.'[41] Peter's endorsement of pseudo-science is given a more
plausible formulation when McCarthy examines language, science
and the unconscious over twenty years later in the 'The Kekulé Problem'. There we find language still as a secondary function, but in this
essay, it is the unconscious which enables us to fuse metaphysical and
scientific depictions of reality.

'The Kekulé Problem'

McCarthy's most direct intervention on the nature of language and
evolutionary science came in his recent popular science *Nautilus* article 'The Kekulé Problem'. McCarthy writes in an explicitly philosophical and scientific register to examine a variety of themes pertaining to
the operation of human language and the unconscious. What bonds
Whales and Men and 'The Kekulé Problem' is McCarthy's concern to
show both the limitations and possibilities of the evolution of human
language. Like the extended speeches in *Whales and Men*, 'The
Kekulé Problem' is speculative in tone. The essay deals with the limitations of language, conscious and unconscious modes of expression,
myth, signalling and the role of evolution. McCarthy's underpinning
observation in 'The Kekulé Problem' is that the unconscious is not a

linguistic phenomenon. McCarthy argues that the 'unconscious is a biological operative and language is not'.[42] In itself, this is not a startlingly original point. We see varieties of this observation in a host of disciplines and sub-disciplines. For example, in phenomenology, the unconscious is not directly accessible to reflective awareness. Here we can recall Jean-Paul Sartre's general scepticism of psychoanalysis.[43] Psychoanalysis generally considers the unconscious as pre-linguistic, with its methodological emphasis on drives and desires. Behaviourism would see the unconscious as a by-product of instincts. Classical philosophical approaches to language configure the unconscious as comprising dispositions and inclinations. For example, Aristotle would classify 'unthinking' dispositions as second nature (*hexis*).[44] Empirical accounts of the unconscious would distinguish between data received from the senses and their formation in consciousness.[45]

What then does McCarthy bring to the table? McCarthy begins 'The Kekulé Problem' discussing the myth of the *ouroboros*. When the chemist Kekulé dreamed of the mythical snake swallowing its own tail, he took the dream image as a eureka solution to a problem he was struggling with in molecular chemistry. McCarthy asks rhetorically why the unconscious did not just tell Kekulé directly that he was looking for a ring structure. The unconscious 'spoke' pictorially, via image rather than speech. Such unconscious thinking, McCarthy reasons, implies a gap between the unconscious and our interior monologue. The unconscious can be obstinately silent for McCarthy, presenting us with symbols, pictures and myths rather than words. For McCarthy, 'the actual process of thinking – in any discipline – is largely an unconscious affair'.[46] Language, as we have seen in *Whales and Men*, is considered as a form of differentiation, describing the plethora of objects we experience in the world. On the other hand, the unconscious ties us to biological processes which we are not reflectively privy to, but which necessarily inform our thinking. What we do with words and our immediate reflective language cannot be the foundational origin of meaning. What, then, does language do? For McCarthy, 'language can be used to sum up some point at which one has arrived – a sort of mile post'.[47]

If all animals are waiting for language, the rapidity of the acquisition and transmission of language in humans is unique. For example, McCarthy draws a clear distinction between 'signalling' and language. Signalling in animals is considered less sophisticated. Even among more sophisticated animals such as bees, chipmunks and some birds, signalling remains restricted to survival behaviours such as warning of nearby predators. For humans, language does have an additional component of substitution, or: 'that one thing can be another thing'.[48] Our signs make explicit things to which they refer. Any instance of language – speech acts, a linguistic thought, a phrase – substitutes for something else picking out a situation. Our sense-making linguistic activities therefore remain tied to the immediate world. For McCarthy, the 'way in which the reality of the world becomes incorporated into our being, while poorly understood, is the salient fact of our existence'.[49] Bluntly put, language makes sense of our immediate environment. Our linguistic capacity to make sense, to render explicit the exterior world, necessarily retains extra-linguistic traces of evolutionary development, because the unconscious is biological.

The failure of language to make explicit deeper biological processes does not undermine the instrumental value of language. For McCarthy, the 'invention of language was understood at once to be incredibly useful'.[50] Language is simply practical: its primary function concerns naming and describing single objects in the world and thus language cannot be self-inaugurated or self-invented. McCarthy here remains an adherent to Ludwig Wittgenstein's theory of language, where 'meaning is use'.[51] McCarthy endorses the context-laden view of language. Language is a sense-making mechanism whose primary task is picking out states of affairs in the world and rendering them meaningful as we adapt to different contexts. If language is restricted to making sense of where one is in the world, and what one does, then it is exceptionally useful in negotiating and problem-solving when confronted with the most pressing tasks of our immediate environment.

There are further points which can be drawn from McCarthy's observations here. Firstly, if language is a point at which one has arrived, a 'mile-post' as it were, then this means language is a transitional and differentiating phenomenon. The ways we gain sense evolve across contexts, describing different objects where advantageous. The language we use develops with the contexts we inhabit, describing and ordering the world as we find it. Consequently, if language is transitional and contextual it must, at least minimally, be malleable. Language changes and adapts, responding to whichever states of affairs are to hand. The point is that we are not generally aware of such contingency. We think language is immediately transparent to reflective awareness, picking out states of affairs in the world with precision and accuracy, but for McCarthy the sense-giving powers of language are limited to adapting to the immediate contexts of the world: 'There is nothing else to describe.'[52] Similarly, 'Problems, in general, are often well posed in terms of language and language remains a handy tool for explaining them.'[53]

If language is dependent on the different contexts and tasks it engages, this does not necessarily imply that the structure or form of language changes. McCarthy is decisive here: 'There are no languages whose form is in a state of development. And their forms are all basically the same.'[54] McCarthy expresses sympathy for the idea of an 'ur-language'.[55] This is the idea that all language is monogenetic, deriving from a single origin.[56] While language may change with respect to idiom, accent and definitions, there remains a general structure of syntax and grammar. Despite language having a capacity to innovate, it remains limited in terms of its structural functions. As language is limited to making sense of the environments we inhabit, its focus on immediate tasks entails that language is automatically unaware of deeper instincts and patterns or how we are constituted by our evolutionary heritage. Therefore, thinking with language must be more than *just* language, as there is a host of other things that we do when we think. The idea that our thoughts can be reduced to linguistic utterances is a simplistic view of metacognition, one delimiting all kinds of reflective activity such as judgements, symbolic recognition, imagistic and visual thinking, as well as the evolutionary dispositions of our animal brain.

The silence of the unconscious

For McCarthy, the unconscious is mostly silent, even resistant to language, imperceptible and non-verbal, impervious to the babble of interior life. With characteristic bleakness McCarthy suggests the unconscious draws on a: 'pool of we-know-not-what'.[57] He argues, 'The truth is that there is a process here to which we have no access. It is a mystery opaque to total blackness.'[58] This begs the question, how is it possible to talk of something immune to expression? When it comes to articulating what precisely the unconscious is, drawing upon McCarthy is not particularly clarifying. He notes that the unconscious knows a great deal. It has a diversity of functions, from the automatic regulation of breathing or scratching an itch, to solving mathematical problems; it may even be solemn or frivolous.[59] That the unconscious is resistant to expression, however, is a positive for McCarthy. The silence of the unconscious has an operative function. The way McCarthy speculates about this is interesting. The unconscious is no doubt there to augment survival, existing alongside the sense-making capacity of language. That the unconscious is recalcitrant to expression injects a degree of contingency into our awareness.

Such contingency serves to ensure we are not absolutely determined by how language responds to our immediate environment.

There is something uniquely human about how the human unconscious works, even if we do share an animal brain with our evolutionary ancestors. It is the conjunction between our invention of language and our own peculiar evolutionary development which characterises being human for McCarthy. McCarthy is keen to draw a sharp distinction between language as something unique to humans and how it operates for other creatures: 'The other five thousand plus mammals among us do fine without it. But useful?'[60] Distinctively, McCarthy sees the unconscious as a 'benign' agent guiding our thinking. The silence of the unconscious has a quasi-pedagogical function, imparting the 'moral compulsion to educate us'.[61] Language gets on with the immediate and pressing tasks of describing our world in all its diversity and nuance, while the more elliptical unconscious connects us, even haphazardly, to our broader evolutionary ancestry. Drawing on the repository of 'we-know-not-what' is valuable, since it means we are not strictly chained only to the pressing tasks of brute survival with which language occupies itself. We can unconsciously draw on a reservoir of myth, foundational narratives, symbols, biological instincts, patterns of struggle, fables and images which can provide us with wisdom, even if only if dimly so. It is because the unconscious is silent that it aids us in our struggles for survival.

Where, then, does McCarthy stand on the relation between the unconscious and our conscious use of language? Firstly, even if McCarthy is acknowledging the relevance of a reservoir of evolutionary dispositions, his position precludes a basic empiricist account of the self. If the unconscious is a by-product of five million years of hominid adaptation, then it is not possible for our minds to be *tabula rasa*, as a behaviourist might conceive. As McCarthy resolutely suggests: 'It is not true of course that we are born blank slates.'[62] Equally, he is not working with a dualistic notion of the mind, where the mind would be an immaterial cognitive process distinct from our material bodies. Both approaches are exempt from the inherited traits of our evolutionary past. As McCarthy cautions: 'You have to be careful about inviting Descartes to the table.'[63] What is left is a view of self that operates between conscious linguistic awareness and dense repositories of evolutionary dispositions and tendencies. This is not an easy alliance. As with the protagonists of *Whales and Men*, we are stuck between the general and the specific, in this case between our animal brain and the linguistic capacities of individual reflective awareness.

To make sense of McCarthy's account of the unconscious, it is necessary to comprehend that our immediate awareness of the world is inflected with a deep repository of multitudinous iterations of evolutionary struggles. If the unconscious is a biological imperative then the way it manifests itself cannot be through language, but only in conjunction with the forms and traces of a long evolutionary past. Hence McCarthy takes the unconscious as having the 'moral compulsion to educate us'.[64] The 'wisdom' of the vast millennia of our mortal survival is functional; however, the unconscious presents this wisdom to us in elliptical and symbolic ways. As evolution requires deep time, and our animal brain retains millennia of information about how we have survived in the past, the unconscious works by testifying, prodding and nudging us through trial and error. It serves as McCarthy's evolutionary version of a guardian angel, as it were.

While the unconscious is biological, it also paradoxically directs us to transform our biological life. The unconscious is necessary for connecting us to a deep repository of survival patterns, patterns which in turn help us to transcend pressing material challenges. This is where the analogy of a benign unconscious stops. If the unconscious must resist expression, remaining opaque to sense-making, then it can only offer guidance in contingent and elliptical ways, offering thoughts, images, patterns, tests and trials to help humans transcend the immediate task of survival. As McCarthy suggests: 'The unconscious wants to give guidance to your life in general but it doesnt care what toothpaste you use.'[65] The path, the unconscious suggests, is broad but 'it doesnt include going over a cliff'.[66]

Evolutionary language

In *Whales and Men* there is guarded scepticism about evolutionary theory. In the 'The Kekulé Problem' McCarthy still does retain some scepticism about evolutionary accounts of language. Language, for McCarthy, is not subject to selection pressures: 'There is little evidence for selection in the shaping of language.'[67] While this view would be challenged by evolutionary linguists, it does hold some sense on a long evolutionary timeline.[68] Language is a relatively recent acquisition on an evolutionary timescale and the ways it is used must be preceded by a mass of evolutionary adaptation. As McCarthy suggests:

> The difference between the history of a virus and that of language is that the virus has arrived by way of Darwinian selection and language has

not. The virus comes nicely machined. Offer it up. Turn it slightly. Push it in. Click. Nice fit. But the scrap heap will be found to contain any number of viruses that did not fit.[69]

As with the characters in *Whales and Men*, McCarthy is not criticising evolutionary processes *per se*, but specifically evolutionary accounts of language that limit language to mechanical function and immediate use. He does not disavow the evolutionary formation of human identity, but instead tries to explain how our evolutionary lineage relates to the acquisition and use of language. Despite the acquisition of language, the unconscious is 'mindless' by definition. Daniel Dennett's book *Darwin's Dangerous Idea* is relevant here. For Dennett, life emerges from non-living matter.[70] Consequently, irrespective of how complex our language becomes, irrespective of how sophisticated our intentional sense-making processes are, they are still rooted in the mindless repetition of evolutionary trial and error. Hence, McCarthy's characters in *Whales and Men* come to accept that life is neither exceptional nor unique and is premised on how the organisation of matter allows genetic variation to take hold through mindless trial and error over the course of millions of years. Such organisation does not disqualify variation. In fact, the variation of traits is essential to allowing different species to evolve. If this variation were not the case, replication would merely clone parental information and evolution could not occur. These processes must remain obscure to linguistic articulation. It is the outcome of generations of biological mindlessness where McCarthy sees humans struggling to cope, caught between animal life and a desire to transcend it.

If the unconscious is not linguistic for McCarthy, it can still complement linguistic awareness. Past evolutionary activity is retained through the unconscious, which presents itself through a variety of thoughts, pictures, symbols, images and judgements, drawing comparisons between the practical tasks that language concerns itself with and the 'lessons' of our evolutionary past. Since the 'unconscious is a biological operative', the functioning of the unconscious must be evolutionary, serving the transmission of biological life.[71] If language arrived in our brain at some point in our evolutionary history, then McCarthy suggests that the brain 'was not expecting it and had made no plans for its arrival. It simply invaded those areas of the brain that were the least dedicated.'[72] If the unconscious is subject to evolutionary imperatives, then the brain is necessarily constrained by our evolutionary history. The brain is certainly a multi-functional organ and yet this does not imply that the brain can do anything.

While the 'virus' of language can change and mutate in innumerable ways, our brain is limited by the sedimented history of millions of years of hominid adaptations. These adaptations are the fruit of evolutionary trial and error, consisting of innumerable dispositions that aid ours and our ancestors' reproductive success.

What makes humans distinctive is the ability for language to change and adapt, yes, but additionally, to transcend selection pressures necessitated by local atmospheric, climatic, natural and geographical conditions. This point is crucial for understanding McCarthy's philosophical disposition. He sees the human being as historical, operating at the intersection of biological striving, as repository of informational memory as well as cultural and linguistic development oriented towards the future. Therefore, what characterises the unconscious is its automatic persistence and a machinic urge to survive. Our evolutionary past is a necessary but not sufficient condition for thinking. It is necessary that evolutionary variation takes place to make us what we are, but this is not enough to explain how we act and make sense of the world. The unconscious speaks to the fundamental and generic parts of our biological status. It is consequently less interested in the specifics of subjective sense-making but instead works cryptically, offering hints and some orientation as we are confronted with the inevitable and objective project of mortal survival.

Our lived existence therefore requires meaningful factuality in tension with the harsh reality of evolutionary struggle. Language helps us cope with the wild revolutions we experience by naming and controlling; evolution also connects us to deeper reservoirs of accident, survival and endurance. Therefore, McCarthy's account of language and the unconscious helps unlock the central themes of his work, namely his persistent preoccupation with the tension between that which endures and that which changes. In literary terms, it is worth remembering that McCarthy is drawn to elemental tropes. He frequently draws on elemental myths, instincts, image and symbol and the way they exist alongside, and direct, moral and psychological thinking. This enables his prose and drama to depict with some acuity the conflicts of sense-making, depicting fraught moral psychologies alongside the archaic and elemental. For example, at the end of *No Country for Old Men* Sheriff Bell ruminates on a stone trough, taking it as a symbol of both endurance and change. At the conclusion of *The Road*, McCarthy uses fire as a symbol of promise and continuity in a bleak and hollow universe. In *Child of God*, McCarthy uses the forest as a backdrop for Lester Ballard's psychological deterioration. In *Blood Meridian*, a mythological violence permeates the novel. The function of these mythic tropes is to bring into relief McCarthy's broader concern, which is to depict human psychology as continuous with a struggle against – and with – the reproduction of life in a material and physical universe. McCarthy's characters persist despite and alongside the Darwinian world they inhabit; they are frequently tragic, subjects of endurance and transformation, attempting to transcend the predicament of existing in a physical universe.

Conclusion

The best way to comprehend McCarthy's non-fiction is to view humans as beings who retain unconscious evolutionary patterns and are also explicit sense-making animals. Beginning with *Whales and Men* and proceeding to 'The Kekulé Problem', I have argued that what is distinctive about McCarthy's writing is his willingness to wed philosophical and literary insights in his own unique form of literary philosophy. In his non-fiction, McCarthy's authorial voice drifts between that of a detached scientist, poet, linguist and metaphysician. His work combines the opaque and mysterious with the mechanical. McCarthy's intervention in evolution and cognitive linguistics is productive for understanding his literary output. The synthesis of evolutionary survival and linguistic comprehension which McCarthy proposes renders intelligible the recurrent themes of his fictional work: specifically, the finite and transient nature of human existence operating against a backdrop of deeper and longer patterns of evolutionary time. The contrast between frail sense-making animals and the deep well of survival instincts engenders the dramatic power of his novels. Humans are precarious, frail, otiose, engaged in persistent sense-making despite the sometimes inscrutable physical and biological processes of the universe. The long arc of the physical universe, as well as evolutionary and geological time, makes his characters at once archaic, mythic and contemporary. McCarthy retains the spirit of a naturalist, albeit a very unusual one, one who adopts a critical distance from the naturalism which he deems necessary for understanding our place in evolutionary history. McCarthy is not a naïve reductionist in his outlook on language. Language is a practical tool for coping with the vagaries of the world. Alongside language, the unconscious reveals mysterious and profound insights about our struggle for biological survival which are not readily apparent. For McCarthy, the silence of the unconscious is an absence at the core of all speech. No linguistic speech pattern is only itself and such patterns remain dependent on the traces of prior evolutionary struggle. If we can cooperate with our unconscious, insofar as what it recommends works, then it can help us connect to universal, generic and primal human experience. Language is our disposition for making sense of our historical dwelling and exists alongside, and through, an overcoming of our basic biological imperatives. McCarthy's writings on language contain some hopefulness despite his usual pessimism. We are evolutionary beings, but we also retain an evolutionary capacity to be wise as we survive. Such evolutionary wisdom might come to lead us away from the abyss we find in *The Road*. While I have outlined here how McCarthy brings literary, scientific and philosophical styles together, it is now necessary to account for how McCarthy's understanding of our linguistic nature informs language as literature.

Notes

1. The title of this essay refers to McCarthy's interview with Oprah Winfrey, where McCarthy suggests that the 'subconscious is older than language'. See 'Cormac McCarthy - Subconscious is Older than Language', YouTube video, 5.24, posted by Sdobric, 19 October 2014, <https://www.youtube.com/watch?v=Qidyx3oXqpY>. For the longer interview see 'Cormac McCarthy Interview on the Oprah Winfrey Show', YouTube video, 8.46, posted by Mohammad Farooq, 8 June 2014, <https://www.youtube.com/watch?v=y3kpzuk1Y8I>

2. For a brilliant ecocritical account of McCarthy's work see James D. Lilley, 'Of Whales and Men: The Dynamics of Cormac McCarthy's Environmental Imagination', *Southern Quarterly* 38, no.2 (2000): 111–22.

3. All references to *Whales and Men* in this chapter may be attributed to the 'McCarthy's Drafts' collection, Box 97: Folders 1–9, the Wittliff Collections, Alkek Library, Texas State University in San Marcos. Although the drafts are not dated, it seems McCarthy wrote this screenplay in the mid- to late 1980s. While earlier drafts are called 'Of Whales and Men', the final draft is entitled 'Whales and Men'. Citation in this chapter abbreviates the title to *WM*. Additionally, since much of the archival material I refer to is from earlier drafts of the screenplay and is thus not always paginated, I will refer to the paginated page where marked and refer to the relevant box and folder number where the draft material is unpaginated. For a more detailed plot summary and a history of McCarthy's writing of the script see Edwin T. Arnold, 'Cormac McCarthy's *Whales and Men*', in *Cormac McCarthy: Uncharted Territories/Territoires Inconnus*, ed. Christine Chollier (Reims: Presses Universitaire de Reims, 2003), 17–30.

4. See Joseph Carroll, *Evolution and Literary Theory* (Columbia, MO: University of Minnesota Press, 1995), and Dennis Dutton, *The Art Instinct: Beauty, Pleasure and Evolution* (Oxford: Oxford University Press, 1995).

5. Cormac McCarthy, *Whales and Men*, Box 97:1. Hereafter cited as *WM*.

6. Ibid.

7. Ibid.

8. Cormac McCarthy, *The Road* (London: Picador, 2006), 93.

9. Cormac McCarthy, *The Border Trilogy* (London: Picador, 2002), 702.

10. Ibid.

11. McCarthy, *WM*, Box 97:8.

12. McCarthy, *WM*, Box 97:1.

13. Ibid.

14. Ibid.

15. The peculiarity of humans having advanced language capability in *Whales and Men* is characterised negatively, whereas animals such as wolves and whales, which vocalise differently, are represented in a positive light since they have a richer communicative capacity. Wolves, which also feature in the draft material of *Whales and Men*, are configured as developed animals that can sense beyond the confines of their locale. They perceive with an immediacy alien to humans, communicating without being restricted to place.

16. McCarthy, *WM*, Box 97:1.

17. Ibid.

18. Ibid.

19. Ibid.

20. McCarthy, *WM*, Box 97:6.

21. McCarthy, *WM*, Box 97:1.

22. Greve, *Shreds of Matter*, 44.

23. Kelly rejects a personal soul for an impersonal one: 'It's not that we have a soul. It's that the soul has us.' McCarthy, *WM*, Box 97:1, 9. Interestingly, in a typed fragment in later drafts of *Whales and Men*, McCarthy engages with pantheistic sentiments regarding the impossibility of localising mathematical points. Within a pantheistic framework, reality cannot be localised to particular points: 'Nothing exists in itself. A point has no measure and it can be described as pure location but location compared to what? . . . It can have no being except where other beings exist.' McCarthy, *WM*, Box 97:9.

24. Stacey Peebles, *Cormac McCarthy and Performance: Page, Stage, Screen* (Austin: University of Texas Press, 2017), 58.

25. McCarthy, *WM*, Box 97:1. This echoes McCarthy's own views. In an interview, when asked about the pessimism of *The Road*, he says that although pessimistic, the central message of *The Road* is: 'that love can even survive even in the most horrible of circumstances'. See 'Interview with Cormac McCarthy (2012)', YouTube video, 6.46, posted by Jacob, 28 September 2018, <https://goo.gl/p1PnV9>

26. Peebles, *Cormac McCarthy and Performance*, 59.
27. Julius Greve, *Shreds of Matter* (Hanover, NH: Dartmouth College Press), 158.
28. Richard Feynman argues: 'Pure mathematics is just such an abstraction from the real world, and pure mathematics does have a special precise language for dealing with its own special and technical subjects. But this precise language is not precise in any sense if you deal with real objects of the world . . .' See Richard Feynman, 'New Textbook for the "New" Mathematics', *Engineering and Science* 38, no.6 (1965): 14. It is no accident that this theme also appears in drafts of *Whales and Men*, given McCarthy's longstanding interest in science and mathematics. Notably, McCarthy worked as a copy editor on Lawrence Krauss' biography of Feynman, *The Quantum Man* (New York: Norton, 2012).
29. McCarthy, *WM*, Box 97:1.
30. Ibid.
31. Ibid.
32. Ibid.
33. McCarthy, *WM*, Box 97:6.
34. McCarthy, *WM*, Box 97:1.
35. At one point on a typed fragment of the early archive material there is a single phrase: 'Gestalten looping' (*WM*, Box 97:1). Presumably, this enigmatic phrase relates to relations and connections between wholes and parts, since a predominant theme of the screenplay is the tension between the universe as a whole and our localised linguistic understanding of it.
36. In the DVD extras of *The Unbelievers* documentary, McCarthy broadly defends the importance of science: 'People who like science are all drawn to it for the same reason. It explains the physical world. What is this stuff? Is it the last word on what reality is, and what the physical world is? I don't know. But if it's not the last word it is at least the best word.' See *The Unbelievers*, DVD, directed by Gus Holwerda (London: Revelation Films, 2014).
37. McCarthy, *WM*, Box 97:1. The use of point brackets in these quotations indicates McCarthy's hand-written marks on the typescript.
38. Ibid.
39. Ibid.
40. Ibid.
41. Ibid.
42. Cormac McCarthy, 'The Kekulé Problem', *Nautilus* 19 (March/April 2017), 31.
43. See Jean-Paul Sartre, *Being and Nothingness: An Essay on Phenomenological Ontology*, trans. Hazel Barnes (London: Routledge, 2003), 74–5.
44. Aristotle, *Nicomachean Ethics*, trans. Christopher Rowe (Oxford: Oxford University Press, 2002), 1099a.

45. Neuro-scientists often demarcate between information included and excluded in consciousness. For example, David Marr in *Vision* (San Francisco: Freeman, 1982) argues there is a host of neuro-computational processes which take place unconsciously between when light photons affect our retinas and the attendant construction of visual images in consciousness. Björn Merker argues that the biological origin of consciousness is linked to evolutionary use. Consciousness provides a stable locale for organising action in the world, but this excludes the sensory and sensorimotor data we experience. See Björn Merker, 'The Liabilities of Mobility: A Selection Pressure for the Transition to Consciousness in Animal Evolution', *Consciousness and Cognition* 14, no.1 (2004): 89–114.
46. McCarthy, 'The Kekulé Problem', 25.
47. Ibid.
48. Ibid. 26.
49. Cormac McCarthy, 'Cormac McCarthy Returns to the Kekulé Problem', *Nautilus*, 30 November 2017, <https://goo.gl/AiFPKM>, para.13:13.
50. McCarthy, 'The Kekulé Problem', 26.
51. Ludwig Wittgenstein, Philosophical Investigations, trans. G. E. M Anscombe (Oxford: Blackwell, 1997), 21.
52. McCarthy, 'The Kekulé Problem', 29.
53. Ibid. 25.
54. Ibid. 29.
55. Ibid. 27.
56. There is not conclusive agreement among evolutionary linguists on this point. On the one hand, the theory is that humans originally evolved from a protolanguage which consisted of primitive sounds such as grunts and other oral noises. On the other, the idea is that our words derive from a more complicated system of grammatical rules and syntax than just primal grunts. See Shigeru Miyagawa, 'Integration Hypothesis: A Parallel Model of Language Development in Evolution', in *Evolution of the Brain, Cognition, and Emotion in Vertebrates*, ed. Shigeru Watanabe, Michel A. Hofman and Toru Shimizu (Tokyo: Springer, 2017), 230.
57. McCarthy, 'The Kekulé Problem', 30.
58. Ibid. 26.
59. Ibid. 31.
60. Ibid. 27.
61. Ibid. 28.
62. McCarthy, 'Cormac McCarthy Returns to the Kekulé Problem', para.13:14.
63. McCarthy, 'The Kekulé Problem', 31.
64. Ibid. 28.
65. Ibid. 30.
66. Ibid. 31.

67. McCarthy, 'Cormac McCarthy Returns to the Kekulé Problem', para.17:14.
68. See Chapter 11 of Steven Pinker's *The Language Instinct* (New York: William Morrow and Co., 1994) for a very good description of the evolutionary origins of language.
69. McCarthy, 'The Kekulé Problem', 27.
70. Daniel Dennett, *Darwin's Dangerous Idea*, London: Penguin, 1995, 48–52.
71. McCarthy, 'The Kekulé Problem', 31.
72. Ibid. 27.

Chapter 2

Literature and Death: McCarthy, Blanchot and *Suttree*

As I argued in Chapter 1, instrumental language is a heuristic strategy for helping humans to navigate the world and for McCarthy, language is accompanied by the silence of the unconscious. This means that there is a mysterious silence at the core of all speech. This muteness may emerge from evolutionary struggles, residual mythological thought-patterns or primal experiences. This silence is the key to understanding.[1] Thus, to appreciate the literary-philosophical dimension of McCarthy's writing, it is necessary to explain how his reflections on language feed into language as literature. McCarthy uses the 'unconscious' as shorthand for 'mystery' or 'silence', as such silence accompanies all the things we do not immediately say, know or comprehend first-hand. It also informs any activities in which humans engage. However, we need to exercise some caution too; this form of poetic silence should not be considered as either bafflement or mystification. To consider it so would amount to saying that the silence that McCarthy acknowledges is comprehensible or may easily be explained away, or that it has a supernatural origin elsewhere. Instead, I will argue that the silence is kept live; our ability to understand the world in linguistic terms is accompanied by an inability to see deeper truths and therefore McCarthy is a distinctly literary-philosophical writer, since the origin and limits of what we know remain intimate with what we do not know. To understand how McCarthy's literature uses the poetic, the lyrical and the philosophical, it is necessary to examine how his work combines our desire to understand the world linguistically in tandem with a deep dialogue with the mute, the silent and the unspoken. The best place to do this, I submit, is in McCarthy's *Suttree*.

McCarthy's *Suttree* is an epic anti-novel, engulfing the reader in a tide of nihilistic deterioration, unconfronted death, teeming negation, loneliness and disenfranchised effluvial life.[2] The power of negation and the function of death have a unique place in this novel. Suttree, the novel's anti-hero, confronts his own death as well as a more expansive cosmic negativity at the heart of all things. The novel itself stages a confrontation between silence, the unconscious and a mysterious emptiness which hums alongside all human action. For the purposes of explaining the literary-philosophical register of *Suttree* I will turn to the literary philosophy of Maurice Blanchot. I will argue that Blanchot's reflections on literature equip us to articulate an original philosophical interpretation of McCarthy. I am not particularly concerned with elucidating how *Suttree* as a literary text represents specific philosophical themes. It is more productive to consider *Suttree* less as a text that offers a catalogue of philosophical themes, where we can elucidate philosophical theme 'x' and 'y', but instead as a form of writing which enacts philosophical questions in a hybrid of literature and philosophy.

More specifically, I will argue that McCarthy's writing in general – and *Suttree* in particular – makes apparent the structure of ontology and ethics in its execution of both form and content. In this sense McCarthy, in his literature, is a thinker who consistently reveals the significance of philosophy for the practice of literature, and in turn illuminates what literature unveils for philosophy. While much commentary on *Suttree* and on the McCarthy *oeuvre* in general places the novel in the context of existential individualism and alienation, I will argue that a more nuanced and philosophical reading of this text is possible through utilising Blanchot's concepts. Examining the proximity of Blanchot and McCarthy offers a hitherto untapped resource for understanding the philosophical implications of McCarthy's fiction, as well as providing a new way to think about his work. The philosophical force of the novel emerges from the very unworking of American idealism and individualism, as will become evident through the novel's presentation of the persistent evacuation of Suttree's subjectivity, which reveals the philosophical kernel of McCarthy's literature: that at the core, all humans are irreducibly mortal and temporal beings. Cornelius Suttree attempts to evade such humanity.

If McCarthy's *Suttree* is a novel of absolute negation, revelling in nihilism, decay and destruction, then Blanchot's reflections on the interrelation of negation, literature and philosophy hint at a distinct ethical orientation in McCarthy's writing. McCarthy does not offer an ethical theory, but a tragic ontology, which sees fundamentally human values emerging in an inevitably violent world. As this chapter will show, this tragic ontology does not preclude evaluating ethical questions or ethical deliberation; it is only that McCarthy is not offering a systematic philosophical ethics such as, say, utilitarianism or deontology. McCarthy's work is founded on an effort to articulate the generically human, as well as the mysterious silence which accompanies and transcends all instances of identity. Such a generic humanity, I will herein argue, can be illuminated via specific elements of Blanchot's philosophical theory of literature. Firstly, this consonance can be identified throughout Blanchot's understanding of the operation of literature. Blanchot sees the literary text operating as an unravelling or unworking of the stability of its own formal structures. 'Unworking' is Blanchot's shorthand for the fragility and interruption of any self-sufficient identity.[3] Secondly, this operation of unworking reveals ontological and ethical concerns about the ethical status of human mortality. Blanchot's understanding of literature tests the capacity and possibilities of the literary work as a response to nihilism. Such an ethics is based on a distinct unworking of anti-individualism, the entrepreneurialisation of the human and their rootedness in immediate networks of belonging.

Blanchot, nothingness and the possibilities of literature

For Blanchot, the very point of the literary text is to resist categorisation. Literature is not the preserve of aesthetics, nor is it a matter of a text holding a comparative rank over other texts, where one text can be quantitatively discerned to be better than another. Philosophically, there is as such no essence to literature. The 'essence of literature is precisely to evade any essential characterization, any affirmation which would stabilize or even realize it: it is never already there, it is always to be rediscovered or reinvented'.[4] The essence of a literary text is traditionally what makes it distinctive and separable from other artefacts; as such, the essence makes the literary artefact what it is. For Blanchot, such a generic classification overlooks the activity of literature. Each literary work has a permanent opacity, singular, specific and resistant to individual comprehension. The very core of a literary artefact, for instance a novel, is the absence at the heart of the text. This is a negative definition of literature. Blanchot offers a paradoxical anti-theory where, 'literature is not only illegitimate, it is also null, and as long as this nullity is isolated in a state of purity, it may constitute a marvellous force'.[5]

We should not approach literature as if there was a covert meaning in the literary text that we just need to decode. Instead, the text is the events, responses and practices which make it more than an item of informational transmission. The null form of the text is for Blanchot an index of its possibility. As Ullrich Haase and William Large argue, Blanchot offers a species of reader-response theory, where each text is an interaction between reader, text and writer. Literary form and content are never activated through a subjective voluntarism. A text has as many meanings as there are readers and events that will respond to it.[6] For Blanchot, the very intransigence to the coding of the literary text is what makes it actively interesting. Such resistance is precisely what opens the possibilities of literature as well as revealing its ethical function. The literary text is always a form of enactment, an opening of possibilities and responses. Blanchot, working in a Heideggerean register, sees the literary text as being actively, materially and historically situated, in a responsive event between author, text and reader.[7] The issue for Blanchot is one of creation. The best literature is opaque and abstract, like the sense of mystery which McCarthy deploys, not because it is at base confusing, but because it inaugurates a space within the historical world, a space that reveals the dimensions of the practical world in which we are embedded, as well as an orientation between past and future.

Literature, for Blanchot, if it is to be anything, must articulate the historical nature of the human being and be actively responsive to the past, present and future; the best literature is literature that has the capacity to illuminate universal human predicaments at various critical, material and historical junctures. Blanchot's literary theory operates in philosophical terms between being and becoming. Eschewing any literary humanism which affirms spiritual wholeness, ahistorical perennial values or imperishable truths, Blanchot seeks to show how literature operates as the precise unworking of such literary preoccupations. Consequently, the ethical dimension of literature becomes apparent: literature is precisely the unworking of the sovereignty of the individual, the idea that character and self are achievements. Most of all for Blanchot, literature makes manifest what is most universal: the existential quandaries of finitude, transformation, historical development, mortality, death and the inexpressible. Blanchot's work – as with McCarthy's – is not so much a species of anti-humanism, but a philosophical corrective to humanism, one that acknowledges the historical, material and temporal density of human experience. Blanchot's intertwining of literature and philosophy is about literature as an event, a singular occurrence where the literary artefact unveils the truth and historical specificity of human possibilities.

Literature operates outside the confines of writer, reader and even to an extent the text's own social context. For Blanchot, the most visceral quality of the literary work is therefore impersonal and neutral (*neutre*). What is written 'belongs to a language which no one speaks, which is addressed to no one, which has no center, and which reveals nothing'.[8] The work does not depend solely on the human world or on networks of human communication. The literary work is wholly indifferent to such issues. It inaugurates itself by devaluing and negating the subjectivity of author and reader. Under Blanchot's consideration the written text works precisely by obscuring its very own origin, the writer, the reader and any supposed 'meaning' residing within the text.

Blanchot is not celebrating negation out of caprice; he is making a distinct philosophical point about the nature of nihilism and nothingness. The other side of the literary text, the part that makes an impersonal literary text relevant to the human sphere, is literature's confrontation with death. In conventional philosophical terms, death is the realm of nothingness. Abstractly, nothingness is the eternal and ahistorical, as this is the domain where nothing can come to be or where nothing changes. Literature, for Blanchot, is valuable because it performs a negation of this 'nothingness'. The literary text makes apparent questions of life and death. Thus, possibility and creation are the other side of negation for Blanchot. The absence at the core of the text requires literature to demonstrate a form of finite survival. The text can be renewed in different contexts and thus surpasses the temporary mortality of humans – the text remains indifferent to our specific mortal life – however, to say that the literary text surpasses our mortality is not to say that Blanchot is endorsing the text as eternal, immutable or ahistorical. As Jacques Derrida shows, mortal existence endures as an 'abidance' that 'does not *remain* like the permanence of an eternity'.[9] The literary text is most evocative when it is a *mélange* of life and death, revealing the mortality of the human as well as divesting us of our subjectivity by opening us to other possibilities. In this way we must think of the literary text in ecstatic terms, operating at the intersection of past, present and future.[10] For Blanchot, the Heideggerean temporal intonation is of huge importance as it means that the literary work is historical, or put another way, it becomes activated in specific spatio-temporal locations.[11] The text is not the time of reading, or the quantitative duration of the material words on a page, but an ecstatic opening defined by the interdependent relation of the past, present and future of the work with regard to reader, writer and historical context.

The dramatic value or success of any work is thus for Blanchot a *mélange* of life and death, power and passivity, death and creation.

Literature which attempts to express this play of absence and presence, death and life, is exceptionally valuable. For example, Blanchot sees Franz Kafka's *The Castle* as a decisive elucidation of the power of absence and possibility within the literary text.[12] The endless search of the surveyor symbolises the reader's pursuit of a meaningful resolution at the core of the text. The castle signifies how literary texts operate with an absence at their core; however, such absence is also what compels us to interpret and engage. The nothingness and absence at the core of the text has its own power. Because the text has a capacity for finite rather than infinite survival, the very absence and negation also reveals possibility. Put abstractly, the literary text is never pure nothingness or pure death but is a way of 'holding open a space for a future that is not the dead repetition of the past'.[13] What the literary text reveals as most universal is how human possibility, value and creation coalesce with a temporal account of human life. Blanchot's ideas presuppose loss and nothingness to be constitutive of what we are. We are haunted by the 'anonymous', by the generic versions of ourselves in the past, present and future. The literary text's primary virtue is the ethical capacity which reveals that what is most fundamental about the human is not that it dies as a subject, but rather that it dies impersonally, that 'one' dies as everyone else.[14]

Blanchot's themes are clearly discernible in McCarthy's novel. Questions of human alienation, death and birth, the foreclosure of ecstatic time, lack, absence and incompletion, bring us to the philosophical dimensions of *Suttree* and how we can conceive McCarthy in a philosophical way. *Suttree* is a novel of unworking, of desubjectification. *Suttree* stages an abject unworking of the individualism of its central character, as well as a relentless unworking of alienated communal ties and bonds. *Suttree* is a great American anti-novel, a novel that renders manifest the absence at the core of the book of America, staging an 'elemental conflict between life and death in the sewage and detritus of American exceptionalism'.[15] McCarthy's philosophical wager relies on Suttree surviving the negative paralysis which defines his existence. Suttree is a lonely figure who exists between various communities and is uncomfortable in them all. Suttree is a figure of stasis, stunted growth and stagnation.

Suttree, form, negation

The philosophical import of *Suttree* as a Blanchotian text can be understood in several contexts and not least in the form of the novel, specifically the way the text is organised around the polluted Tennessee River. Movement, flow and transformation are embedded in the unfolding of the story and manifest Suttree's struggles with becoming and death. In addition, the topography of Knoxville, a hollow foundationless city, indicates Blanchot's anonymous void which besets all dramatic *personae* with 'ontological anxiety'.[16] The thematic of birth and death, the intersection of life and death and the threat of the feminine are ubiquitous throughout the text. Finally, and in opposition to a characterisation of Suttree as an existential voluntarist, the ethical and philosophical stakes of the novel require the evacuation of Suttree's subjectivity in his confrontation with death. *Suttree*, rather than offering a valorisation of the self, presents a central character that must come to terms with the negation of himself. The self with which Suttree battles is a symptom of nihilism, represented in the form of his dead twin. Suttree needs to integrate death into his character by the end of the novel. If there is a 'redemptive' thrust to the novel, it is that Suttree can discern and live along with a mortal past, present and future despite the relentless generational pressure that besets his human origins. Furthermore, within the text the idea of a secure self always features in the context of exchange. In other words the self becomes a unit of currency, interchangeable, a cheap attempt to stave off death, whether in relation to Suttree's drunken orgiastic relations with his community of outcasts, in exchange with nature in his anti-pastoral wanderings in the mountain, in terms of bourgeois quasi-security with Joyce, or in the pastoral idyll he briefly experiences with Wanda.

In formal terms, the structure of the novel oscillates between birth and death. This can be evidenced in the manner in which the material world unravels any attempt Suttree makes to assert his own lonely self-reliance. Suttree maintains an uneasy concord with the ebb of the river. He haphazardly fishes, gains minimal sustenance and nourishment, exists in a ramshackle houseboat on the threshold of water and land, and thus is at odds with both the inside and the outside of society. However, the river does not offer Suttree a vision of his sovereign individuality and nor does it, as it does for Huckleberry Finn, offer an alternative to the world of convention. The used-condom-strewn river unremittingly confronts Suttree with images of stunted life and birth. The river as the chief figurative engine of the narrative functions in the same way as Blanchot's mysterious negativity, delimiting the possibility of any resolved meaning and any possibility of Suttree's triumphant self-assertion. The river disperses meaning in the orbit of unpatterned meetings, events and occurrences.

At the outset of the novel, we find Suttree fishing for carp while a dead body is 'fished' from the river. Later in the novel, the river confronts Suttree with a monstrous natality when a dead baby emerges from the river, 'Bloated, pulpy rotted eyes in bulbous skull and little rags of flesh trailing in the water like tissue papers.'[17] Hence, while Suttree is relatively at ease on the river in the beginning, the river constantly reminds him of the homunculus dead twin at his core. His ease in gliding above the polluted river is a mixture of life and death. Suttree, the fisherman of men, is bereft of salvation and the possibility of immortal life. Any life, even the most abject, is mixed with material decay.[18] Suttree notices 'with a feeling he could not name that the dead man's watch was still running'.[19] Time goes on. Becoming is the true reality that even death cannot stop. McCarthy is here reminding us that what Suttree cannot confront is that he is of a past, a present and a future. Suttree's escapism throughout the novel is his absorption in the present, as manifested through the world of Knoxville and the river.

In the formal structure of the novel itself, we see the emptiness and the void of consumer utility. *Suttree* provides us with a narrative of equalisation and impersonalisation. The figures of entrepreneurialism and the Protestant ethic of hard work, as represented most obviously by Suttree's own father, are unworked in a levelling gesture, one that sees patriarchal pomp, masculine self-assertion and unscrutinised self-belief negated via contact with the teeming world of the denizens and pariahs of Knoxville and the McAnally Flats.[20] Suttree's detestation of the community of the patriarch, which his father occupies, presents the possibility of another vision of the world, a beginning, one other than a world reified into the illusory perpetuity of economic success and efficiency. Consolidating such a notion, we see the logic of unworking in the ontological structure of the novel. What most obviously demonstrates McCarthy's Blanchotian aesthetic is the way the material world erupts and spews forth death in the form of cadavers, tombstones, industrial and human waste. In *Suttree*, death has a life of its own. The caves under the city are covered in slime, figuratively sticking the hollow core of Knoxville in place. The Tennessee River itself presents a constant reminder of slime, excrement and death. As congealed as the river may be, it is intransigently carrying its own will to survival, presenting a mocking and festering vision of Suttree's crystalline stasis in a world without future, wholly present, alongside a denied and contested past. Suttree's rejection of his dead child testifies to his incapacity to allow birth to come to fruition.

The traces of death are traces of an unreconciled past. McCarthy's literary achievement in *Suttree* is to show that the world of others, of previous generations, always leaves traces which impinge on present awareness in multiple ways beyond our immediate comprehension. Hence the novel deploys a regular eliding of first- and third-person narration. The lack of clear demarcation between first and third person, the regular use of Joycean stream of consciousness, the hallucinatory synthesis of madness and sanity all serve to intertwine the thoughts of Suttree with the lives of past and future worlds. 'Suttree' can only be Suttree to the extent to which his first-person narration is interrupted by the movement of the world that he forsakes and cannot integrate into his own existence. In Blanchotian terms, the formal structure of the novel represents the excess of death that Suttree cannot integrate into the coordinates of his own consciousness. The persistent insertion of the material world into his own consciousness performatively unworks Suttree's stubborn attempts to assert his own self-sufficiency. Both the inner world and the outer world, as much as the fate of Knoxville and Suttree, are the same. In some sense, the entire novel is McCarthy's reflection on the desubjectification of the human being.

Such desubjectification, it must be noted, is not a dehumanisation. As with Blanchot, the philosophical force of McCarthy's *Suttree* is that he is presenting another idea of what the human is. Human life is perpetually accompanied by the mute, the silent, the mysterious elements of impersonal and generic processes which exist alongside first-person subjective comprehension. There is as such no 'state' or 'object' called the human, only the acknowledgement, in an existential sense, that we are what we are not. Thus, *Suttree* is a novel of losers and failure: McCarthy attempts to understand the extent of this profound loss at the core of the human. Suttree himself engages in different activities throughout the novel to transcend his death. Suttree's desire to avoid confronting death does not resolve itself in a vertical religious transcendence. Instead, McCarthy aims to retain a sense of mystery alongside the reality Suttree inhabits. Suttree is a wanderer, looking for something that is not there. He attempts transcendence in rejection of his family and the ordered world of the American bourgeois, in alcohol, in the camaraderie of the pariahs, in domestic harmony with Joyce, in hallucinogenic trips, in the river itself, in his love affair with Wanda and in his hallucinatory trip with Mother She.

The persistence of such ontological uncertainty is evident in the precarious structure of Knoxville itself. His trip with Harrogate into the caves beneath in an act of risky self-sacrifice – and thus self-renunciation – is at the same time a trip into the core of the possibility of the novel. Positioned about halfway through the novel, Suttree finds the void, an ineluctable absence, where his character begins dimly to discern the intransigent presence of death. The anonymous absence at the core of the text, at the core of the City, at the core of Suttree's psyche, exists in a *mélange* of life and death. Nothingness breathes through any human construction, revealing the irreducible temporal facticity of our mortal life, 'In the damp and alveolar deeps beneath the city [. . .] Everywhere a liquid dripping, something gone awry in the earth's organs to which this measured bleeding clocked a constantly eluded doom.'[21] The city has a form of death at its core; nothing breathes through nothing. This is the death Suttree fears. It is the impersonal negation at the heart of all things about which Blanchot speaks.

What Suttree begins to discover is that there is no radical separation of death and life. As Blanchot would have it, the core of the novel and thus the core of Suttree's selfhood withdraws the nearer he gets to the impersonal absence at the centre of the text. This negativity transforms itself into something positive. The fundamental impermanence at the core of the city, in Blanchotian terms, compels Suttree to narrate, however confusedly, the interdependence of past, present and future, and also to present the impossibility of concluding narration itself. The impersonal void at the core of the text, represented by the 'filthy basilica' beneath Knoxville, reveals the possibility of something essentially human: survival in mortal time. Harrogate sets the tone for this spatial and temporal dislocation: 'He began to suspect some dimensional displacement in these descents to the underworld, some disparity unaccountable between the above and the below. He destroyed his charts and began again.'[22] Suttree's *catabasis* into the underworld begins to awaken recognition of something other than his immediately present self and selfishness. He dimly begins to discern that he is now not just of the present; he is not just of the current order of things. His rescue mission of Harrogate is remarkable for two reasons. Firstly, he notes no sound but a distant timeless dripping, the mute and vast nothingness, which is 'without boundary' and as 'large as the universe and as small as anything that was', and which is punctuated by the relentless 'sound' of time itself.[23] Secondly, at this moment, in the depths of the underworld, Suttree hears phantom noise and sees the spectral torchlight of children, which he ignores and returns to the surface. Throughout the novel, children symbolise futurity and possibility for Suttree. They represent possibility, birth, creation, regeneration and a sense of the possibility of a community of others. Again, this is not creation in a theological sense – the abyss beneath Knoxville is after all an unholy church – but in the philosophical sense. Children are generational markers who demonstrate the irrevocable interdependence of the past, present and future. At this point, the only child Suttree has his mind on is Harrogate. Harrogate's 'salvation' is Suttree's 'salvation'.

Suttree and the death of creation

Suttree, as well as many of the other characters in the novel, is, as Richard Sennett puts it, subject to a corrosion of character.[24] Suttree has no temporal arc; this absence is defined by a deficit of narrative. The story of Suttree is thus in Blanchot's terms an anti-story, a novel of unreconciled characters, without place or belonging in a world grimly repeating a dead past in the face of relentless change. It is the incapacity to confront the historicity of human life that drives the tragic force of Suttree. Such incapacity to confront the historical existence of the human is consolidated by McCarthy's anti-pastoralism. *Suttree* is anti-Edenic in composition, as demonstrated from the outset by the bathos of Harrogate, 'the moonlight melon-mounter', and his stunted sexual copulation with a watermelon.[25] This is important, because as well as demonstrating the fundamental alienation and homelessness of the characters, it illuminates the perversion of creation and thus of possibility. If time is a marker of both death and creation, then the characters of *Suttree* are fundamentally without time and thus remain imprisoned in a mortal purgatorial lot. As much as Suttree is embedded in the past, Harrogate remains tied to the repetition of his scams. Beyond *Suttree*, in McCarthy's other fiction we find similar sentiments, specifically with characters out of step with the movement of history, unreconciled to their own mortal origin. The Parham brothers in *The Border Trilogy*, the sheriff in *No Country for Old Men*, Culla Holme in *Outer Dark* and effectively all of humanity in *The Road* are at odds with their birth and their origin, alienated from the unfolding of history.

McCarthy makes the same direct philosophical point in *Cities of the Plain*. The ontological status of human existence, for McCarthy, requires history as the condition of human development; it is the acknowledgement of the temporal arc of human affairs which is essential to what we are:

> The world of our fathers resides within us. Ten thousand generations and more. A form without history has no power to perpetuate itself. What has no past can have no future. At the core of our life is the history of which it is composed . . . [26]

In philosophical terms, the conditions of the possibility of existing require, in Heideggerian terms, an ecstatic relation between past, present and future. The only way there can be a future is if there is a past, and the only way there is a past is insofar as it generates a future.

The tragedy of Suttree, and the difficulties which beset his existence, is that he remains absorbed and entangled in the material present and immediacy of his world. Suttree struggles to elevate himself to the recognition that he is an exemplar of all humans. This is Blanchot's anonymous neuter at the core of all texts. Every text is a story and every story confronts singular humans with universal predicaments and, as such, with the negotiation of further narration. It is only when we can negate our individual, self-sufficient selves that we gain insight into a sense of ourselves as exemplars of all humans. In this way, Suttree corresponds to the cold comfort that Billy Parham receives at the end of the *Cities of the Plain*, when he recognises 'that a man's life was little more than an instant and that as time was eternal therefore everyman was always and eternally in the middle of his journey, whatever be his years or whatever distance he had come'.[27]

In terms of McCarthy's proximity to Blanchot, we see that McCarthy's fictional worlds are not efficient, they are not smooth, and the utility of modernity tends to bring its own curses. The anti-Edenic theme demonstrates the impossibility of a primary peace from its inception. The world is violent to its roots, a negation that is a contingency and excess that compels human action as the foundation of any good and evil. For McCarthy, there is originary violence at the depths of all existence, providing a literary aesthetic to view *Suttree*, which is at odds with the gilded 1950s age. For McCarthy there is 'no such thing as life without bloodshed [. . .] the notion that the species can be improved in some way, that everyone could live in harmony, is a really dangerous idea'.[28]

In fact, the entirety of *Suttree* presents an unworking of this notion, especially through the representation of the unsavoury underbelly of American capitalism. Commerce and trade are associated with putrefaction and corruption. In what is McCarthy's most political and class-conscious novel, *Suttree* is a vision of an America that works unworked, in the Blanchotian sense. The philosophical lampooning of work, combined with the productive power of uselessness, finds its zenith in Harrogate's character. Harrogate is Suttree's idiot twin and his surrogate. Harrogate offers the only real hope of 'salvation' that can counteract both Suttree's own dead child and his double anti-twin. There is a 'salvation' possible for Suttree in Harrogate. His care for Harrogate is as for a child. He is a 'good boy' on Suttree's hearing of his incarceration at the end of the novel. Harrogate represents underdeveloped growth and possibility.

As a satire of the American self-made man, it is Harrogate's indefatigable diligence which is continually his undoing. His comic attempts to realise the American Dream lock Harrogate in the present, unable to transcend his existence, perpetually remaining the 'city rat' whose main achievement is constructing a bourgeois paradise from bric-a-brac. The slapdash entrepreneurialism of Harrogate only ever remains a form of underdeveloped creativity and ultimately leads to a destructive end. What he brings into existence is essentially combined with failure. Harrogate mirrors Suttree's absorption in the present, devoted to the now. He is benign, yet also impish and demonic, mixing destruction and creativity, flitting from one get-rich-quick scheme to another. His philosophical function in the novel acts as a destabilisation of the self-assuredness and self-perpetuity of typical narratives of American success. His innocence, however, is combined with destruction. He offers a critique of the entrepreneurial self that brings comic relief to the excesses of Suttree's extreme brooding and solemn existential gravitas. Despite his sex obsession, the perpetual rebirth of his scams and the recycling of his character, Harrogate is a figure that Suttree persistently cares for, counsels and attempts to steer on the right path, and therefore he presents Suttree with the possibility to unwork and repudiate his wilful luxuriance and self-absorption in his own isolation. Harrogate maintains within the orbit of Suttree's existence notions of contingency, the possibility of creation, and most importantly the thought that things can be otherwise. Harrogate challenges Suttree's immediate self-absorption with an ever-present sense that possibility is always to hand. Thus, he is in Blanchotian terms possessed of a unique negative capacity.

Suttree, history and the fateful feminine

In addition to Harrogate's character, Blanchot's logic of the sharing of death is nowhere more evident than in Suttree's persistent rejection of women and children. The experience of the fatal feminine is code for the possibility of past and future, of a fraught but generational solidarity, the trials of others, the mortal designation of life and the irreducible acknowledgement of a fraught generational solidarity. Suttree, son of Grace, rejecter of his patriarchal lineage, remains in conflict with the possibilities of maternal life.

In general, female figures within *Suttree* can rightly be seen corresponding to hackneyed types such as grieving wife, prostitute, mother, succubus and nymphet, acting largely as mere functionaries illustrating Suttree's psychological state.[29] This representation of women is most discernible with regard to marginal female figures. Suttree recoils on numerous occasions when women confront him with sexual possibility. Sexual possibility can double for natality. Natality in *Suttree* denotes the intersection between past, present and future. The problem in the novel, however, is that for Suttree, life is always split from death. Death is his death and thus signifies his inability to reconcile the present with possibility. After the bar room brawl, he finds himself in hospital flirting with a nurse. The nurse rooms in an 'old morgue', and when she indicates her availability, Suttree quickly leaves. Also, Suttree recoils from Aunt Alice's elderly friend who flirts with him.[30] Suttree has a one-night stand, cruelly abandoning the girl in his houseboat to help Leonard's scam to bury his dead father.[31] The literary function of women in *Suttree* is thus as meaning-bearers for creation, possibility and the sense that life is the temporal duration which Suttree is failing to come to terms with and actively bridles against. Suttree's stunted growth within the broader structure of the novel is particularly manifest in his relation with Joyce. In spring when there is a thawing of relations with Joyce, there is not rebirth but death. Suttree notices that Joyce gains weight, that she is a self-harmer, her ablutions and cleansing become grotesque, her douche bag is like a bladder.[32] Joyce and Suttree's domestic parody illuminates Suttree's general discomfort towards female and transgendered characters. Joyce's internals become external; the material forcefully irrupts onto Suttree's self-regard, denoting the ethical and philosophical thrust of the novel.

While the representation of women is weak, once we philosophically contextualise this representation, we can see McCarthy making another point.[33] It is persistently the rejection of the feminine by Suttree, in conjunction with the rejection of children, that is the major impediment to any deepening of his understanding of the human condition. There are several instances where this becomes apparent, not least in his problematic and contested relationship with his dead twin, as well as with his own dead child and abandoned partner. When visiting his Aunt Martha – prior to which he rejects a baptismal ceremony – Suttree is confronted with the generational lineage of his own mother's line through some old photos that Martha shows him.[34] Martha – named for the Biblical witness of Lazarus's rebirth – presents Suttree with the impasse of life, death and becoming. Lazarus is an appropriate reference here. As Blanchot shows, Lazarus, a figure of life *and* death, is precisely what Suttree resists.[35]

The dead child in the photograph which is shown to Suttree at this point 'appears sinister, like the fruit of forbidden liaisons'.[36] This child presents a double bind. Suttree becomes subject to an allergen and as such rejects his own past, the possibility of the future, as well as the interdependence of the three. The woman-child-Suttree function allows McCarthy to show how an alternative generational solidarity may emerge. The photograph-cum-negative is emblematic of a stasis of the before and after. There is, for Suttree's psychological wholeness, nothing worse than a child. The child represents the threat of being absolutely determined by others. For example: 'The old musty album', reeks of 'the vault, turning up one by one these dead faces . . .'[37] Here Suttree glimpses his philosophical origin. He is the 'artifact of prior races'.[38] The equation of his sense of 'I' with a relic bespeaks the stasis of his identity at the nexus of generational change. Furthermore, his maternal lineage becomes constructed wholly in the negative when conjoined with the dead child in the photograph, 'Bloodless skull and dry white hair, matriarchal meat drawn lean and dry on frail bone, a bitter refund ashen among silk . . .'[39] The mother is bluntly figured as a piece of dead meat. We should not, however, take this literally. It is possible to understand this as necessary for an expression of the philosophical stakes of Suttree's rejection of time, possibility and generations. The dead past is alive; death itself is present and cannot be overcome but has its own form of life. This truth is unpalatable to Suttree and drives his own self-destruction and existential quandary.

The most overt representation of McCarthy's negation of self-valorisation is evident in Suttree's rejection of patriarchy, as represented in his encounter with the sheriff after he gate-crashes his son's family's funeral preparations. The sheriff, the repository of absolute meaning and law, presents Suttree with no alternative, 'That's where you are wrong my friend. Everything's important. A man lives his life, he has to make that important.'[40] The meeting with the sheriff is bookended by violent and abrupt attacks by the mother of his child and a random youth he meets.[41] At this point, Suttree is as such lost between the child as the symbol of lost potential, and the unquestioning authority of the sheriff, which denotes Suttree's inability to connect the future and the past, as well as his inability to see potential in an acceptance of death. Immediately after, McCarthy directly draws attention to the relentless passing of time, marking the intransigent punctuation of

Suttree's life with time and mortality: 'There is a gap in the iron of one tire and above the meaningless grumbling of the wagon it clicks, clicks, with a clocklike persistence that tolls progress, purpose, the passage of time.'[42] Suttree's powerlessness to see time as a form of becoming as well as a form of negation defines the tragedy of the recurring motif of women-children. The span and duration of life is only ever stasis for Suttree. Suttree is atemporal and embedded in the now. During Suttree's wandering he comes across an abandoned slave plantation, outside which 'Old paint on an old sign said dimly to keep out. Someone must have turned it around because it posted the outer world. He went on anyway. He said that he was only passing through.'[43] This symbol defines the confusion of the past, present and future. The present is out of joint, inside and outside is no longer demarcated, human borders are arbitrary. For Suttree, there is no orientation of the past and present. The decaying Southern plantation is of the present, it has not passed, everything is incarcerated in a rotten festering now.

McCarthy's most extended consideration of Suttree's potential recovery in relation to the feminine comes through the figure of the woman-child Wanda. The visceral and material, rather than the spiritual, becomes McCarthy's focus in his construction of an anti-Eden. Suttree's introduction to Wanda is conjoined with a moment of bathos, where possibility and creativity are coupled with material bodily excretions: 'Through the fog Suttree was presented with a bony pointed rump. She pissed loudly in the river and rose and went in again.'[44] For a brief period in the novel, Suttree experiences a sense of wholeness and tranquillity as he is 'struck by the fidelity of this earth he inhabited and he bore it sudden love'.[45] The aesthetic is one of unity and harmony that sustains an ersatz immortality. The intimation that Suttree impregnates Wanda leads to the 'hiss of meteorites through the blind stellar depth'.[46] Of course, the whole point of the Garden of Eden is that it does not end well: Biblical retribution in the form of a flood kills Wanda. Wanda represents youth, regeneration and revival, the future and possibility, as well as some sense that Suttree can integrate the death of his own child. However, Suttree remains tied to the present and the mechanical during his sojourn with Wanda. He reads car manuals and she reads *Mildred at Home* in a vision of unreal quasi-domesticity.

The death of Wanda is thus absolutely necessary within the aesthetic of the novel; if Suttree is to gain philosophical knowledge about the human condition, he must puncture the uneven, dissymmetrical and self-contained fantasy he occupies with Wanda. The period with

Wanda is represented as whole. Tranquil and temporal life is experienced only on Suttree's own terms. Hence, the diabolical harbingers Vernon and Fernon undermine Suttree with a monstrosity other than himself. Vernon and Fernon are simpatico, displaying a 'happy acceptance of their sameness'.[47] They are interchangeable, confronting Suttree with the possibility of a sinister reconciliation with his own self. Rather bluntly, Vernon and Fernon demonstrate the monstrosity and solipsism of self that is present to itself. They confront Suttree with an easy and comfortable stasis and sameness and thus, paradoxically, they are manifestations of the brute individualism that represents the hindrance to Suttree's recovery. Vernon and Fernon's world is directly atemporal, both 'despise a wristwatch', and thus the death of Wanda becomes inevitable. Where there cannot be time, the possibility of life cannot happen, the world must come to an end, so Suttree's psychic self-containment becomes visible in the Biblical flood which kills Wanda.[48] Suttree always stumbles when faced with female characters as they represent birth, reproduction, newness and are simultaneously marked by irretrievable loss.

The logic of natality as negation comes to full fruition through Suttree's relations with Mother She. Mother She is Suttree's Diotima, the ender of plagues. The folk-healer succubus marks, from Suttree's perspective, the *telos* of Joyce's transformation into a grotesque, which directly confronts Suttree with the ethical necessity of negating his own self-sufficiency and isolation.[49] While critics are rightly cautious about McCarthy's pejorative language regarding female genitals, there is another way of reading Suttree's encounter with Mother She and the 'sexual nightmare' he experiences after he takes her potion.[50] The encounter with Mother She functions as another index of the Blanchotian absence at the core of the text and Suttree must break through the other side of his own negation: 'He was being voided by an enormous livercoloured cunt with prehensile lips that pumped softly like some Levantine bivalve. Into a cold dimension without time without space and where all was motion.'[51] Mother She denotes the ultimate negation of Suttree's own self; Suttree must give an anti-birth to himself. Suttree is his own afterbirth.

Certainly, Mother She is a grotesque, but grotesques, too, can generate possibility. Mother She is after all a prophetess, a figure who exists between the past, the present and the future. Suttree's failure to relate to women is an index of his failure to reconcile with creation. Mother She instigates his *anabasis*. Philosophically, the literary function of Mother She is to make apparent to Suttree firstly a Blanchotian evacuation of his own subjectivity, secondly the acceptance of negation and thus death at the core of his life, and thirdly a core humanity where all vestiges of Suttree's narcissism are undermined through his absolute abjection. The encounter with Mother She leads Suttree to expunge his own innards, signifying an integration of his own hollowness. In the context of Nietzsche's death of God, Suttree is an anti-Christ-figure, of the world, of matter, of death and more at ease with his own monstrosity.[52]

Ultimately, as we will see in the conclusion to this chapter, it becomes unsurprising that the figures of women and children offer a palliative to Suttree's own self-destruction for a character as self-destructive as he. For a character that exists on the threshold of death, the function of women and children in the novel is decisive for challenging Suttree's one-to-one relationship with death and thus with himself. McCarthy forces Suttree to the ultimate existential question, why live? *Suttree* is McCarthy's philosophical reflection on the question of suicide. For example, Suttree's anti-Thoreauian *catabasis* into a monstrous and indifferent nature sees him emerging as an indistinct figure of what Giorgio Agamben calls 'bare life'.[53]

As Blanchot argues, suicide, as an act of pure voluntarism, attempts to arrest the movement and historical development of life. Suicide marks a decision, in itself an absolute incision, bringing to an end both the past and the future. Suicide is a punctuation; a separation of life and death. As Blanchot suggests, suicide is the ultimate moment of voluntary self-control, confronting death and forsaking life. Suttree's *anabasis* can only emerge when he figuratively becomes living-death, when death and possibility are not separated. McCarthy remains consonant with the central Blanchotian reflection that death is not separate from life but radically entwined with it:

> Death must exist for me not only at the very last moment, but as soon as I begin to live and in life's intimacy and profundity. Death would thus be part of existence; it would draw life from mine, deep within. It would be made of me and perhaps, for me, as a child is the child of its mother.[54]

Suttree wilfully performs a slow suicide across the text; his desire for self-control and independence is precisely the condition of his own destruction. The more the novel progresses, the closer Suttree comes to wilful self-destruction. In a literary sense, Suttree's suicide, precipitated by his diminished care of the self, would be required to bring an aesthetic unity to the novel, where he becomes the ultimate 'American existentialist'. Suicide would be the absolute rejection of convention for untrammelled individualism, the affirmation of rebellion, insubordination and liberty.[55] However, something else happens. Suttree does not in the end terminate his existence and thus does not exist in a self-contained sphere between life and death.

Suicide, for Blanchot, is the most rational and instrumental of all events, making of death a tool, the zenith of human efficiency.[56] More than anything, suicide works; it works efficiently, it is the ultimate means to an end. For McCarthy, Suttree's failure to end himself in his own protracted self-destruction reveals his acceptance of the intermingling of life and death, of the necessity of unworking. Suicide would be the ultimate affirmation of pure nothingness and death. Suttree, in the final analysis, avoids such a fate. He learns that all death is not just his death. The negation of the self, the death of the self, allows Suttree to discern possibility and creation. The death of Suttree is not his death; it is also the death of others, as well as the life and narration of others. Other stories begin where Suttree's story ends. His aloneness is ultimately monstrous. *Suttree* is a novel about others, because Suttree is never alone. Even when he is alone, he is haunted by himself. The suicidal arc of the text is about a one-to-one relationship between death and Suttree: death individuates Suttree. The dramatic unity of the novel is entirely dependent on Suttree overcoming this individuation, of seeing death as shared where death is the death of all others and is thus impersonal. This is where McCarthy directly corresponds with Blanchot's understanding of death, where Suttree, as the novel progresses, becomes radically de-individuated, aware of human origins, limitations and possibilities.

Conclusion

Throughout the novel, Suttree strives to cling to the vestiges of manifest destiny and fails; this failure is the negation that gives birth to a newer Suttree (represented by his recognition of a different type of double in the eye of the child in the final pages of the novel, as opposed to his twin and the torrid doubles that stalk him throughout). The ideal of self-sufficiency and self-reliance that is so relevant to American identity is wilfully displaced by McCarthy, and this is what makes the novel idiosyncratic and rare within American literature. Its aesthetic achievement, indeed its ethical force, resides in performing a philosophical-literary resistance to the sovereignty of the individual. The emancipatory force of *Suttree* is its recognition of the absolute evacuation of wilful subjectivity towards a horizon of a generic humanity. Questions of community, belonging, loss, loneliness and an unyielding anti-individualism haunt the novel. See Suttree's declaration, 'I am Suttree, there is one Suttree'.[57] This proclamation might be taken as an affirmation of a voluntaristic existential individualism, revealing Suttree's desires for personal integration and the achievement of his 'own centre'.[58] Alternatively, from a Marxist perspective, Suttree lapses back into bourgeois individualism.[59] In another way, it has been argued that Suttree is a novel about transcending death.[60] None of this offers the full story. As Douglas Canfield notes, Suttree is not in pursuit of 'obsessive uniqueness'.[61] Conversely, it is philosophical questions of the negation of the self, mortality and its consequences that are the fulcrum of the text and that make *Suttree* philosophically interesting and ethically relevant.

Blanchot's acknowledgement of the literary text's resistance to categorisation dovetails with McCarthy's *Suttree*. If the literary text is an exercise in delimiting the sovereignty of the self, *Suttree* corresponds to this logic. McCarthy gives literary form to Blanchot's insight that there is an impersonal universal dimension of human existence that haunts us from our inception. Suttree's liberation is not one of voluntaristic self-assertion, but instead it remains a freedom that is very precarious, where the contingency of the world gives birth to ethical possibility. During Suttree's sexual nightmare, we see Suttree haunted by a procession of the dead.[62] The return of the dead, that haunting of life by the dead, of the survival with death, is the cornerstone of McCarthy's literary-philosophical position. McCarthy's work in general is an attempt to illustrate the essentially human, irrespective of self-regard, historic period, or identity. What McCarthy suggests is most human is, however, essentially paradoxical. The human is historical and temporal, irrespective of the period he is in. All humans have specific narratives, but those specific narratives are transcended by a shared mortality. Suttree discovers this at the close of the novel: 'I know all souls are one and all souls lonely.'[63]

McCarthy's Suttree acknowledges a vulnerable and chaotic world. This is an ontological commitment: *omnis malignia discordia*.[64] Following Blanchot's logic, *Suttree* is a novel of depersonalisation and universalisation. Towards the close, Suttree renounces his own self-regard: 'I said that I would take my own part against the slander of oblivion and against the monstrous facelessness of it and that I would stand a stone in the very void where all would read my name. Of that vanity I recant all.'[65] Where does this leave us? What positive ethical and philosophical insights can be extracted from McCarthy's worldview? *Suttree* is not a celebration of the abject for the sake of it. At the very end of the novel, the skeletal contours of Knoxville finally become manifest. The anti-Knoxville appears as a city made of old bone, indicating how Suttree rejects the static and deathly. There is no redemption, but there is a wary compromise with human mortality, and human complicity in the dynamics of the worlds it inhabits. Suttree, in the Nietzschean sense, is reconciling himself with creation; he is realising the power of possibility. Stasis, sameness is McCarthy's shorthand for pure nihilism. To become human, one must negate this nothingness. In simpler terms, the evacuation of Suttree's self throughout the novel coalesces in the human complicity in the birth of the universe, in the sensuous world, in matter, in the ghosts of others and ourselves and the generations with which we negotiate our existence. Suttree bears witness to another type of creation, the historical formation of human life alongside the historical formation of the world, 'for life does not come slowly. It rises in one massive mutation and all is changed utterly and forever. We have witnessed this thing today which prefigures for all time the way in which historic orders proceed.'[66]

I have argued in this chapter that any time Suttree is faced with his own individual mortality, there is a woman or child on the scene. In the epilogue, we see McCarthy combine several symbols of death, life and possibility, in the form of hunter, eunuch, child and water-bearer. Suttree walks down the street, 'until there was nothing left for him to shed. It was all gone. No trail, no track.'[67] Suttree's depersonalised self exists as a weak and gentle hunter of traces and tracks of the past. Also, there is a sleeping eunuch. The sleeping eunuch marks the quelling of Suttree's resistance to the future. And most significantly, Suttree receives water from a young boy, symbolising a tentative reconciliation with possibility. The young boy defines the intersection of future and past. Rather than the Tennessee River being shorthand for contamination and decay, water now becomes a gentle symbol of gratuity, potential and hope. Suttree sees his reflection and double in the eye of the child.[68] The anti-Suttree is refigured. The anti-Suttree was never his double, but philosophically a monism, that is, an absolute and pure self-expression of the self. If the dominant images of the final pages of *Suttree* are hunter, eunuch, child and reflection, then Suttree in the eye of the child is the Suttree where the perishability of life coexists with possibility and potential.

Suttree, in an attempt at self-assertion and self-reliance, is a being without transcendence, of past, present and future. Suttree's problem is that he is absolutely determined and ahistorical. If persistent McCarthyian themes are generations, alienated generations and people trapped in ahistorical loops, then by the end of the novel it is no accident that Suttree, the fisherman, reaches a partial reconciliation with water. So too, as I have shown, the ethical and philosophical stakes of *Suttree* depend on Suttree's inability to overcome being anchored to the world. Suttree ends as a 'between', an ecstatic elongation of past, present and future. Suttree at this point exhibits a defiant readiness, because he can now confront the obstinacy of death whose 'hounds tire not'.[69] It is thus fitting that the last words of the novel are 'Fly them'.[70]

Notes

1. Garry Wallace, *Meeting Cormac McCarthy Plus 9 Notable Essays of The Year* (Independent: CreateSpace Independent Publishing Platform, 2012), 15.
2. I use the term 'anti-novel' in the sense that *Suttree* offers a reflexive undermining of the conventions of the novel. *Suttree* is obviously not the first or only novel to do this. I will herein argue that what is distinctive about how *Suttree* subverts the conventions of novel can be understood more clearly following the philosophy of Maurice Blanchot.
3. Maurice Blanchot, *The Unavowable Community*, trans. Pierre Joris (Barrytown: Station Hill, 2000), 5–6.
4. Blanchot, *Blanchot Reader*, ed. and trans. Michael Holland (Oxford: Blackwells, 1995), 141.
5. Blanchot, *The Work of Fire*, trans. Charlotte Mandell (Stanford: Stanford University Press, 1995), 301.
6. Ullrich Haase and William Large, *Blanchot* (London: Routledge, 2001), 18–19.
7. Blanchot, *The Space of Literature*, trans. Ann Smock (Lincoln: University of Nebraska Press, 1990), 54.
8. Blanchot, *The Space of Literature*, 26.
9. Maurice Blanchot and Jacques Derrida, *The Instant of My Death/ Demeure: Fiction and Testimony*, trans. Elizabeth Rottenberg (Stanford: Stanford University Press, 2000), 69.
10. Blanchot, *The Space of Literature*, 30–1.
11. Ibid. 205.
12. Ibid. 78.
13. Lars Iyer, *Blanchot's Communism: Art, Philosophy and the Political* (Basingstoke: Palgrave-Macmillan, 2004), xi.
14. Blanchot, *The Work of Fire*, 320.
15. John Cant, *Cormac McCarthy and the Myth of American Exceptionalism* (London: Routledge, 2009), 106.
16. Verneen Bell, *The Achievement of Cormac McCarthy* (Louisiana: Louisiana State University Press, 1988), 89.

17. Cormac McCarthy, *Suttree* (London: Picador, 2010), 368.
18. Douglas Canfield, 'The Dawning of the Age of Aquarius: Abjection, Identity, and the Carnivalesque in Cormac McCarthy's Suttree', *Contemporary Literature* 44, no.4 (Winter 2003): 670.
19. McCarthy, *Suttree*, 10.
20. Ibid. 13–14.
21. Ibid. 315.
22. Ibid. 316.
23. Ibid. 332.
24. Richard Sennett, *The Corrosion of Character: The Personal Consequences of Work in the New Capitalism* (New York: Norton, W. W. & Company, 1999), 47–8.
25. McCarthy, *Suttree*, 38.
26. McCarthy, *The Border Trilogy: All the Pretty Horses / The Crossing / Cities of the Plain* (London: Picador, 2007), 1026.
27. McCarthy, *The Border Trilogy*, 1027.
28. Richard B. Woodward, 'Cormac McCarthy's Venomous Fiction', *New York Times Magazine*, 19 April 1992.
29. In addition to pejorative representations of women, the question of abjection may also be extended to questions of race. For the most nuanced and thoughtful account of race, see Noemí Fernández Labarga, '"No gray middle folk did he see": Constructions of Race in *Suttree*', *The Cormac McCarthy Journal* 18, no.2 (Fall 2020): 128–46.
30. McCarthy, *Suttree*, 233, 522.
31. Ibid. 300–1.
32. Ibid. 486–7.
33. Christopher Walsh, *In the Wake of the Sun: Navigating the Southern Works of Cormac McCarthy* (Connecticut: Newfound Press, 2010), 192.
34. Thomas D. Young, 'The Imprisonment of Sensibility: *Suttree*', in *Perspectives on Cormac McCarthy*, ed. Dianne Luce and Edwin T. Arnold (Jackson: University Press of Mississippi, 1999), 101–2.
35. Blanchot, *The Space of Literature*, 196.
36. McCarthy, *Suttree*, 152.
37. Ibid. 154.
38. Ibid.
39. Ibid. 155.
40. Ibid. 189–90.
41. Ibid. 195.
42. Ibid. 196.
43. Ibid. 164.
44. Ibid. 370.
45. Ibid. 427.
46. Ibid. 432.
47. Euan Gallivan, 'Cold Dimensions, Little Worlds: Self, Death, and Motion in *Suttree* and Beckett's Murphy', in *Intertextual and Interdisciplinary*

Approaches to Cormac McCarthy, ed. Nicholas Monk (Albuquerque: University of New Mexico Press, 2002), 152.

48. McCarthy, *Suttree*, 433.
49. Ibid. 545–6.
50. Ibid. 542.
51. Ibid. 545–6.
52. Ibid. 548.
53. Giorgio Agamben, *Homo Sacer: Sovereign Power and Bare Life*, trans. Daniel Heller-Roazen (Stanford: Stanford University Press, 1998), 88.
54. Blanchot, *The Space of Literature*, 125.
55. Ibid. 95.
56. Ibid. 99.
57. McCarthy, *Suttree*, 557.
58. William C. Spencer, 'The Seventh Direction, or Suttree's Vision Quest', in *Myth-Legend-Dust: Critical Responses to Cormac McCarthy*, ed. Rick Wallach (Manchester: Manchester University Press, 2000), 107.
59. David Holloway, *The Late Modernism of Cormac McCarthy* (Westport, CT: Greenwood Press, 2002), 140.
60. Bell, *The Achievement of Cormac McCarthy*, 67.
61. Canfield, 'The Dawning of the Age of Aquarius', 681.
62. McCarthy, *Suttree*, 548.
63. Ibid. 553.
64. Ibid. 557.
65. Ibid. 499.
66. Ibid. 554.
67. Ibid. 565.
68. Ibid. 567.
69. Ibid. 568.
70. Ibid.

Chapter 3

Spirits in Cinderland: *Blood Meridian*'s Nietzsche

Blood Meridian is renowned for its spectacle of violence. The novel can easily be considered to reveal McCarthy at his most fatalistic and nihilistic. Indeed, it is difficult to appraise the novel as anything other than a cynical, nihilistic and resigned acceptance of the inescapable reality of war, with *Blood Meridian* seducing the reader with an aesthetic ballet of murderous mayhem, revelling in a grotesque phantasmagoria of gore and spilt innards. This is a fair assessment to some extent; *Blood Meridian* is not a moral book. In no way does the novel provide prescriptions on how to behave well. It offers very little in the way of guidance to humans pursuing meaning, purpose and flourishing. Thus, nihilism is unquestionably at stake. However, to suggest McCarthy endorses nihilism is mistaken. While there is little if any moral reprieve from the relentless brutality found within *Blood Meridian*'s pages, it does provide a philosophical thought experiment, a literary provocation, forcefully probing how readers might cope or liberate themselves from the most adverse of conditions.

In the same way I argued in Chapter 2 that *Suttree* actively resists classification, in *Blood Meridian* the implacable force of violence present actively resists any potential for moral or literary classification. Violence, war and the overweening superciliousness of Judge Holden ensures that the novel has no moral fulcrum whilst actively nullifying meaning. This resistance to moral and literary classification is compounded by Judge Holden's totalitarian sovereignty over the novel. The rhetorical power of the Judge looms so large that the reader may be seduced by his perverse moral logic. Outstripped only perhaps by Vladimir Nabokov's Humbert Humbert, Judge Holden is one of literature's great seducers. The Judge's joy in cruelty titillates and entices the reader with the pleasures of amorality, domination and consequence-free violence. *Blood Meridian*'s Judge Holden challenges any reader with the metaphysical hypothesis that reality itself is war, which in turn offers the reader a glimpse of the joy of the unlimited freedom of the tyrant. If the cosmos itself is inherently violent, constituted out of struggle and war, it follows that morals and principles themselves must also be cruel and savage, since they are inextricably derived from that very reality. Things can be no other way. The question is, does McCarthy provide any alternative to Holden's nihilism?

In *Understanding Cormac McCarthy*, Steven Frye argues that *Blood Meridian* offers only very transitory alternatives to nihilism, in that questions of 'meaning, purpose, and value' yield 'answers only in bright but fleeting glimpses'.[1] More significantly, Vereen Bell's landmark 1983 study explains McCarthy's 'ambiguous nihilism'. Bell argues that with McCarthy, 'ethical categories do not rule, and moral considerations seem not to affect outcomes', so 'the action and events are defined by caprice and incomprehensibility'.[2] For Bell, McCarthy's early literature performs a nullification of any moral universe, where relief from the menacing spirit of violence and cruelty is acutely brief. Bell concludes that the nihilism in McCarthy's earlier novels is ambiguous, providing 'questions while supplying no answers'.[3] Regrettably, Bell does not further develop these specific insights on McCarthy's nihilism, in terms of either psychological or cultural effect. It is therefore necessary to expand Bell's initial insights on McCarthy's earlier novels.

My premise is that McCarthy confronts nihilism nowhere more clearly than in *Blood Meridian*, and he does so in ways that can provide a clear response to Bell's observations about McCarthy's preceding work. Additionally, there is some critical attention devoted to Nietzschean readings of Judge Holden. These readings usually focus on his moral relativism, his valorisation of strength and will, the worship of war, the absence of God and the brutal implementation of the most rapacious forms of capitalism. Leo Daugherty has suggested that McCarthy in novelistic form goes as far as Nietzsche in philosophy.[4] Dana Phillips suggests that the Judge's rhetoric is a compound of Nietzschean and Spenglerian motifs.[5] Russell Hillier, too, describes Judge Holden as 'a self-styled Nietzschean superman'.[6] Similarly, Eric Williamson sees in Friedrich Nietzsche a direct philosophical complement to Judge Holden's savagery.[7] While Williamson offers one of the more sophisticated comparisons of Nietzsche's influence on *Blood Meridian*, his reading still draws on predictable interpretations of Nietzsche as an exponent of extreme individualism and amorality. Here McCarthy is cast as using Nietzsche instrumentally, for the purposes of warning against the deleterious consequences of a full-throated enactment of Nietzschean philosophy. In this reading, McCarthy in effect sets up Nietzsche to knock him down, in order to offer more virtue. The sense that McCarthy is doing battle with Nietzsche in *Blood Meridian* is replicated elsewhere. Emphatically, Denis Donoghue suggests, 'Nietzsche is Judge Holden's philosopher, not McCarthy's'.[8] Jay Ellis also offers a glimpse of how McCarthy's work struggles with Nietzsche, suggesting that the scholarly placing of Nietzsche and Judge Holden in tandem derives from an anxiety that both are 'invalidating morality'.[9] Of course they are, but in different ways, and thus my argument will show that we can read McCarthy's putative Nietzscheanism in a positive light.

This chapter will comprise four sections. The first will describe how *Blood Meridian* works formally and stylistically in articulating an intersection of ethics and ontology. This will be necessary because both the Judge and the kid construct different responses to this nihilistic universe. I will then proceed in the second section to provide a summary description of Nietzsche's account of active and passive nihilism. This will enable me to go on to explain in the third section how Judge Holden corresponds to what Nietzsche calls passive nihilism; I will argue that the Judge exhibits distinct traits of how Nietzsche classifies passive nihilism in the context of instrumentalism, superior morality and hierarchical violence. In the final section I will describe the kid as offering a constructive response to nihilism.

To understand the philosophical dimension of *Blood Meridian*, it is essential to understand how active and passive nihilism unfold for these characters, which will in turn expand our understanding of the philosophical concerns of McCarthy's novels. Overall, I will show that *Blood Meridian* can be understood as offering a cogent representation of Nietzsche's accounts of active and passive nihilism. This analysis will further enable me to outline how McCarthy conceives of the relationship between metaphysics and ethics. If nihilism implies a repudiation of philosophy, metaphysics and ethics, it is necessary to confront *Blood Meridian*'s representation of metaphysical collapse and amorality in order to explain the degree to which McCarthy thinks we can extricate ourselves from such a predicament.

War is all: the ontology of *Blood Meridian*

Donoghue perceptively argues that the dramatic potency of *Blood Meridian* emerges from a form of metaphysical undifferentiation. The idea is that the presentation of objects, cartography and the material world within the novel are foregrounded, whereas character, psychological agency, moral reflection and plot are secondary, derived from the novel's portrayal of the violence of nature itself.[10] There is an unnerving equality to how all objects and items in the novel are posed. Things – human, plant, animal, meteor and architecture – all blend, remaining unindividuated within McCarthy's 'optical democracy', where 'that terrain of all phenomena were bequeathed a strange equality and no one thing nor spider not stone nor blade of grass could put forth claim to precedence [. . .] and a man and rock become endowed with unguessed kinships'.[11] As Donoghue remarks, *Blood Meridian* has all objects, action and events correspond to McCarthy's neuter austerity. Consequently, McCarthy does not permit the reader to adjudicate on the moral status of any deed carried out by the characters. Any moral force or reckoning is co-opted through the novel's portrayal of existence itself. If all things are presented equally, then all things are good and bad indifferently. This formal style generates the novel's sharply stifling and oppressive atmosphere, one befitting the uncertainties of Judge Holden's moral relativism, where all acts are equally good and bad. The Judge's pernicious influence looms so large over the novel that he stifles all possible forms of alternative or exit, making character and reader interdependent on the Judge's noxious paradigm. This is particularly the case with the kid.

It is philosophically necessary that the kid is inextricably and metaphysically entwined with Judge Holden. That the kid develops under Judge Holden's perverse tutelage is dramatically necessary to allow the novel to scrutinise the scope through which one might transcend and liberate oneself from a needlessly cruel cosmos. Even if one inhabits the worst possible world, under the most domineering, dysfunctional and abusive pressures, *Blood Meridian* can provide some mitigated therapy. The kid's character brings some succour given his persistent desire to extract himself from his quandary as the novel progresses. Furthermore, the function of the dialectical interdependence of Judge Holden and the kid serves to illustrate McCarthy's rejection of simplistic moral binaries. Their symbiotic relationship also undermines a host of other simple dichotomies. As well as good and evil, *Blood Meridian*'s optical democracy and neuter austerity undermines any separation of matter and spirit, subject and object, self and other, or civilisation and nature. We find a particularly pointed example of McCarthy's rejection of Manichean thinking in his depiction of the wanton violence in the overrunning of a precarious settlement:

... all the horsemen's faces gaudy and grotesque with daubings like a company of mounted clowns, death hilarious, all howling in a barbarous tongue and riding down upon them like a horde from a hell more horrible yet than the brimstone land of christian reckoning, screeching and yammering and clothed in smoke like those vaporous beings in regions beyond right knowing where the eye wanders and the lips jerks and drools. Oh my god, said the sergeant.[12]

Here, irresistible violence swamps any markings of differentiation and civility. In this scene, the opposition of nature and civilisation is overswept by an indistinct force.

As Harold Bloom suggests, the 'violence is the book'.[13] This is a world without purpose, hope and redemption. The abyssal desert, scant vegetation backdropping the orgiastic violence, confines the reader to a claustrophobic and entangled mesh. However, the force of McCarthy's ontological 'democracy' makes it impossible for the kid to liberate himself. As opposed to a world where we may be saved through divine foundation, the metaphysics of *Blood Meridian* definitively suggests there is no underlying order or pattern to come to the rescue. The cruellest acts exist on the same plane as kindness, innocence and virtue, in the same sense that the kid's more redemptive traits are entwined with his own and the Judge's monstrosity:

If much in the world were mystery the limits of that world were not, for it was without measure or bound and there were contained within it creatures more horrible yet and men of other colors and beings which no man has looked upon and yet not alien none of it more than were their own hearts alien in them, whatever wilderness contained there and whatever beasts.[14]

McCarthy defines alienation and alienated life as the norm rather than the exception. Even more, beyond the limits of our world, there are infinitely new monstrosities awaiting.

Blood Meridian's lyrical hellscape demands of the reader violent passage through the worst excesses of war and violence. In a departure from the tragic tradition, there is no guarantee of any cathartic purification by the novel's *denouement*. Any possible connection to the glory and nobility of the epic is prohibited. The existential test the novel inflicts on the reader is whether they should acquiesce to the bloody and implacable logic of Holden's worldview, or construct alternatives to the worst iterations of life beyond good and evil. The novel uses the kid to place the reader in a position of moral compromise. The kid provides the novel's only sustained form of resistance to Holden. Despite *Blood Meridian*'s inexorable amorality, it is too simplistic to suggest that McCarthy is therefore endorsing either amorality or its inevitability. More accurately, McCarthy is examining how humans cope and struggle in a nihilistic world. *Blood Meridian* is a type of anti-Bible, effectively offering a version of David and Goliath. On the one hand we have the Goliath of Judge Holden's nihilism and on the other, we witness the kid's struggle to disentangle himself from Holden's dominion. Although complicit in the senseless scalping and murderous violence which the Glanton Gang inflict on Native Americans and Mexicans, we find in the kid a soul at stake, a David who faces down and attempts to extricate himself from the behemothic and toxic influence of Judge Holden.

As readers we are consigned to this metaphysical nightmare, inseparable from the wilderness forces that propel us. *Blood Meridian*'s weird metaphysics acknowledges that estranged inhumanity is still humanity. This estrangement is not absolutely determined, however: the kid's character, though incompletely and unsuccessfully, attempts to deviate from Holden's predetermining metaphysics. And as I will proceed to argue, this shows how McCarthy, through the kid, provides a more constructive Nietzscheanism.

Nietzsche matters: unravelling Holden's 'Nietzscheanism'

Friedrich Nietzsche's characterisation of active and passive nihilism illuminates the moral stakes of *Blood Meridian*'s core characters.[15] Nihilism describes the crises of meaning, purpose and direction precipitated by the death of god.[16] For Nietzsche, nihilism is not simply about the fact that the cosmos is without foundation in the broadest possible sense; the death of god also has innumerable pernicious consequences for the cultural, political and psychological projects of humans. The reality of metaphysical nihilism morphs into passive nihilism, or in psychological terms, when the consequences of a foundationless universe engender disappointment, self-abnegation and cruelty, and in the political and cultural sphere, resentment, resignation and cynicism. Nihilism, in its psychological iteration, transforms individuals into mere passive recipients of the external world. In addition, individuals become unable to garner any meaning from external moral principles. Consequently, contrary to conventional accounts of Nietzsche, the self becomes excessively inward, introspective, hyper-focused on one's own subjectivity as the only reliable guide to truth.[17] In summary, nihilism makes the self passively determined by history, rather than taking an active part in shaping how history unfolds in any meaningful way.

Active nihilism, on the other hand, is defined by a positive response to the exhaustion of all the possible outlets of meaning we find in passive nihilism. What Nietzsche calls *amor fati* is an argument for the acceptance of the futility of principles and ideals.[18] If we do not reject external moral foundations, we find ourselves channelling our psychological resentments into new false gods and idols in order to find some sure footing in an empty universe. Or, as Nietzsche puts it, we wallow in 'some supreme form of domination and administration'.[19] Active nihilism requires a joyful acceptance of becoming, where historical becoming has no goal or grand unity. All that remains are the actual events of history or, in other words, the occasion of truth itself. Disbelief and belief in eternal metaphysical worlds fail to acknowledge the 'reality of becoming' as the only reality.[20] For Nietzsche, the death of god tempts us with false prophets, false truths and idols that anaesthetise our ability to discern our own possibilities. And when it comes to false prophets, there are none more terrifying than Judge Holden.

The transvaluation of all values which Nietzsche instigates is designed as a therapy for all the practices of self-denial and resentment stemming from the loss of idols and ideals. *Amor fati*, eternal recurrence, the *übermensch*, affirmation, embodiment and sincerity are Nietzsche's putative antidotes to 'the ways of self-narcotization'.[21] This is a term for the practices of passive nihilism. Nietzsche names a variety of such practices including, but not limited to, cruelty, hatred of the prosperous, obsession, mechanised living, petty indulgences, mystical escapism and tribal fanaticism.[22] Placing these idols in the ascendancy forces humans to determine themselves in weak and narrow ways. We allow ourselves to become determined according to meagre ranges of possibility. On the other hand, active nihilism requires that human beings discern themselves truthfully, existing historically as temporal beings, understanding that they are unfinished and can exist with possibilities in view. Rather than being psychologically insular, for Nietzsche, the sincerest self can engage in productive acts which both accept and determine the fate in which it finds itself.

One can either affirm that humanity is a species of becoming, or one can become seduced by the deadening decline of static idols. Active nihilism thus indicates a type of dispositional power. Here one needs to comprehend oneself as a form of power, tendency or ability to do. Put simply, one is characterised by activity rather than passivity. This becomes a sign of strength for Nietzsche, with active nihilism necessitating the overcoming of existing conventions, whether legal, political or social, since all 'previous goals have become incommensurate'.[23] The primary virtue that Nietzsche extols in this context is that of courage. Rejecting existing values is dangerous, filled with risk and temptation by the dominant idols of the day. It should be noted, however, that active nihilism is not an end-stage one can reach. Rather, it is a transitional stage where one accepts the truth of a foundationless universe, whilst discerning the limited perspectives of conventional moral idols. In such a situation, one is demanded to proceed truthfully alongside one's historical fate. One can do good as well as evil beyond good and evil. This point firmly separates Nietzsche from Judge Holden since for Holden, a universe beyond good and evil only obliges us to do evil.

The question of naturalism is another point at which we can unravel Holden from Nietzsche. Nietzsche is often considered to advocate a naturalistic ethics.[24] If Nietzsche conceived of himself as a physician of culture inaugurating a therapy for nihilism, then Judge Holden clearly represents what Nietzsche designates as the nihilism of scientific materialism.[25] For Nietzsche, nihilism denotes very vulgar forms of positivism and materialism, which reject the historical and spiritual dimension of humanity in favour of a crudely materialistic view of life. Holden, as I will argue, elevates this materialistic view of life to its absolute 'apogee'. This is certainly Nietzschean in tone; Nietzsche's genealogy of morality does assert that our values and ideas have a 'base' origin, an origin we do not generate ourselves, that instead they originate in the historical forces and processes which precede the constitution of our values.[26] However, to say that such a genealogical conception of morality is equivalent to crude philosophical materialism would be mistaken. Philosophical materialism rests on the proposition that reality is reducible to, and composed by, basic units of matter. For Nietzsche, such an atomic conception of matter overlooks the question of how life emerges from inanimate substances or material.[27] As such, how does the interaction of material processes contribute to the emergence and existence of life? The problem for Nietzsche is that philosophical materialism conceives of matter without purpose, value and meaning.

In response, Nietzsche offers a more radical materialism, one that attempts to unite both the epistemological and ethical dimension of values. Famously, he achieves this through the doctrine of the will-to-power, where the basic material units of the universe are constituted through drives and impulses. This is a primeval form of experience, where all material things have a rudimentary will-to-power.[28] This will-to-power subsists as the passion or drive to persist and continue. Put another way, anything which exists has a drive to survive and seek out possibilities. Life emerges from the interaction of material things and our thoughts, actions and beliefs emerge through the lived world that we inhabit.

For Nietzsche, the question of nihilism is central to considering how we respond to this world as will-to-power. Either we permit ourselves to be passively determined by material processes as Judge Holden does, or we actively affirm the living materiality of a world in process. For Nietzsche, there is no stark demarcation between organic and inorganic life: all that matters is the desire to persist. Thus, the ethical stakes of Nietzsche's radical materialism hinge on both accepting and confronting the conceptions of our physical conditions. This is where we can distinguish Judge Holden from Nietzsche. Holden wilfully does not confront the predicament our natural constitution bequeaths us, but instead sacralises natural forces as the moral pivot of the universe, whereas Nietzsche asks us both to accept and transform the reality of our material constitution. The most important thing to understand about Nietzsche's critique of scientific materialism is that our ideas and thoughts do not emerge from the spiritual plane but from the material one. Nietzsche does not reject materialism *per se*, but he does reject a crass reductive materialism. Thus, while Nietzsche may be described as a materialist of the body or embodiment, he cannot be described as a mechanical materialist; to describe him thus would be merely to substitute a slavish worship of God for an equally slavish sacralisation of matter, which is precisely what Judge Holden does.

In *Blood Meridian*, it is easy to discern themes of active and passive nihilism at work. This is particularly the case in the pairing of the Judge and the kid. Both Holden and the kid operate in tandem, dramatising the consequences of active and passive nihilism. In both we find a fraught interdependence, as Judge Holden suggests: 'I recognized you when I first saw you and yet you were a disappointment to me. Then and now. Even so at the last I find you here with me.'[29] Both characters present literary explorations of the possibility of moral dispositions beyond good and evil, without the luxury and safeguard of conventional morality. McCarthy boldly poses the Nietzschean question: how exactly can we be just, if radical violence and chaos are the ultimate origin of our existence? *Blood Meridian* is an elongated meditation on the monstrous fact that humans are both good and evil. That it is impossible to separate these different moral dispositions shows McCarthy as a sophisticated Nietzschean whereas, as I will proceed to argue, Judge Holden is an unsophisticated one. McCarthy is not extolling a vulgar Nietzscheanism, one which recommends that we ought to be bad, self-creative and ruled by self-interested impulses. Instead, McCarthy demonstrates a much more subtle Nietzscheanism, one which works with the hypothesis that if we are beyond good and evil, then we are beyond evil also. The kid, who despite being pegged by the haunted Sproule as 'wrong all the way through', still has a soul at stake, represents the human's capacity to mitigate and renounce cruelty in the face of the ineradicable cruelty that constitutes our character.[30]

Judge Holden as passive nihilist

It does not require a great deal of examination to defend the claim that Judge Holden is the fulcrum of *Blood Meridian*'s nihilistic moral vacuum. The litany of cruelty, murder and manipulation which Judge Holden wreaks throughout the novel testifies to this. However, what is more interesting is the moral poses he adopts when engaging in ferocious violence. The cruelty of his acts is consistently accompanied by extolling the value of his activities. In one sense, Judge Holden is not amoral. While he certainly does amoral things, his actions are still quite markedly couched in a moral rationale and a language of values and metaphysics. In fact the Judge is an arch-moraliser, albeit a moraliser who transforms his values into exceptionally callous acts. His 'superior' morality is zealously Darwinian: might makes right, so casual cruelty is the only barometer of virtue. At the same time, throughout the novel, Judge Holden continually offers a moral apology of his worldview. We find evidence of this when he adjudicates a gun dispute:

> The judge smiled. It is not necessary, he said, that the principals here be in possession of the facts concerning their case, for their acts will ultimately accommodate history with or without their understanding. But it is consistent with notions of right principle that these facts – to the extent that they can be readily made to do so – should find a repository in the witness of some third party. Sergeant Aguilar is just such a party and any slight to his office is but a secondary consideration when compared to divergences in that larger protocol exacted by the formal agenda of an absolute destiny. Words are things. The words he is in possession of he cannot be deprived of. Their authority transcends his ignorance of their meaning.[31]

Judge Holden, as a Judge, resides both inside and outside the law. In the above passage we find him defending his moral cosmology with inflated legalese in a register both principled and transgressive. This legal jargon is founded on a preposterous morality of relativism – those taking part in legal proceedings are not privy to the facts of a case – yet Holden still mounts a distorted appeal to the putatively higher moral authority of history and absolute destiny. This appeal loosely corresponds to a sub-standard Nietzscheanism. However, this appeal does not, as Nietzsche does, attempt to transcend the phases of passive nihilism; instead, it cynically extols the worst values whilst masquerading them as the best. The Judge, too, has his idols.

The Judge rejects civilised virtues yet replaces them with his own external set of principles. Just prior to the preceding quotation, we find him appealing to a postmodern hodgepodge of disparate authorities including:

> the children of Ham, the lost tribes of Israelites, certain passages from Greek poets, anthropological speculations as to the propagation of races in their dispersion and isolation through the agency of geological cataclysm and an assessment of racial traits with respect to climactic and geographical influences.[32]

That Holden requires such a diffuse grounding for his 'principles' exposes the vacuous relativism he commends. For Nietzsche, revealing the hypocrisy of our existing morality is critical to let the future exist, to self-recognise ourselves as temporal beings, as beings with a past, present and future. But for Judge Holden none of this matters, since any authority is as good as any other, so ultimately what happens to the future is not an issue for him. In fact, he is largely concerned with reducing all things to the present. All that counts is cruelty perpetrated in the moment. A world without possibility is a salient if not defining feature of nihilism; Holden's pompous moralising serves to undermine possibility itself by revelling in dubious ethical standards.

The Judge's moral relativism is further bolstered by his mechanistic outlook. Judge Holden exalts a deeply instrumental view of human nature: people are valuable only insofar as they are useful vehicles to advance his warped version of history on a whim. Others are valuable only for their immediate use-value in advancing his higher cause, not for what they can become, or the extent to which they might actively determine themselves or overcome the blind impersonal processes of nature. All things are equally a means to the end that is war. As with his moral pronouncements, Holden's instrumentalism is also couched in value-laden terms specifically related to a vigorous determinism. The only world Judge Holden can discern is one of vulgar materialism, where it is impossible to elevate thought beyond the crude material world: 'Books lie, he said. God dont lie. No, said Judge Holden. He does not. And these are his words. He held up a chunk of rock. He speaks in stones and trees, the bones of things.'[33] Judge Holden's crude amalgamation of matter and spirit, or more strongly, the reduction of God to matter, denotes the passivity of his nihilism. The supposedly superior values he offers are utterly reactive, defined by the caprice of the 'gods' of material processes. Holden revels in a dearth of transcendence; there can be no exit or escape when all possibilities are foreclosed. There can be no alternative to Holden's impish moral contention that humanity's greatest achievements and endeavours are wrought from the same base origins of war and violence. The mere assertion of the moral value of instrumentalism should not be taken with any more depth than any juvenile utterance about the relativity of values. Therefore, it is again important to underscore that McCarthy is not endorsing Holden's worldview, even if we can still acknowledge that the creation of Judge Holden's terrifying appeal is a distinct literary achievement.

Judge Holden's passive nihilism is further evidenced through his cavalier mixture of the spiritual and rational. The Judge certainly could be viewed as a quasi-Nietzschean figure; however, his nominally Nietzschean view of nature is constructed ambiguously. McCarthy characterises him as containing elements of both the supernatural and natural, the rational and irrational, the scientific and sacred.[34] He is, though, more devil than Nietzschean *übermensch*. During the pursuit of the Glanton Gang aforementioned, Judge Holden resembles a Victorian naturalist, taking notes, observing flora and fauna, collecting plants and observing geological formations. The combination of preternatural ability and concrete manipulation of the environment illustrates Judge Holden's supernatural domination of material elements. It is notable that after recording each item in this way, he destroys it.[35] All that can be classified and counted is to be swept away. Such record-keeping, however, is not an indicator of chaos, but instead a marker of control, objectification and order, as if Holden asserts himself as a demi-god of chaos. Just as a cynical nihilist shelters from the disappointment of ideals and reality, Holden's cataloguing serves to underline a seething desire to dominate and own nature, which is why the 'freedom of birds' profoundly offends him.[36] While McCarthy consistently presents Judge Holden as preternatural in appearance – a twenty-four stone bald enigmatic albino carrying a gun inscribed with '*et in arcadia ego*' – his mastery of nature belies this otherworldliness. His competence in rendering the natural environment pliable indicates another dimension of Holden's passive nihilism which is appropriate to the Victorian period in which the novel is set, and to his vulgar mechanism, where nature is effectively a machine to be used.

We can detect further evidence of Judge Holden's 'spiritual materialism' especially when considering the part of the novel in which the Glanton Gang, low on ammunition, are pursued by Native Americans. The Judge leads the gang to mountain caves filled with bats. He subsequently sets up a kiln and manufactures gunpowder by distilling nitre from guano and powdered charcoal mixed with saltpetre, creek water and the gang's urine. This consequently enables the gang to massacre their pursuers. It is worth taking the time to understand both the theological and scientific dimensions of this scene, as McCarthy offers up the Judge as a mixture of a distorted spiritual and scientific synthesis. In a volcanic hellscape, Holden dominates matter, concocting gunpowder from sulphur and brimstone, a 'devil's batter' for the purpose of murderous slaughter.[37] The ex-priest Tobin draws a parallel between Judge Holden and 'sinners so notorious evil that the fires coughed em up again'.[38] Such observations ought not imply that we take any of Holden's geological, theological and geographical speculations seriously. Holden is a parody of a self-made renaissance man. As Tobin relates:

> Mayhaps he aint to your liking, fair enough. But the man's a hand at anything. I've never seen him turn to a task but what he didnt prove clever at it . . . God the man is a dancer, you'll not take that away from him. And fiddle. He's the greatest fiddler I ever heard and that's an end on it. The greatest. He can cut a trail, shoot a rifle, ride a horse, track a deer. He's been all over the world. Him and the governor they sat up till breakfast and it was Paris this and London that in five languages . . .[39]

The fiddle foreshadows Holden's final victory dance, but we should also remember that a fiddler is also a confidence trickster.

Throughout *Blood Meridian*, Holden indulges in constant geological and geographical speculation; the material world, however, is only there to be subordinated or used to advance his bellicose theology. Geological formations and the processes of material nature are wholly pliable, existing only to serve the purposes of domination.

The use of faeces and urine to concoct gunpowder only more force-fully reminds us that any noble goal or sense of common destiny is secondary to Judge Holden's nihilistic acceptance that material processes exist for the sole purpose of exploitation and control. Judge Holden's nihilism is thus defined through letting nature be itself and the task of humans is only to emulate this viciously Darwinian nature. Indeed, the only metaphysical avenue available, according to Judge Holden, is elevation of ourselves to the spirituality of war. Thus, Holden's instrumentalism and materialism have their own sacred logic and still subscribe to a superior 'moral code', albeit one that only serves as an instrument to abet his perverted materialism, expanding his corrosive destruction of the psychological realm to all of nature.

Judge Holden's nihilistic mix of the sacred and the material can also be discerned in his glorification of war. Here the passive nihilistic element is quite obvious, as found in the worship of destruction. Holden exults in war as the ultimate profession:

> War endures. As well ask men what they think of stone. War was always here. Before man was, war waited for him. The ultimate trade awaiting its ultimate practitioner. That is the way it was and will be. That way and not some other way.[40]

This spiritual reverence for war works on both an ontological and ethical level. In an ontological sense, war is the cosmos. In an ethical sense, accepting war as the fundamental metaphysical grounding of all that exists determines that the greatest spiritual status humans can ever achieve is one that unquestioningly accepts war as the father of all and king of all.[41] Therefore, if war is the ultimate productive force in the universe, then any effort to ennoble the human condition can only ever be another manifestation of war itself. Judge Holden goes so far as to suggest that engaging in the activities of war reveals humanity's truest nature. Within the sinister moral logic of his metaphysics, the human being can only reach its ultimate expression when it apes the viciousness of the material world. Anything else is delusional. The significance of Judge Holden's outlook on war and the attendant value of violence reveals the brute instrumentalism at the core of his thinking. It also reveals the simplicity of his philosophical position. Holden's nihilism is defined by classifying war and violence in purely instrumental and deterministic ways. Nature can only be as it is: humans must serve at the altar of war; things can never be otherwise. War and violence only operate as means to the end of war itself. Indeed, Judge Holden only celebrates means since war is holy; if we do not engage in war then we are effectively nothing other than matter.[42] We therefore have no choice but to accept the brutal truth of violence since this is just the way things are. But how seriously should we take these philosophical pronouncements?

Like McCarthy's other psychotic killer, Chigurh in *No Country for Old Men*, Judge Holden is a postmodern rationalist, committed to a weak simulacrum of reason and enlightenment, rather than a purveyor of any deeper truth. Despite the rhetorical flair McCarthy attaches to the Judge's proclamations, we should remain more than cautious of assigning any deeper significance to his utterances. For example:

> Whatever his antecedents he was something wholly other than their sum, nor was there system by which to divide him back into his origins for he would not go. Whoever would seek out his history through what unravelling of loins and ledgerbooks must stand at last darkened and dumb at the shore of a void without terminus or origin . . .[43]

When the Judge argues that we are without foundation or that our origins are impure, this is not consonant with what Nietzsche argues, since for Nietzsche, to be foundationless is an opportunity for creativity, possibility and transformation. The extent to which such utterances are not a manifestation of a coherent philosophical position is clear. If Judge Holden is archetypal, the archetype that best suits him is that of the trickster, or an 'old hoodwinker' as Tobin describes him.[44] Largely, Judge Holden's speeches and sermons resemble nothing more than the tedious ramblings of the psychopath. Ultimately, at best, Judge Holden's pontificating amounts to a banal transgression of the naturalistic fallacy, where we state that if something is the case then it also ought to be the case; at worst, it offers only the platitude that since humans are animals at heart, we are therefore morally obliged to behave like animals.

That Judge Holden elevates such banal moral observations to a grandiose cosmological level underlines his nihilistic cynicism by precluding the possibility of any ethical transformation from the outset. If, for Nietzsche, the psychological indicators of passive nihilism are a revelling in signs of corruption, decay and despair, then Judge Holden is the exemplar. His prognosis of the human condition revels in resignation, meaninglessness and chaos, rather than actively confronting the order of nature. This is not to say that Judge Holden and what he represents is uninteresting, or that his shtick is not an accurate depiction of the self-aggrandisements and techniques of the callous psychopath. Quite the contrary; McCarthy's study of Judge Holden incisively reveals acute strategies of domination and cruelty, particularly in the ways those under his sway remain tied, dependent and left to rationalise their place in his universe. This in turn reveals the subtleties of McCarthy's perspective on the philosophical status of human beings more broadly and the nature of domination specifically.

Judge Holden's pronouncements on war reveal the complicity of his violence with a stark instrumentalism. That he elevates violence to a metaphysical status only serves to bring more sharply into relief the fact that he too is governed by the Gods of utility. Judge Holden imagines violence in a way which only works if we conceive of violence as equivalent to the most pernicious version of Darwinian struggle: that is, if we understand Darwinism in the very limited sense of social Darwinism. Here, Judge Holden's character can be taken as a perfect symbol of the ruthless competition necessary in a struggle for survival. Who better than Judge Holden and the Glanton Gang's unimpeded exploitation of the scalp market to confirm the view that species compete and struggle violently, with only the fittest surviving? However, this only offers a very limited account of the nature of violence in an evolutionary sense and provides further evidence as to how the Judge transforms natural processes into idols.

In evolutionary terms, violence has an obvious and specific function, but contrary to Judge Holden's worldview, it is not a necessary one. Violence is certainly a biological mechanism, in the sense that violence can have a use-value for survival; this is the realm of violence in which the Judge wallows. One can easily imagine resorting to violence to procure food or in self-defence, as is predominantly the case with all forms of biological life, and often in the human realm. However, this is not necessarily the case for humans. Violence can also diminish our capacity to survive and is therefore not necessarily instrumental for the prolongation or propagation of the species. In short, we often do not need to be violent, although we certainly have the disposition and capacity to be so. That human beings are violent is so obvious it is barely worth restating. But whether we must be violent is entirely another matter. Judge Holden's character firmly supports the thesis that because we can be violent, we must be violent because morality is just a by-product of war and violence. In his speech on war, he states: 'Moral law is an invention of mankind for the disenfranchisement of the powerful in favour of the weak.'[45] Thus, the Judge claims that morality is inherently violent and exists to assert the powerful over the powerless. The trajectory of the kid's character development testifies to this.

The kid clearly has a capacity to be violent and is continually violent, but this does not necessarily indulge the distinction between being necessarily violent and having a capacity for violence. This will become important, as I will show, in differentiating the kid from the Judge. It is clear that McCarthy wants to separate the violence of the Judge from that of the kid. The ending of the novel shows us this. In a book that spares the reader no other detail in its portrayal of lurid gore, we are left to imagine the last violence that is perpetrated on the kid. It would be tempting to say this conscious omission on McCarthy's part shows that there is no moral redemption, that we cannot transform the deeply violent processes which constitute us; however, to do so amounts to endorsing a superficial Nietzschean-ism. For Nietzsche, while we cannot detach ourselves from violent natural processes, neither are we absolutely determined by them. What we find in the opposition of the Judge and the kid is that the Judge represents violence as essentially destructive. The Judge effec-tively naturalises violence, suggesting that violence, because natural, is also therefore good. The consequence of natural violence is that it becomes self-fulfilling, generating ever more violence in a repetitive, cyclical, relentless expansion, as we find with the Judge's metaphys-ics. The kid's character, however, demonstrates the possibility that violence, albeit ever present and inescapable, might also be produc-tive, capable of doing work and seeking out the creation of things of enduring value.[46] The kid carves out some things of temporary value despite his violent predispositions, such as his loyalty to Tobin, ran-dom acts of mercy and his disruption of Judge Holden's invocation of the necessity of violence.

Judge Holden's indulgence in passive nihilism leads to consider-ing natural violence itself as the zenith of human development and achievement. To assert that he elevates war to cosmological signifi-cance is to remain wilfully enthralled to metaphysical presuppositions, since he draws equivalence between a specific human activity – war – and inflates it to an ontological explanation of all that exists. In terms of literary quality, this is necessary for McCarthy to infuse the Judge with a distorted and narcissistic anthropology; humans are the worst, and the worst of our activities is a fitting model for describing the cosmos. But this anthropology is politically instru-mental. The violence Judge Holden inaugurates, while couched in vainglorious theological terms, is no more than a political device for controlling groups and individuals. His misanthropic view of the human as inherently violent nonetheless highlights his political and theological prejudices. Here his passive nihilism is as value laden as that of any two-bit preacher. Indeed, we first encounter Holden turning a congregation against a rival two-bit preacher, the Reverend Green, whom he accuses of being an imposter.[47]

For all the grandiose sermonising, Judge Holden's metaphysics of war offers little more than a version of the doctrine of original sin. All humans are born impure and sinful. While baptism is the conventional remedy for this, Judge Holden attains spiritual sanctification through his worship of war, at one point even precipitating a dark baptism where the Glanton Gang bathe together, with the waters turning gory and bloody.[48] The function of Judge Holden's baptismal theology is to maintain and impose sovereign rule. Ostensibly, Judge Holden is anarchic, wilfully disrupting all the markers of political civilisation; however, within the ersatz political configuration that is the nomadic Glanton Gang, the Judge preaches disorder to enforce the gang's acceptance of his existing social order. Hence,

> war is the truest form of divination. It is the testing of one's will and the will of another within that larger will which because it binds them is therefore forced to select. War is the ultimate game because war is at least a forcing of the unity of existence. War is god.[49]

The idea that chaos is the truest expression of divinity, alongside the Judge's veneration of war, underlines the instrumentality of his violence. This thought is an assertion of a dubious fact and, as we have seen, something that Judge Holden cheaply clothes in the respectability of the language of naturalist exploration. As such, Judge Holden ignores other Darwinian impulses, where species survival is of the utmost importance. If humans are inherently violent then this also implies that we are always a danger to one another. This might be potentially true, but it is neither necessarily nor actually true. For Judge Holden, the only authority is senselessness, but it is an authority nonetheless. Hence, nothing he says is of value, nor can it be taken seriously.

For Nietzsche, after we experience the void which the death of God imposes on us, the danger is that we substitute our desire for metaphysical foundations with human idols such as religion, convenience, science or political ideology. In the Judge's case, we find the ultimate expression of this mix of scientific, ethical and religious idols. The resentment that arises from the hollowness of such idols leads to the unleashing of destructive impulses such as envy, cruelty and bitterness. Judge Holden's cruelty manifests itself in a childishly cruel fetishisation of war and violence. The spiritualisation of war reveals Holden's underlying fascism, where for all the cynical and brutal acts he perpetrates, for all the adoration he espouses of violence and combat, he can still be characterised by naïvety and idealism. This naïvety explains his intense interest in the young, who as symbols of possibility and growth are his philosophical rivals. This also explains the Judge's wearing of kidskin boots, his vendetta with the kid, his paedophilic desires as shown when he sits naked next to a cowering twelve-year-old girl, and indeed why McCarthy draws his physical appearance to resemble that of a giant infant.[50] Judge Holden's character, however menacing the violence he unleashes, remains suffused with a naïve idealism for the purity, spirituality and simplicity of violence, for the idea that violence is natural, bolstered by a naïve understanding of the moral consequences of a deterministic universe. Judge Holden's idea that life is worthless, that all that comes to be ought to perish, is as naïve a supernaturalism as the most conventional of religions. The Judge passively accepts that violence is entwined with nature. However, passive nihilism, for Nietzsche, does not oblige one to be necessarily cruel.

The kid as nihilist

To wonder whether the kid is moral or not is wrongheaded. The temptation is to think that the kid retains or develops morals despite the overwhelming influence of Judge Holden. But the kid is fundamentally compromised morally, both directly and tacitly. Throughout the novel the kid participates in or, at the very least, tacitly consents to disturbing acts of rape, mutilation and genocide. Whether the kid develops morally is beside the point. The kid cannot be sequestered from the actions and carnages of the Glanton Gang even if he exhibits signs of mercy throughout the novel. For example, we see that the kid does not put the wounded Shelby out of his misery, giving him an outside chance of life; later, the kid gives a young boy who might attack him a chance to walk away. Even more intensely, we see him exercise mercy when he spares the life of the Judge himself when with Tobin. The purpose of these small acts of non-violence is not to show that he has morally redeemed himself, but instead to show that moral character is contingent rather than determined.[51] The kid's antipathy to Judge Holden remains defined by Holden. This is philosophically necessary within McCarthy's depiction of a nihilistic universe, since to overcome nihilism, one must be exposed to the worse excesses of nihilism in the first place.

If, for Nietzsche, passive nihilism is the most intense form of pessimism and cynicism, then active nihilism is characterised by an opening towards possibility, futurity and novelty. For Nietzsche, passive nihilism entails that humans grow fatigued and alienated from even the possibility of value, the result of which is psychological weariness, moral exhaustion and a wilful obscuring of the origins of nature. While passive nihilism signals decline and deterioration – subscribing to the basic proposition that the world is meaningless – active nihilism engages with the shepherding-in of something novel and transformative. Active nihilism, for Nietzsche, asks us to go through the necessary transition from passive nihilism to understanding the world in terms of possibility and becoming. If Judge Holden represents, as I have argued, a foreclosing of possibility, then what the kid represents is the possibility of building something new. Hence the kid remains more of a type than a character. Notwithstanding Sarah Borginnis's view, I agree with Joyce Carol Oates's assessment that the kid is the closest we can find to a sympathetic character in *Blood Meridian*, one with whom we are not meant to identify in any way except just to perceive him.[52] If the kid represents a type, then this begs the question as to what precisely he typifies?

The best way to answer the question of type is by understanding the kid as a form of active nihilist. Inasmuch as Judge Holden, as I have argued, represents the nullification of possibility, potential and the future, the kid represents the possibility of birth, becoming and transformation. If Holden asserts that the human is determined and can become nothing other than it presently is then the kid, as a child, is essentially 'unfinished' and open to growth, opportunity and renovation. McCarthy's imperative on the first page of the novel, 'See the child', should be taken very seriously. Also, at the outset of the novel, McCarthy describes the kid as educationally undeveloped: 'See the child. He is pale and thin, he wears a thin and ragged linen shirt [. . .] he can neither read nor write.'[53] If the active nihilist, as Nietzsche holds, is devoted to transfiguring the human's morally compromised nature, of renewing life in the face of a deathly nihilism, then the kid, who is an efficient and effective killer, defines the human's capacity to renew itself despite the worst cosmological fate and even despite humanity's irredeemable nature. That the kid's birth – born under the astronomical omen of a meteor shower – led to the death of his mother, emphasises the complications of life and death as staged in the novel, further displaying his fate in bloodshed as well as a potential for renewal. Elsewhere, in perhaps one of the most gruesome images of the novel, the kid and Sproule confront a tree hung with dead babies that are 'larval to some unreckonable being'.[54] Both Sproule and the kid are left stunned by this chilling vista, which marks their desensitisation at a point in the novel when they are most under the Judge's rule. Desensitisation implies a deadening and as outlined, is consistent with the effects of passive nihilism which Nietzsche describes, namely psychological exhaustion, alienation and emptiness. The effect on the kid is anaesthetic – rather than aesthetic, in the more traditional sense of the term – since a confrontation with this apparition of monstrous birth prohibits any potential of resistance and renewal, or the reconsideration of any existing values.

In addition to the desensitising force of the novel's events, the Judge actively attempts to anaesthetise any links between past, present and future, severing the possibility, indeed the value, of understanding the human as a historical being across the span of a life with an ability to hold a covenant between generations. The broader goal of the Judge's deeds is to force the conception that the human being is always and already metaphysically dead and is as such nothing other than a living corpse. Holden's aim is wholly nihilistic, since he reduces the human being to its most atemporal iteration, a corpse denuded of vitality. This is particularly obvious when the Judge proposes a Darwinian theory of education:

> So what is the way of raising a child? At a young age, said the judge, they should be put in a pit with wild dogs. They should be set to puzzle out from their proper clues the one of three doors that does not harbor wild lions. They should be made run naked in the desert . . . The way of the world is to bloom and to flower and die but in the affairs of me there is no waning and the noon of his expression signals the onset of night.[55]

The implication of the Judge's pedagogy is that there is no place for parental guidance or teachers. As such, children should parent and give birth to themselves against the cruelties of wild nature. His ideas are reminiscent of Spartan rearing practices; the Judge thinks the ideal form of education is found where no historical intersection can be permissible, between the historical, the current and the impending. Since the kid has no mother, is the child of a schoolteacher and has reared himself, he is thus the model child for the Judge. However, what Judge Holden cannot countenance is the kid's adolescent resistance. The significance of the kid's rebelliousness cannot be overstated, since he is rebelling against the ultimate transgressor.

The Judge develops a distaste and scepticism towards the kid's aptitude for mercy, considering the kid's vestigial kind-heartedness as mutinous, seditious and undermining of the gang's holy mission to propagate war: 'I spoke in the desert for you and you only and you turned a deaf ear to me. If war is not holy man is nothing but antic clay.'[56] The term 'antic clay' is hugely evocative here. It illustrates Judge Holden's moral mission. The conjoining of 'clay', a material term, and 'antic', a temporal term, demonstrates that what the Judge deems most apostate is that humans can consider themselves as material beings, both ancient and modern, as well as old and new simultaneously. The Judge is effectively barring the possibility of Nietzsche's constructive values, where tradition and novelty exist simultaneously. In the Nietzschean sense, the kid is beyond good and evil, retaining, by the end of the novel, a capacity to do both good and bad. It is not simply the case that the kid rebels against a malign surrogate parent by becoming more virtuous or redeeming himself by adopting the opposite values of a parent figure. No, McCarthy offers a more nuanced perspective on the moral consideration of intergenerational conflict. The kid, as an active nihilist, opens the possibility of concord between past and future.

Though the kid is largely mute and taciturn for most of the novel, towards the finale he unburdens himself with a strange urgency.[57] The kid provides a confession of his litany of crimes after being arrested in a tavern, a penitence his jailer-confessors consider mad due to the kid's exposure to so much violence and 'acts of blood'.[58] The significance of this act is not the self-assignment of guilt, or a renouncement of his psychopathic tendencies; instead it should be read more productively, as an overturning of a very particular moral order, which is that of Judge Holden. Holden's metaphysical schemes are as contingent as any other nature-based moral system. Consequently, the Judge views the kid as treasonous. The kid deviates from Holden's holy mission to propagate war: 'There's a flawed place in the fabric of your heart. Do you think I could not know? You alone were mutinous. You alone reserved in your soul some corner of clemency for the heathen.'[59] The kid, a psychopath in his own right, does not present a moral alternative to Holden's cosmology; rather, the kid is flawed and impure, retaining some trace of decency which besmirches Holden's closed view of nature. The Judge, too, can dimly discern alternative paths to his totalitarian ideal, prophesying a future when war will be abandoned for other trades and activities, a time when: 'war becomes dishonored and its nobility called into question [so] those honorable men who recognize the sanctity of blood will become excluded from the dance'.[60] The kid precipitates in Holden a sense that his own values too are becoming lost and, thus, meaningless.

Of course, Holden does not make the Nietzschean transition, preferring to remain a pure warrior, 'the last of the true' rejoicing in nihilistic chaos.[61] For Nietzsche, nihilism is corrosive, but is also a positive indicator of how tradition permits novel forms to arise.[62] The anomaly that Holden can't countenance is not so much the minor evidence of moral principles which the kid exhibits; it is, rather, that the Judge cannot tolerate that the kid might retain the hint of an ethical alternative. The kid's rejection of Judge Holden 'poisons' the sealed totality of Holden's metaphysics, simply by the persistence of his resistance and capacity for survival. The kid is a survivor and that which survives endures, which is why Holden finds the human capacity to go on so distasteful. This is important because, as I have already argued, *Blood Meridian* is not a moral book, and neither does it indulge in moralising. This is essential to the aesthetic of the novel: the flat ontology of McCarthy's 'optical democracy' entails that morals exist on the same plane as existence. It is Judge Holden's error to think that this ontology implies that humans are purely evil. The kid is thus not a symbol of moral principles, but that human nature itself can be harnessed for ethical transformation. Certainly, we can assume the kid does not survive, that he is ultimately ignominiously murdered in a bathroom. Nonetheless, what is significant is the capacity to survive, to persist and create, which is important and which is what the Judge forsakes for a cult of death and negation.

In their final meeting, the theme of active versus passive nihilism comes to a head. The kid tells the Judge that he 'aint nothin'. This can be read in several ways. In the mouth of the kid, we can read this as the kid simply puncturing the Judge's inflated sense of self. However, there is a double negation present, where the proposition also effectively states that the Judge is something rather than nothing. To say that the Judge is something, a statement to which he acquiesces: 'You speak truer than you know',[63] is in keeping with his pretentiously diabolical character. In addition, there are distinct theological resonances of fullness and plenitude, where the Judge, akin to Lucifer, elevates himself to the status of God, where there is no exterior to him, nor to the theology he represents. However, another reading is possible, where in fact the Judge agrees with the kid, and that he is 'something', created just like anything or anybody else. Thus, the kid, with a courageous indifference to the Judge's philosophical meanderings in their final encounter, illustrates that the Judge cannot

elevate his mantra of destruction and negation to cosmic exception-
ality. This provides the kid with a small victory, since the Judge is
as much an aberration and an accident as anything else, and he also
shall pass. And hence the novel ambiguously ends with the Arts: the
Judge dances and fiddles away the night, since all that is left to him
now is creation.

As we have seen, for Nietzsche, creation is ineluctably concerned
with the future. Throughout *Blood Meridian*, the Judge is at war
with the future. By attempting to let the future be, the kid retains
the seeds of liberation from extant traditions: hitherto ruling ideals
as well as their nihilistic inclinations. Ultimately, the kid represents
distinct elements of Nietzsche's constructive rejection of nihilism.
The kid, howsoever haphazardly, tries to reject the dominant certainties which have endured in his awful culture. In opposition to
Judge Holden's worship of the instrumental, the present and his hostility to the future, the kid attempts to prioritise the temporal rather
than the eternal, creation and creativity rather than apparent truths,
the transformative over the immutable. If, for Nietzsche, truth is a
mobile army of metaphors, then the kid acquiesces to the knowledge
that reality itself is a form of historical becoming.[64] The danger for
Nietzsche is that the truth of such becoming is suffused with negation,
change and contest, and it is extremely difficult to disentangle change
from the changes also necessary for enacting brutality, cruelty and
hostility. The kid as an active nihilist eventually attempts to combat
the cult of confusion, despair and alienation which is promulgated by
the Judge. However, rather than rejoicing in the wanton destruction
engendered by the Judge's moral order, the kid becomes a different
conduit of negation, one which is palpably demonstrated by both
the kid's undermining of the Judge's idols and by his propinquity to
death, which dominates his life from his birth onwards. The symbolic
proximity of the Judge and the kid is utterly essential in revealing
the tortured complication of the human condition. McCarthy is thus
much more than a vulgar Nietzschean. He realises, and convincingly
presents in novelistic form, the intractable difficulties of constructing
resistance and affirmation alongside our undeniable worst instincts.

Conclusion

Blood Meridian begins and ends with a meteor shower. Stars falling
to earth hint at the themes discussed in this chapter. The novel begins
and ends with the heavens made material. Whether deliberately or

otherwise, McCarthy firmly places us in the world after the death of God. Contrast the meteor showers which bookend the novel with the Judge's feat of brute functional strength when tossing a grounded meteorite.[65] The Judge, too, returns the meteor to earth. The Judge's casual bravura gives witness to his purely instrumental efforts to negate human capacity itself, and the inability in any way to elevate ourselves above a godless world.

In the kid and in the Judge, *Blood Meridian* presents two distinct responses to nihilism. Judge Holden is a version of passive nihilism because he accepts reality as it is. The kid is an active nihilist as he eventually engages in a tawdry project to overcome his predicament. Judge Holden represents the wilful celebration of negation and destruction. The kid represents the predicament of inhabiting and actively overcoming the vicious logic of the Judge's universe. The consequence of Judge Holden for philosophy is thus twofold. He evokes eerie syntheses: in the Judge we find a blend of rationalism and romanticism, spirit and matter, order and chaos. He elevates his voluntarism to mythic and metaphysical levels. For McCarthy, Judge Holden is certainly an avatar of war and wanton destruction. However, he is also a trickster and charlatan and thus any moral gravitas attributed to him is only provisional.

Judge Holden does represent the most pessimistic articulation of McCarthy's fatalistic views of the cosmos. The cosmos is war and the ontology of the novel expresses this reality. Superficially, McCarthy could be said to fall foul of what philosophers call the naturalistic fallacy, where what ought to be the case is derived from what is the case. However, it is more accurate to say that McCarthy in *Blood Meridian* is examining how good might be possible even despite values emerging from violence, self-interest and war. If such is the inescapable nature of the cosmos, then it follows that any available moral responses can only be framed negatively. The Judge looms so large that any effort to distinguish civility and moral progress outside the conflictual nature of reality is exceptionally arduous. Indeed, it is fair to say that the Judge is the monstrous manifestation of the negative consequences of moral progress.[66]

Still, the kid, despite his nihilistic tendencies, remains essentially unfinished and undetermined, thus retaining a shred of the desire to improve morally. The fate of the kid mirrors the fate of the reader, as we grapple with exposure to Holden's nihilistic maelstrom of cruelty, negation and destruction. Consolidated by McCarthy's impersonal narration, the ontological presentation of the novel's action demands and forces the reader to confront a nihilistic and treacherous universe, one wholly indifferent to human pursuits of meaning, aspiration or hope. Hence the novel's epilogue presents a resistance to Judge Holden, to the things he makes, to turning all life into an instrument, a thing which can be put to war. After all, Judge Holden is not an absolute nihilist. He does not grant to himself the simplest option for conjoining himself with the primordial ooze which his own suicide would bequeath him, and thus he is no more immune to being created than anything else. Judge Holden has his own dysfunctional moral compass, one anchored in self-assertion, elevating his strange peccadillos to metaphysical grandiosity. Nietzsche described nihilism as a 'belief in unbelief'.[67] When one does not have the strength for renewal, one resorts to coveting someone who commands severely. For Nietzsche, this could be 'a god, prince, class, physician, father confessor, dogma or party conscience'.[68] And who better than Judge Holden to be a bearer of all these professions? Nihilism amounts to a desire for certainty, albeit the certainty of nothingness as opposed to the existential condition of uncertainty.

The novel's brief and enigmatic epilogue provides a resistance to the viciousness of Judge Holden, a resistance which rests in acts of construction, in civilisation, in beginning again and again. The epilogue has an unnamed man working on a plain at dawn, punctuating holes in the ground, sparking 'fire out of the rock which God has put there'.[69] Behind, the man is pursued by wandering bone searchers who progress:

> one by one that track of holes that runs to rims of the visible ground and which seems less the pursuit of some continuance than the verification of a principle, a validation of sequence and causality as if each round and perfect hole owed its existence to the one before it . . .[70]

And then they all move on again. Bloom is correct to suggest that the last word does not fall to the Judge; the dawn is a contrast to the novel's eponymous sanguinary meridian as well as the 'evening redness' of the novel's alternative title, a space which the Judge dominates, to be sure, but does not own. McCarthy firmly places us in the twilight of the idols, with the Judge cast as the greatest idol of all.

The epilogue shows that while the Judge endures and dominates the landscape, a new Prometheus may be rising to go up against him.[71] Although deliberately opaque, it is possible tentatively to suggest that the epilogue draws together the themes we have discussed in this chapter. A hole is, after all, a form of emptiness and nothingness. That McCarthy has discrete holes punctuating the Judge's blood meridian bespeaks an active negation. Humans continue to build and create despite the Judge's supposed triumph of nothingness. The slaughter of the preceding pages concludes with a modest salvation. The man is building and creating something with rudimentary technology: it could be an agricultural fencepost, it might be for military activity, an omen of the incoming telegraph system, indeed it could be anything from the imminent future of the novel's time-period. It is most likely he is constructing, in McCarthy's own words, a fence for an 'embryonic wall' for 'a burial scene'. This mixture of birth and death, possibility and actuality, hope and finality brings together the themes which I have argued are present throughout the novel. However, the literal meaning is uninteresting: what the epilogue symbolises is a spirit of endurance and indebtedness, of the capacity for survival in the face of the most searing nihilism. All that is left after the onslaught of the preceding pages is the indefatigable persistence of human becoming. Since each round and perfect hole owes its existence to the one before it, it can be surmised that all the tiny little negations of humans connect to what precedes them and in a Beckettian way, point to a future, where all that is left to do is move on.

Notes

1. Frye, *Understanding Cormac McCarthy*, 23.
2. Bell, 'The Ambiguous Nihilism of Cormac McCarthy', 31–2.
3. Ibid. 41.
4. Leo Daugherty, 'Gravers False and True: *Blood Meridian* as Gnostic Tragedy', in *Perspectives on Cormac McCarthy*, ed. Dianne C. Luce and Edwin T. Arnold (Jackson: University Press of Mississippi, 1999), 170.
5. Dana Phillips, 'History and the Ugly Facts of Cormac McCarthy's *Blood Meridian*', *American Literature* 68, no.2 (June 1996): 442.
6. Russell Hillier, 'The Judge's Molar: Infanticide and the Meteorite in *Blood Meridian*', in *They Rode On:* Blood Meridian *and the Tragedy of the American West*, ed. Rick Wallach (Bakersfield: The Cormac McCarthy Society, 2013), 60.
7. Eric M. Williamson, '*Blood Meridian* and Nietzsche: The Metaphysics of War', 265, 271.
8. Denis Donoghue, 'Reading *Blood Meridian*', *The Sewanee Review* 105, no.3 (Summer 1997): 418.
9. Jay Ellis, *No Place for Home: Spatial Constrain and Character Flight in the Novels of Cormac McCarthy* (New York: Routledge, 2006), 153.
10. Donoghue, 'Reading *Blood Meridian*', 409–10. On this topic, see also Dianne Luce's very informative short essay 'The Bedazzled Eye:

Cormac McCarthy, José Y. Gasset, and Optical Democracy', *The Cormac McCarthy Journal* 17, no.1 (Spring 2019): 64–70.

11. Cormac McCarthy, *Blood Meridian* (London: Picador, 1989), 247. Hereafter *BM*.

12. Ibid. 52–3.

13. Harold Bloom, 'Interview: Harold Bloom on *Blood Meridian*', AV Club, accessed 19 May 2020, <https://www.avclub.com/harold-bloom-on-blood-meridian-1798216782>

14. McCarthy, *BM*, 138.

15. Nietzsche provides a typology of the different phases of nihilism. See Friedrich Nietzsche, *The Will to Power*, trans. Walter Kaufman (New York: Vintage, 1968), 17–19. Hereafter *WP*.

16. Friedrich Nietzsche, *The Gay Science*, trans. Walter Kaufman (New York: Vintage, 1974), 181.

17. A common view of Nietzsche is that he unquestioningly celebrates individualism. My point is that such a characterisation of his philosophy is far from clear or obvious. Nietzsche offers a much more nuanced account of human subjectivity than the trite epithet to 'be yourself'.

18. See Nietzsche, *WP*, 14–15.

19. Nietzsche, *WP*, 12.

20. Ibid. 13.

21. Ibid. 20.

22. Ibid.

23. Ibid. 18.

24. For a systematic account of Nietzsche's naturalism, see Brian Leiter, *Nietzsche on Morality* (London: Routledge, 2002).

25. Nietzsche, *WP*, 33.

26. Nietzsche, *On the Genealogy of Morals and Ecce Homo*, trans. Walter Kaufman (New York: Vintage, 1989), 25.

27. Friedrich Nietzsche, *Beyond Good and Evil*, trans. Marion Faber (Oxford: Oxford University Press), 35–6.

28. This idea does not correspond to cruder versions of pan-psychism, where material elements can perceive in a conscious way.

29. McCarthy, *BM*, 328.

30. Ibid. 66.

31. Ibid. 85.

32. Ibid. 84.

33. Ibid.

34. Rich Wallach does a very good job of providing the literary-historical background of the ways in which science, values and spirituality intersect in his essay, 'Sam Chamberlain and the Iconology of Science in Mid-19th Century Nation Building', in *They Rode On:* Blood Meridian *and the Tragedy of the American West*, ed. Rick Wallach (Bakersfield: The Cormac McCarthy Society, 2013), 38–45.

35. McCarthy, *BM*, 144.

36. Ibid. 199.
37. Ibid. 131.
38. Ibid. 130.
39. Ibid. 122–3.
40. Ibid. 248.
41. This is a reference to the Heraclitan dimensions of *Blood Meridian*. We can say McCarthy definitively had Heraclitus generally in mind when composing *Blood Meridian* and more specifically, that he saw the Judge as an iteration of Heraclitan philosophy. In the archive material, McCarthy quotes Heraclitus directly: 'War is the father of us all and our king. War discloses who is godlike and who is but a man, who is a slave and who is a free man. – Heraclitus—See other translation Let the judge quote this in part and without crediting source.' McCarthy, *Cormac McCarthy Papers (1964–2007)*, Box 35: Folder 1. One might surmise that Nietzsche's philosophy, given his fondness for Heraclitus, can be extended in the same way to the Judge. However, things are not so simple. Heraclitus was, for Nietzsche, a thinker who balanced contest and rule. The natural destructive traits of humans were to be held in check through rule-governed contests. This was a sign of strength, since it mitigated the unleashing of war, annihilation and chaos. Judge Holden defines that chaos in *Blood Meridian*, so we should note that the Judge's Heraclitan proclivities are not necessarily Nietzschean ones. For a well-researched and insightful account of the links between McCarthy and Heraclitus see Ian A. Moore, 'Heraclitus and the Metaphysics of War', in *Beyond Reckoning: Philosophical Perspectives on Cormac McCarthy*, ed. Chris Eagle (London: Routledge, 2017), 93–108.
42. McCarthy, *BM*, 370.
43. Ibid. 309–10.
44. Ibid. 252.
45. Ibid. 250.
46. I am thinking here specifically of Hannah Arendt's critique of Franz Fanon. Arendt distinguishes between power and force. Violence for Arendt is essentially instrumental, whereas force is not solely natural and is connected to human activity and creation. Also, while violence is more individual and connected to strength, force is social and plural, connected to the creation of purpose and action. See Hannah Arendt, *On Violence* (New York: HBJ Publishers, 1970), 37.
47. McCarthy, *BM*, 6–7.
48. Ibid. 167.
49. Ibid. 249.
50. Ibid. 79, 275, 335.
51. Ibid. 207, 321.
52. Joyce Carol Oates, *In Rough Country: Essays and Reviews* (New York: HarperCollins, 2010), 155.
53. McCarthy, *BM*, 3.

54. Ibid. 57.
55. Ibid. 146.
56. Ibid. 307.
57. Ibid. 305. See also Lydia Cooper's interpretation of the relation between the confessional and nothingness. Lydia Cooper, *No More Heroes: Narrative Perspective and Morality in Cormac McCarthy* (Baton Rouge: Louisiana State University, 2011), 73.
58. McCarthy, *BM*, 305.
59. Ibid. 299.
60. Ibid. 331.
61. Ibid. 327.
62. Nietzsche, *WP*, 69.
63. McCarthy, *BM*, 331.
64. Nietzsche, 'Truth and Falsity in an Ultramoral Sense', in *The Philosophy of Nietzsche*, ed. Geoffrey Clive, trans. Oscar Levy (New York: Mentor Books, 1965), 508.
65. McCarthy, *BM*, 240. Notably, McCarthy juxtaposes the Judge's feat of lifting the meteorite with an infanticide.
66. In the archival draft material of *Blood Meridian*, McCarthy misattributes to Henry James the following: 'There is a deep truth in what the school of Schopenhauer insists on – the illusoriness of the notion of moral progress. The more brutal forms of evil that go are replaced by others more subtle and more poisonous.' (Henry James – An Address to the Harvard Divinity Students in 1884).' McCarthy, *Cormac McCarthy Papers (1964–2007)*, Box 35: Folder 2, 12. The point is clear: McCarthy is drawn to a standard point present in both Nietzsche and Schopenhauer, that moral progress is no guarantee of precluding the creation of future evil and as such, moral progress is an idol in itself. The original quotation is from William James, not Henry James, and can be found in William James's essay 'Dilemma of Determinism', Uky. Edu, accessed 20 May 2020, <https://www.uky.edu/~eushe2/Pajares/JamesDilemmaOfDeterminism.html>
67. Nietzsche, *The Gay Science*, 289.
68. Ibid.
69. McCarthy, *BM*, 337.
70. Ibid.
71. Harold Bloom, 'On Violence, the Sublime, and *Blood Meridian*'s Place in the American Canon', last modified 16 October 2019, <https://lithub.com/harold-bloom-on-cormac-mccarthy-true-heir-to-melville-and-faulkner>

Chapter 4

In the Shadow of the Forms:
The Sunset Limited as
Educational Encounter

Introduction

In February 2016, during a victory speech at the Nevada Republican Party caucus, the United States presidential candidate Donald Trump said: 'We won with young. We won with old. We won with highly educated. We won with poorly educated. I love the poorly educated.'[1] Candidate Trump's speech made conspicuous the acute tension between those with and without advanced education. Also in 2016, a key predictor of the United Kingdom's Brexit vote was a gap in educational attainment. While these two political events are obviously not synonymous, a clear commonality is the educational divide within the electorate.[2] In 2006, Cormac McCarthy published both *The Sunset Limited* and *The Road*. While *The Sunset Limited* has received less critical attention than *The Road*, this drama is equally important for understanding McCarthy's philosophical interests. The play's torrid atmosphere examines how the cherished self-certainties of two men are entangled in, and undermined by, mutual wariness and scepticism. McCarthy's drama generates a mood of incessant alienation, staging a confrontation between the supposedly educated, in the guise of a university professor, White, who is dismissive of superstition and ignorant know-nothings, and the supposedly less educated, Black, who considers White to be deficient in both meaningful and spiritual experiences. *The Sunset Limited* is a philosophical conversation between White, who is both formally educated and jaded, and Black, who despite having less formal education has a schooling developed from the streets, penal institutions or the so-called 'university of life'. That McCarthy was wrestling with the fraught relationship between the formally educated and uneducated over a decade prior to the democratic disruptions wrought by Trump and Brexit testifies to his prescience as an author, especially in recognising a significant fault-line which would emerge in two significant major (self-styled) democracies: the United States and the European Union.

As well as a dialogue on education, *The Sunset Limited* is also a philosophical encounter. Most overtly, as I will argue in this chapter, the drama contains distinct Platonic elements whereby the characters test received opinions and scrutinise congealed dogmas to educate their counterpart. This chapter examines how the play adopts Platonic themes. In short, *The Sunset Limited* asks whether it is possible for two polarised perspectives to transcend the things they take for granted in order to achieve a meaningful account of the good. Can two such dissimilar men in fact find common ground? The extent to which accord is desirable or possible for Black and White is where the philosophical wisdom of the play emerges. *The Sunset Limited* illuminates how the apparent educational asymmetry of the two characters in fact reveals a more profound solidarity, albeit a solidarity which is tragically forsaken. *The Sunset Limited* plays its own distinct part in helping us understand the philosophical dimension of McCarthy's literature, as the play demonstrates his general strategy of viewing humans as intersecting between spiritualism and materialism, matter and meaning, despair and hope.

Plot as philosophical encounter

The plot of *The Sunset Limited* is straightforward. It takes place in an apartment containing two men called White and Black. Black has just saved White from attempting to take his own life by jumping in front of a commuter train called The Sunset Limited.[3] Black locks White into his apartment for his safety. The plot is subsequently driven by Black's conversational efforts to convince White that life may be meaningful enough that he could choose to keep living. White attempts to convince Black of the opposite. Both characters reveal aspects of their lives throughout the conversation. For example, Black has murdered someone in a prison fight, whilst White did not attend his father's funeral. Midway through the play they eat a meal which Black cooks. White becomes reanimated and after the meal he proceeds to defend his nihilistic outlook more staunchly. By the end, Black lets White out of the apartment, presumably to pursue his death. Black says he will keep trying to save him, but White still leaves. The play which began with a question: 'So what am I supposed to do with you Professor', ends with a question. Black is left asking his God, 'Is that okay?'[4]

As the plot unfolds, the overarching opposition of religion and rationality, ignorance and education are matched with the oppositional colour-coding of black versus white, light versus dark. We also see, at least superficially, that Black is an optimist and White is a pessimist. Black is spiritual and religious; White is atheistic and an evolutionary materialist. Black is ostensibly emotional; White is ostensibly rational. Black is proficient in mathematics; White is proficient in art and culture. Black is for life; White is for death. Black thinks we are morally obliged to help people; White thinks this is pointless. Such sharp asymmetry heightens the oppositional tension, forcing the men's contrasts to the foreground and exacerbating the play's insurmountable irresolution. Such oppositional framing makes tangible the tragic absence of any commonality between Black and White. However, while the plot of *The Sunset Limited* is simple, such simplicity does belie the more complex entanglements it stages between the two protagonists.

What is striking about McCarthy's dialogue is that the plot places irreconcilable characters in a position where they inflect and influence each other's perspectives and opinions. Both characters are like the two sides of a rail track, on the same journey while holding completely separate tastes, values and moral preferences. The philosophical significance of the play emerges from the way both characters might overcome the immediate asymmetry that defines their respective moral worldviews.[5] While the characters are ostensibly antagonistic, there seems to be a deeper solidarity in evidence. For example, Black and White evoke the tactics and strategy of a game of chess.[6] The ambiguity of war and peace is perfectly captured when White accuses Black of seeing everything in black and white, to which Black responds, 'It is Black and White.'[7] This could equally be read as the dogmatic assertion of polar antagonism or the expression of the unity of Black *and* White – and thus the yearning for a deeper unity.

That *The Sunset Limited* has philosophical concerns is obvious. Throughout the play, Black and White examine an assortment of philosophical and theological questions such as evolution, religion, theodicy, nihilism, meaning and the possibility of an afterlife. The play, bookended such as it is by two questions, functions as a thought experiment on the human ability to transcend the chasm of rationality and religion. But do Black and White teach each other anything in the course of the play?

Platonic education in *The Sunset Limited*

Plato's dialogues are all examples of educational encounters, whereby Plato's chief protagonist Socrates tried to bring people from a state of ignorance to a state of knowledge. As such, Platonic dialogues were a form of *paideia*.[8] Similarly, the extent to which *The Sunset Limited* is successful depends on whether philosophical dialogue can educate two polarised positions out of intransigence. Both protagonists adopt a mentor-mentee role; both struggle to find common ground and both, more often than not, try to achieve the upper hand. By the conclusion, it is unclear whether either has taught the other something significant, beyond some general knowledge about different topics. For example, Black teaches White about food and John Coltrane; White teaches Black about evolution, culture and rationality. However, the extent to which they have dialogued their way to a meaningful relation is unclear.

Martin Heidegger helps us understand the pedagogical stakes of overcoming opinion, by contextualising Plato's famous allegory of the Cave as not just an epistemological theory, but as an educational allegory. Heidegger reads Plato's allegory of the Cave as an exercise in liberation. Plato's Cave is about the transformation of the human being, leading us away from darkness to the light, in a move away from the murky world of opinion and half-truths. The move from darkness to light is equivalent to the task of philosophising, where humans are led towards an authentically unhidden realm. For Heidegger, the Cave allegory shows that for Plato, the nature of truth is not absolute. Instead, truth is empowering and enabling, helping humans to see the reality of their historical situation, with all its urgencies and priorities. Such a reality requires the human being to be a questioner and inquirer into its own historical origin and destination. Heidegger sees the extent to which humans can continually transform themselves to live and understand truth.[9] This is directly relevant to *The Sunset Limited*. Black's apartment is an allegorical Cave in which both characters are locked for the duration of the play.[10] The crux of the play depends on whether Black and White can forego their fixed opinions and illuminate each other.

In *The Sunset Limited*, it is in the extent to which the characters can overcome their entrenched positions that it becomes possible to see a meaningful pedagogical and philosophical encounter taking place. Applying Heidegger's distinctive understanding of Platonic truth is insightful for understanding *The Sunset Limited*'s pedagogy. Heidegger argues that education cannot be recited in formulae or rote expression. Throughout *The Sunset Limited*, Black and White do fall into the recitation of formulaic expressions of their respective spiritualism and rationalism. Even if they affirm their beliefs with passionate zeal, their beliefs remain just that: belief and opinion, which they take to be knowledge. Thus, each man has a propensity for solipsism; each is self-contained in the formation of his own life-narrative, which circularly informs his own character and which he assumes to be the true and the good. The extent to which both Black and White reach insightful wisdom about themselves depends on the possibility of educating each other about something other than themselves.

Such educational 'otherness' is a central motivation of all education. For Heidegger, *paideia* is not education in terms of character building or character reinforcement.[11] While Heidegger thinks Plato is responsible for undermining the true nature of education, he also thinks Plato's doctrine of truth is based on the intimacy of *paideia* and ignorance. In other words, an educational situation requires exposing the limits of our character formation to alternative forms of thought, where the things which build character are enriched through exposure to what they are not. This basic opposition is crucial to the function of *The Sunset Limited*. Black's and White's character formation and mutual enlightenment emerge by being exposed to the other's perspective, by undermining their existing preconception and intellectual shibboleths. *The Sunset Limited*, by demonstrating the incompleteness of each character's education, replicates Heidegger's appraisal of Plato; education is a paradoxical situation, drawing sustenance from a state of knowing and unknowing.

Heidegger's point can also be consolidated by considering Plato's own theory of knowledge, where the decisive prerequisite for educational transformation is the presence of an ideal standard regulating and dampening humans' habitual tastes, opinions and dispositions. Put simply, for Plato, there needs to be some common goal to which educators refer in order to achieve a broader enlightenment.[12] This is why Plato's Socrates famously chastised the Sophists, or the false educators, those given over to idiosyncratic rhetoric and trivial pomp. In a sense, the same logic operates in *The Sunset Limited*. Black and White are, initially at least, tragically sophist, both entranced and enchained by their own rhetoric. Both are filled with self-certainties, apparent knowledge, brash expertise, but both lack a sense of that which transcends their respective positions. And this mutual enlightenment, I will proceed to argue, is the primary philosophical expression within McCarthy's play.

Within Plato there is a fundamental rejection of opinion. This is evident in the allegory of the Cave, as well as in the metaphor of the divided line.[13] Implicit to such a rejection of opinion and common sense is a rejection of tradition. It would be erroneous to see the rejection of tradition as an elevation of the moral conscience of the individual. Plato is not a modern liberal who thinks the individual should be protected by, or from, the State. For Plato, knowledge of the good has an objective rather than subjective character. As such, Plato's whole work is about the depersonalisation of our selves. And in *The Sunset Limited*, Black and White for the most part speak with certainty and are jointly dismissive of each other's philosophical identities, finding it difficult to attain a consensus of common purpose or discourse.

Plato rejects trusting one's own senses, intuition and moral sentiments as a valuable judge of the best in life. In his *Meno*, knowledge requires moving from opinion to truth, whereby we draw manifold different perspectives together into one 'standard'. Socrates, in the *Meno*, demonstrates that real education is not about a crude transfer of information. It is not as if those who learn can be filled as a receptacle. For Plato's Socrates, excellence and a flourishing life is teachable and a natural disposition of humankind. The *Meno* shows that if virtue is only specific, localised or particular, it cannot relate to a general standard.[14] Such a standard of the good is the aggregate of all the different and manifold things in our lives and the lives of others. All things seek some good, and the totality of the good is impossible without understanding the connection of different opinions and beliefs. For example, Plato's *Meno* is about the human ability to educate oneself away from the specific towards the general. Furthermore, it is about the emancipatory necessity of seeing how common purpose resides in particular perspectives. The 'standard', that which makes all the relative identities the same, is the *eidos*, or the shape or form. The standard is the thing around which all the manifold changes coalesce.[15] This is not an end in itself; it is the goal towards which all things move.

In the *Republic*, Plato calls this process of conversation, discussion and interlocution a 'synopsis', or the drawing-together of the varied characteristics of a phenomenon. I am less interested here in Plato's ontology or metaphysics than in the pedagogical consequences

of his thought. For my purposes, *The Sunset Limited* functions philosophically by offering an analogous synopsis of Black's and White's
perspectives. For Plato and for McCarthy, we see that the effort
to construct a synopsis is essential for pedagogical dramatics. For
example, in Plato's *Meno*, this happens with the young slave boy that
Socrates teaches. The boy begins without knowing how to complete
constructing Pythagoras's theorem. Socrates awakens the pre-existing
dispositions of the boy, helping him transcend the self-conception he
inhabits as a slave, unwittingly believing that he is in a world where
he cannot learn. By dint of learning how things must be, the slave
boy comprehends that what he believes is apparent rather than real,
since he comprehends that what he takes to be true is only a limited
perspective. The synoptic drive requires drawing together both the
strange and the familiar, which in turn awakens a desire for learning. In *The Sunset Limited*, both White and Black view each other as
infantile and unformed. In McCarthy's play, Black and White engage
in a struggle and both make the effort to elevate their interlocutor
despite their intractable views. Here we can detect, at least minimally,
a common good. They are motivated by some obscure good and both
sincerely will a version of this good. While their unique standards
are peculiar to themselves, both are motivated by a desire to seek out
the good, even if they disagree on the way to find it. While it might
be argued that White does not will the good because of his fatalism,
he does, however, dimly yearn for a perverse form of goodness, even
if grimly found in the release of death where there is: 'only hope in
the nothingness', or when he subscribes to a 'religion which prepares
one for death'.[16] Black and White thus do hold in common the fact
that they are both exemplars of a standard towards which life ought
to strive, despite their spiritual differences. The logical prerequisite
of Black's and White's respective desires, of one's desire for life and
the other's desire for death, is that they both are desiring some good,
irrespective of their psychological insularity.

The Sunset Limited is also very much about the limits of faith and
conviction, the indefatigability of belief and its tragic consequences.
Plato's dialogues also are often premised on overcoming a pedagogical hierarchy between Socrates and his interlocutor to achieve equality beyond opinion. In the *Meno*, as mentioned, Socrates famously
helps a young slave boy to solve Pythagoras's theorem by construction. Socrates attempts to demonstrate that the boy is not determined
by his identity as a slave and attempts to elevate him into a position of equality through demonstrating how all people can access
knowledge irrespective of circumstance. In the *Meno*, wisdom and

virtue are general rather than specific. On this point McCarthy follows Plato. McCarthy's *The Sunset Limited* attempts to show a universal human experience rather than the individual beliefs of a theist and an atheist. In a way, both Black and White can adopt the mantle of Plato's Socrates. For Plato and for McCarthy, on this point at least, the good requires a synthesis; it is the exposure of Black's and White's perspectives to each other that brings about the possibility of concord. For Plato, the good is that which all things seek and desire.[17] McCarthy follows Plato up to a point, as deeper wisdom is found in the ability to perceive the one in the many. The good does not reside in specific faiths, or in Black's and White's beliefs and testimonies, but instead can be viewed as a 'whole', or the way in which both positions mutually inform each other.

Black in White: overcoming asymmetry

In *The Sunset Limited*, Black and White alternate in the role of Socrates. However, neither White nor Black persuades the other of their distinctive perspectives and they fail to reach a synopsis of their views. For example, Black repeatedly calls White 'honey' and a 'good lookin man'.[18] For his part, White attempts to sway Black with money. These two failed attempts at educational seduction show that in *The Sunset Limited* there is ultimately no educational conversion, although the play does hint at the possibility of transformation. Tragically, the two players remain rhetoricians, resorting to seducing the other to their views. To maintain that this play revels in asymmetry would be mistaken. On closer examination, the play is as much about the possibility of overcoming stark opinion as it is about irreconcilable pieties. While *The Sunset Limited* is superficially full of asymmetry, it also attempts to illuminate a deeper symmetry shared by both protagonists.

The Sunset Limited is a thought experiment in meaningful pedagogy. By meaningful pedagogy, I simply mean the capacity for a dialogue to engender an enriching transformation of the relevant interlocutors. If humans exist within the confines of their world, education is the ability freely to transcend determination by the limits of that world. But do the starkly opposed antagonists of *The Sunset Limited* reciprocally liberate each other? The extent to which Black and White become friends, teach each other something of worth, or even save each other is unclear by the play's denouement. Black may very well have failed to save White. *The Sunset Limited* is accordingly a pessimistic play, especially as exemplified through White's general fatalism and Black's failure to redeem White.[19] Ultimately, *The Sunset Limited* has no resolution and the arguments each character presents to the other cannot really be said to compel and persuade them to the other's point of view.

However, despite the ostensible pessimism of the play, we can begin to see several things that draw Black and White together. Firstly, the educational disparity brings them together. Their respective educational and socio-economic experiences have entrenched both men within their own perspectives. Secondly, violence unites Black and White – White in terms of the violence of his suicide attempt; Black in terms of the prison violence he has experienced. Black was in a place where White now is. Having nearly died, Black was cut up and chained to a hospital bed, in a state of living death, anticipating his own execution.[20] Thirdly, Black and White have certainty in common. The ability of the central protagonists to educate each other depends on their ability to overcome their biases and opinions through realising the limitations of their respective worldviews. While both men pose a certain worldview, as with many of McCarthy's characters, their self-interpretation is fraught and unsure. As such, the main obstacle these characters have to educating each other is themselves.

It is necessary to resist the temptation to see Black or White as being in the ascendancy; that is, it is important to avoid reading the text or performance with a preference for the perspective of either protagonist.[21] This is because the play is not an exercise in rational or spiritual proselytisation. The stark conversation of Black and White operates dialectically. It is the interdependence, the ebb and flow between the characters' interactions, which is meaningful, not their respective positions. In fact, I would go so far as to say that it is the extent to which both characters transcend their respective religiosity and atheism that makes the play one of McCarthy's most philosophically interesting works. The power of *The Sunset Limited* precisely resides in its ability to elucidate the unifying force of negating cherished perspectives and received dogmas. We find a rejection of Black and White's mutual certainties evidenced in McCarthy's subtle undermining of stereotypes.

Overcoming stereotypes helps underline the symmetry of the play. Superficially, one could say that Black and White conform to well-trod cultural types. After all, there is little more hackneyed than the oppositional confrontation between night and day, black and white, good and evil. McCarthy's characterisation of the play's two protagonists could even be perceived as trading in cheap stereotypes. Black is a poor black person living in a ghetto alongside drug addicts and thieves; he has been to prison but holds considerable 'street-smarts'. Conversely, White is a respectable middle-class professional, has been to college and is an intelligent and cerebral professor, devoted to a life of the mind, exuding deep familiarity with the artefacts of high culture. For example, White's taste for classical music by Beethoven is juxtaposed with Black's preference for popular art in the form of John Coltrane's jazz. However, my argument is that these oppositions are secondary rather than primary. As White explicitly states, he is the: 'professor of darkness. The night in day's clothing.'[22] White's statements provide us with a clue to McCarthy's deeper purpose, which is that the protagonists' adoption of the mantle of superficial types, when examined more closely, actually reveals a closer kinship, as both protagonists reflect traits of their opposite.

The subversion of obvious stereotypes becomes more apparent in the way both characters inflect, inhabit and haunt each other. Thus, what we take as the characters' individual opinions and perspectives are much more complicated and entwined than may initially seem apparent. We discover, for example, that Black, like White, was a vocational teacher of sorts while imprisoned. Black started a ministry before release, in contrast to his fellow convicts who 'just wanted it for their resumé'.[23] And this is not the only symmetry detectable in McCarthy's general subversion of clunky stereotypes.

We also see such a subversion in the nominal belief and non-belief of each character. While Black extols spiritual transcendence, his character also contains a heretical dimension. For example, while Black enjoys the spiritual direction of the Twelve Steps programme of Alcoholics Anonymous, those very rules, steps and directions are rejected. For Black: 'I hadnt set there too long fore I figured out that the God part was really all the part they was. The problem wasnt that they was too much God in AA it was that they wasnt enough.'[24] Black's religious affirmations are therefore thoroughly idiosyncratic, personal and incompatible with doctrinal commandments. Furthermore, Black admits, in the ultimate heretical expression, that he probably does not believe the 'literal truth' of the Bible.[25] When White casually dismisses Black by saying: 'Well I'm sorry, but to me the whole idea of God is just a load of crap',[26] Black demonstrates his ease with the blasphemy: 'Oh Lord have mercy oh save us Jesus. The professor's done blasphemed all over us. We aint never gone be saved now.'[27] Black is therefore a maverick spiritualist with an auto-hermeneutics of his own and for all he professes to be at ease with the spiritual realm, he is also a figure of doubt.[28] He says as much when asked if he is a heretic: 'I aint a doubter. But I am a questioner.'[29] That certainty and questioning are entwined indicates Black's questioning spirituality, with both White and Black in the place of Job.

Conversely, White's atheism is also ambiguous. Despite his obvious rejection of theism, it cannot be said that White offers a simplistic atheism. White's atheism contains a critique of conventional atheism; he asserts the philosophical dead-end of epistemological efforts to disprove God's existence. The 'village atheist' is a fool for White, trapped in a circular argument: 'And I loathe these discussions. The argument of the village atheist whose single passion is to revile endlessly that which he denies the existence of in the first place.'[30] White's atheism is more radical since it is also posed in a vocational way. White is messianic in his vision of the futility and suffering of the world and this view gives him his despairing meaning.[31] White's perspective is stripped of belief and thus he claims to hold a superior form of atheism: 'My own reasons center around a gradual loss of make-believe. That's all. A gradual enlightenment as to the nature of reality. Of the world.'[32] Despite White's rationality and logic, he too is possessed of a covert religious sentiment. For all the differences between Black and White, both are motivated by a desire to get to the heart of reality.

It is also the case that White's appreciation of high culture further demonstrates his entwined identity with Black. For White, art was instrumental to his salvation. White is a consumer of culture. The pedagogical capital he has accrued is built on a passive relationship to cultural artefacts, rather than conceiving them in a way that allows them to educate and edify himself. White's love of: 'Cultural things, for instance. Books and music and art. Things like that' are premised on a self-oriented messianism.[33] They exist only to save him: 'The things that I loved were very frail. Very fragile. I didnt know that. I thought they were indestructible. They weren't.'[34] White ultimately acknowledges that his infatuation with art was trivial rather than substantial. Although his path to enlightenment is fatalistic, he still professes to have strained to reach transformative truth bordering on the redemptive, even if it is ultimately moot. This provides further evidence of how McCarthy uses *The Sunset Limited* to subvert some stereotypical philosophical oppositions, specifically the philosophical binary of reason and emotion. White purports to conform to what really is a formulaic version of rationalism; like his idea of the rational and logical, however, much of what he professes is an assertion of pure voluntarism. White's supposed objective picture of reality is in fact highly subjective. White does not reach Platonic wisdom; he remains trapped in the personal, which clearly leads to his justification of his own non-existence. White deems his suffering more elevated, more real and therefore more of a candidate for cosmological insight than the suffering of others. White has a saviour complex, even if motivated by a cynicism which deems humanity's best option to be collective suicide.

What is distinctive about McCarthy's characterisation of White's rationalism is that although largely unsympathetic, White still represents an unusual spiritual rationalism, preaching about the logical inevitability of the church of nothingness: 'Show me a religion that prepares one for death. For nothingness. Theres a church I might enter.'[35] Once one subjects White's supposed rationality to deeper scrutiny it becomes clear that it is not rationality at all. His rational assertions are clichés, simulations of rational argument; what he proposes is well-rehearsed but emotional nonetheless, even if he endorses the primacy of the intellect. He feels the proximity and inevitability of death and substitutes his own emotions as if they were an objective standard for all humans. For instance, White clearly views the inevitability of death in emotional terms. Death is emotional and intimate; White understands it in terms of feelings such as joy, fear, love, torment, betrayal, loss, suffering and pain:

> If you could banish the fear of death from men's hearts they wouldnt live a day. Who would want this nightmare if not for fear of the next? The shadow of the axe hangs over every joy. Every road ends in death. Or worse. Every friendship. Every love. Torment, betrayal, loss, suffering, pain, age, indignity, and hideous lingering illness.[36]

White, in his own distinctive way, is a purveyor of religiosity. White's personal atheistic preferences in his view coincide with the totality of reality itself and thus his personality is psychologically equivalent to that of a deity: 'I don't regard my state of mind as some pessimistic view of the world, I regard it as the world itself.'[37] White's cosmic nihilism and rationalism exhibit their own messianism and faith, providing us with further evidence of the mutual intermingling of Black's and White's perspectives.

There is further evidence of the ways in which each character reflects the other. While White's cold rationalism is all feelings, one can equally say Black's emotional spiritualism is peculiarly rational. For example, Black exhibits mathematical proficiency throughout the play. He says: 'I'm a number man' prior to calculating the number of curses White has heaped on his fellow commuters over twenty years of commuting.[38] Earlier, Black impresses White with his ability for mental arithmetic.[39] For a Platonist, the alliance of mathematics and spirituality is unsurprising. However, what is interesting is that Black sees mathematics in very earthly terms. His numerical talents are associated with food, diet, theft and gambling: 'Numbers is the black man's friend. Butter and eggs. Crap table. You quick with numbers you can put the mojo on you brother. Confiscate the contents of his pocketbook. You get a lot of time to practice that shit in the jailhouse.'[40] Furthermore, Black sees salvation in material and sensuous terms as much as White sees artistic and cultural experience in transcendent terms: 'He said you could have *life* everlasting. Life. Have it today. Hold it in your hand. That you could see it. It gives off a light. It's got a little weight to it. Not much. Warm to the touch.'[41] In addition to understanding immortal life in sensuous terms, Black sees salvation construed in the material terms of craft and industry. Black says:

> At the deep bottom of the mine where the gold is at there aint none of that. There's just the pure ore. That forever thing. That you dont think is there. That thing that helps to keep folks nailed down to the platform where the Sunset Limited comes through.[42]

His faith is infused with material and sensuous life, which is a contradiction in terms, since salvation and immortal life must be immaterial rather than material. Black is haunted by White's atheist materialism, as much as White is haunted by Black's spirituality. And herein lies the crux of their symmetry.

What is important is that McCarthy has clearly put these two opposing characters into dialogue with each other and the dialogue demonstrates their symmetry and what they hold in common, even if they are radically divided in terms of access to the social capital of education. While *The Sunset Limited* appears to express a radical asymmetry, it is in fact motivated by a struggle to find symmetry and commonality. The subversion of types which McCarthy effects shows how characters have the capacity to share common ground even if they are fundamentally fixed in their opinion. This is why *The Sunset Limited* hinges on the success of an educational encounter. The existential test of McCarthy's play resides in seeing how knowledge and ignorance might be mutually informative. In terms of their oppositional identities, both men are full of certainty. The play is meaningful only to the extent that the light of their own truths is illuminated by either character coming to accept the possibility that their own positions are provisional, contingent, limited, and subject to scrutiny and scepticism. Ultimately, the educational encounter that we find in *The Sunset Limited* is Platonic in its incredulity against opinion and the self-certainty of knowledge.

The pedagogical dimension of *The Sunset Limited*

As a representation of education, *The Sunset Limited* offers a critique of educational institutions in the context of a broader critique of institutions within the play. Here we can see another, deeper symmetry come to the fore. Both Black and White are fundamentally critical of the same institutions, even if they come from different sides of them. For example, like Cornelius Suttree, White's father is a State official, in this case also a government attorney. And the institution of law and government is rejected by White in an absolute way when White admits he did not attend his father's funeral. Black is a representative of religious institutions even if, as I have already noted, his religiosity is complicated. More acutely, Black represents a critique of American penal institutions. Black has undertaken his own educational journey by way of his time in the American prison system. This is certainly an education, albeit an education premised on discipline, punishment and coercion. Educational institutions have not at all improved the lot of either character. Black's prison experience does not improve his material prospects. He lives in a poor neighbourhood, gets robbed and tries to save those who do not want to be saved. White's advanced education has not improved his outlook and offers no immunity to the violence he visits upon himself.

The deepening critique of educational institutions is more obviously present in White's professorship at a university. White is a representative of higher education but remains unsatisfied with the life of relative affluence and comfort which university employment provides, even while rebelling against it. He even draws an inflated and fatalistic comparison between his institution and the worst possible type of institution, that is, the concentration camp: 'The things I believed in dont exist any more. It's foolish to pretend that they do. Western Civilization finally went up in smoke in the chimneys of Dachau but I was too infatuated to see it. I see it now.'[43] White's university employment has not allowed him to discern how education can take one beyond the personal by depersonalising one's own suffering. White does not like his colleagues and assumes they do not like him. Additionally, for him the educational process is equivalent

to making the world personal: 'It is personal. That's what an education does. It makes the world personal.'[44] This is a solipsistic view
of education, but it is understandable given how White's attempted
suicide overshadows the dramatic arc of the story.

In the end, *The Sunset Limited* remains a pessimistic play. There is
no real resolution or moral triumph at the end and there is no obvious impression that Black or White persuade each other of the merits
of their own opinions, which they both hold in high regard, nor that
public institutions have the capacity to lessen their suffering. This
somewhat anarchic pessimism is ameliorated, however, through the
depiction of the ways in which Black and White inject uncertainty
into each other's mindsets. Both have some success in disrupting
each other's perspective: for example, Black concludes the play asking whether God is there since he fails in his mission to save White;
White, for his part, is continually shocked by Black's perspicuity and
vernacular intelligence. These disruptions allow McCarthy to reveal
a deeper humanity.

This helps the two men transcend their subjective stances towards
a more universal view of human experience. In the end, we do not
know if White in fact succeeds in taking his own life, despite how
certain he is of his choice and the way he professes it with messianic
zeal. Also, in the last line of the play, we are left with Black feeling
unsure of whether his deity is listening. It would seem the only certainty is uncertainty. This sceptical position, however, is necessary
in order to illuminate the educational dimension of the play. *The
Sunset Limited* is a Socratic play and it demonstrates the antagonistic entanglements of a true educational encounter, one where there
is a struggle to bring about mutual enlightenment. More accurately,
The Sunset Limited is about the failures of education. As such, the
stalemate which occurs at the conclusion of the play does not deliver
resolution, nor is there a pedagogical conversion where one character is convinced and transformed by the other's arguments. All that
the characters share is left unsaid.

As well as the general scepticism the play holds for institutional
power, there is a more immediate question of education springing from
the direct encounter between Black and White. It is commonplace to
suggest that an obstacle to an enlightening educational encounter is the
obstinate selfhood of the teacher. Both protagonists adopt a mentor-
mentee role in *The Sunset Limited*, and their selfhood impedes the possibility of having a transformative pedagogical encounter. The extent
to which they transcend this selfhood within their immediate encounter offers the possibility of discerning things which are lasting and of

value. Within the comfortable confines of their own personas, Black and White remain asymmetrical in their respective opinions. However, as they probe and test each other, McCarthy shows the extent to which their perspectives at least have the potential to find a more meaningful truth. Education, in the Platonic sense, requires *metanoia*, or a turning of the soul. Therefore, *The Sunset Limited*, from an educational vantagepoint, is interesting to the degree that the two characters can transcend their own opinions, self-narration and even self-mythologising to access a deeper symmetry.

Pedagogy of the expressed

The task of the educator, as we saw for Plato, is to create an egalitarian *ethos*; that is, the teacher must create the right moral atmosphere in which the student can be enabled to flourish. Education is essentially a form of growth, a process where student and teacher can mutually build on their existing skills. This was the message of the *Meno*, as I have shown: the slave boy develops his existing capacities and undermines the initial hierarchical relation between teacher and student. The achievement of equality is in turn enriching for the teacher, who by bringing out the best in people also brings out the best in themselves. By coming to know the standard of the good, the good grows within us and becomes the reality of our lives. What kind of moral atmosphere is created, then, in *The Sunset Limited*?

By the play's conclusion it would seem that the possibilities of a transformative teaching encounter are ended. It seems obvious that White will carry out his plan to kill himself, an absolute act that proscribes all further educational growth. Likewise, Black looks as if he is satisfied in his religious identity even if feeling momentarily disappointed by the lack of guidance he receives from God. In *The Sunset Limited* we fail to see how each pupil's transformation of their nature might be enriched by the light of the good. However, we do see that in the play, educational growth comes from the encounter itself, not from reference to external forms, political arrangements or pre-established forms. A point where McCarthy deviates from Plato is discernible in the role of recollection. In Plato, to recollect is a form of rebirth. Any pedagogical relation is what is known as *maieutic*. Philosophy itself is about reproducing forms of cultural life that are enduring and correspond to the eternal.[45] McCarthy sees pedagogical enlightenment in more historical terms, embedded in the activities, events and encounters of different protagonists. Where McCarthy's and Plato's educational insights do align is through the idea that an educational encounter itself can bring about equality, or the glimpse of a fundamental humanity. This is evident in the symmetry of Black and White which I have already outlined, but also in the fact that their strident positions are more equal than they suspect. McCarthy presents us, in *The Sunset Limited*, with essentially two Socratic characters.

The dramatic task of Socrates in the Platonic dialogues is to be disquieting. Socrates prods and probes his interlocutors into transcending their biases, the things they take for granted, to illicit a meaningful self-interrogation and self-transformation of the self. For Plato, education is a type of conversion, the *metanoia* discussed above. In *The Sunset Limited* this conversion is played out formally rather than in the psychological development of characters. Black begins in the ascendancy and White ends in the ascendancy. The move from Black to White presents a synopsis of the human condition; its conservative impulse is represented by Black and a creative, innovative impulse is symbolised by White. The play thus attempts to express the varied nature of the human condition.[46] Again, it is certainly not the case that McCarthy is asking the reader to come down on the side of the religious proclamations of Black, or to align with the atheistic leanings of White. The play performs and stages from the confines of expertise, or Black's and White's supposed 'subject-specialism'. It is only insofar as Black and White move out of their respective comfort zones that they near the stakes of philosophical education.

Black and White do have things in common and *The Sunset Limited* does present some oblique moments of pedagogical transformation. If true pedagogy requires a transformation of one's character, then such transformation requires uncertainty about the status of one's opinions. This is a necessary precondition for educational development. Despite Plato often being cast as the great rationalist, he very much thought that irrationality, while not good, does have a practical function in developing humans. For example, in Werner Jaeger's interpretation of Platonic education, Jaeger argues that an obdurate human irrationalism is useful since it provides humans with an inexhaustible font of renewable energy to ensure the good is kept in question.[47] Jaeger sees the intimacy of rationality and irrationality as being equivalent to a union of *eros* and *paideia*. A truly educational encounter requires the combination of divergent elements in order to see things of universal validity. Jaeger describes it, in a less abstract way, as the 'lively awareness of all the concrete facts of the life in which he is living'.[48] Jaeger draws his interpretation from Plato's *Symposium*. Desire, for Jaeger, is about the metaphysical yearning for wholeness, a yearning for something it is impossible to reconcile from an individual perspective. Therefore, *The Sunset Limited* may be firmly read within a Platonic tradition with one important caveat. For McCarthy, the sun of Plato's Cave remains limited, not absolute: it is a sunset, after all. The union of meaning which Black and White crave is impossible to attain on a spiritual level. Instead, the commonality they share is their experience together.[49]

McCarthy's *The Sunset Limited* shows two broken, fragmented men who are splintered across class, culture and, above all, by an educational divide. Both have a profound yearning for unity – Black for the unity of spirit, White for the peace that nothingness brings. This split corresponds to the foundation of Platonic love, where the human is a fragment striving for reunification with the other half that complements them. Plato's *Symposium* is very much about humans continually seeking to retrieve a lost whole.[50] McCarthy does deviate from Plato here, however. While the Platonic encounter requires leading our desire for unity, meaning and belonging towards recollection of the lost whole we already had, McCarthy is more radical: he views our capacity to educate others as requiring the realisation that there is no previous unity to recuperate. All we can do is bring together the radically disparate and divergent perspectives which constitute what we are. The 'one' can only remain a mixture, whereas Plato sees education as stimulated by the perpetual drive towards an unobtainable eternity. McCarthy's dialogue, while clearly in the Platonic tradition, does not see any hope of an ahistorical unity, since we draw only from the historical materials that constitute the development of our character. In *The Sunset Limited*, Black and White are men of no importance. Neither is successful, or at least their pursuits of material acquisition do not lead them to an enriching place. Black and White try to educate each other, but they have no cosmic standard or pre-established harmony to yearn towards.

The lives of Black and White cannot be explained solely on psychological grounds, nor on their biographical self-narration. Black and White are joined in a common tragedy, one where their loftiest endeavours and self-conceptions cannot transcend the inevitability of death, or The Sunset Limited and all of its 'terminal commuters'.[51] Both disappoint each other, failing to elucidate the truth as they perceive it. This disappointment makes palpable the lack which constitutes their lives. Both men exist in a state of common mournful unfulfillment. For Plato, the only way to overcome the mournful lack at the core of ourselves is by reasoning, examining and testing our way to the truth. The moral and pedagogical lesson of *The Sunset Limited* is that Black and White need each other – if only their arguments could become dialogue rather than monologues. And it is through contestation, conflict and antagonism that one can at least try to reason one's way to a distinctive life, to an examined life, to a life that is not pointless or ordinary, where one can discern what one really needs.[52]

There is, however, one clear moment where Black and White do attain a form of consensus, albeit temporarily. This is evident when Black provides White with some stew, bread and coffee and they both eat. This meal is the whole axis of the play. There is an obvious Christian resonance to it. The scene is a type of Eucharist, where radical opposites break bread with each other. They come together for a moment of respite over a meal, during which communion becomes possible. Prior to Black and White dining together, White has been extolling the 'primacy of the intellect'.[53] When he shares a meal with Black, they finally agree on something, which is the process of culinary innovation.[54] Innovation implies renewal and White, despite his preference for the intellect, has missed how eating, a bodily function, reanimates him, providing him with sustenance and energy to argue against Black for the remainder of the play. The meal provides both men with reanimation and renewal, a communal experience offering both of them agreement, accordance and some humour. Although a very temporary respite from the bleakness, a sense of possibility is tangibly present. Since eating is a universal necessity, the symbolic function of the meal gives both men something they share beyond their own individual viewpoint and that is how easy it is to share a sense of survival and common destiny.

This meal demonstrates McCarthy's mitigated Platonism. Both protagonists are a mixture of matter and meaning, embodiment and rationality. This scene shows how an ordinary event – even the most material of things, such as eating a meal – allows meaning to be transformed. The meal does not guarantee psychological or spiritual resurrection, but McCarthy does show how disparate identities can be drawn together. The meal provides an expansive context of meaning, one where change is not *just* a matter of the physical and biological processes of the digestive system being satiated, nor the individual opinions of Black and White, but more significantly, how shared possibility emerges in a context of common survival. Necessity brings about a temporary togetherness, which is so proximate to an essential survival function that it demonstrates McCarthy's concern to show that any form of salvation remains a synthesis of matter and meaning.

If anything, this meal shows why *The Sunset Limited* is an important piece of work for understanding the philosophical elements to McCarthy's literature. McCarthy's characters serve to render explicit how matter becomes discourse, that is, how material processes come to articulate themselves. The Platonic parallel is clear: our embodied selves seek and bear meaning. Here in the most material form of all, where food is ingested, the material concerns of human discourse transcend individual appetites and desires towards understanding the urgency of shared experience: one where the past, the present and the future are gathered together. In *The Sunset Limited* the respite is only temporary, rejuvenation is only partial, but such partial meaning does not preclude the importance of this moment. Here both men, even if unconsciously, are willing the good of the other and thus have insight and understanding of their fellow humans and the things they hold in common.

Conclusion

The Sunset Limited is about education and the possibility that one can teach and coach another towards meaning. The philosophical problem the play poses is not about the factual accuracy of the atheist's or the theist's worldview, but is a rather more radical question, which is how diametrical opposites generate a moral atmosphere of equality. The opposition between the nominally academically educated and uneducated is radically altered by McCarthy. Both Black and White offer each other a meaningful encounter, but only to the extent that they might allow themselves to expand their own philosophical identity. The tragedy of the play is that in the final reckoning, they do not. Black remains in his very modern Platonic Cave at the end, while White is more than likely going to take his own life. Indeed, White is the one who leaves this particular Cave, but without a Socrates to guide him towards the sunset. This is a play about radical differences, polarised opinions, and where reconciliation might be possible. On the surface *The Sunset Limited* appears to be about differences, but it is really a play about similarities. Both characters are led away from their moral sentiments. Therefore, it is erroneous to suggest that the play comes down on the side of either atheism or theism. It is instead a play about a dialectical encounter, one where each protagonist injects disquiet and irresolution into the other to a point at which they verge on teaching each other something.

The conundrum of *The Sunset Limited* is felt in the effort to bring together spiritual and material interpretations of the world. Neither discourse is sufficient. In *The Sunset Limited*, McCarthy again tries to understand the human as a being that is cultural and material, at once material and transcending those very material processes which constitute us. Through the language, culture and society of the characters, the play begs the question as to how far an educational encounter between two people can transcend institutions, politics, culture and language itself. McCarthy's play, in a Socratic vein, puts education in dialogue with ignorance, belief with unbelief, matter with spirit, knowledge with error – and thus any resolution remains inherently elusive. This is because these things, matter and spirit, belief and unbelief, are never absolute but always inform each other. The reversals and paradoxes that Black and White elicit from each other achieve a mix of the tangible and the intangible. Really, the target which McCarthy and Plato both have in their sights is the notion of unquestioned belief and opinion.

Black and White have their dogmas. One of Plato's points is that the student must have a desire to learn. You cannot really force the student to learn. It is only by channelling desire into productive and creative practices that you can stimulate educational development. The ruses, prodding and stratagems with which Black and White engage each other leave them in a state of *aporia*. Both reach a state of disquiet and they experience manifold contradictory ideas together. In a way, the reality is that they have a common struggle. Both fight for each other's souls. In Plato one must have a yearning, a desire, a cognitive longing to transcend our habitual dispositions in order to connect to reality. In *The Sunset Limited* that reality remains on the side of conflict, in the productive antagonism of conflicting positions. So although the text has Platonic resonance, wisdom and insight remain tied to the lived experiences of the characters in this world.

Student and teacher are elevated above the material world in order to see the truth of humanity's common problems. It is only within a situation, an event, or a face-to-face lived encounter, rather than experience mediated through institutions, that McCarthy shows how Black and White have the possibility of reaching some accord. It is Black's and White's potential ability to overcome their personal identity which would allow them to achieve an impersonal vision, one not obscured by their personal predilections and attachments. This impersonality is the bedrock of the educative process, one that can allow us to participate and see excellent things that make life worth living. *The Sunset Limited* explores this more than anything. Is it possible for one human to save another? If Black and White can shift their own moral psychology towards a view of what is important, meaningful and good, then they can educate each other. McCarthy is pessimistic about the easiness of stepping outside one's psychic reality to comprehend humanity's common fate, and yet his dialogue shares with Plato the urge for the characters of their dialogues to transcend their individual and contingent human nature. McCarthy is not as utopian as Plato, as the means for educational self-transcendence take place in small, face-to-face and direct educational encounters rather than via the comprehensive political therapy Plato prescribes.

Notes

1. 'Donald Trump Nevada Watch Party & Victory Speech', YouTube video, 5:28, posted by 'Bright Side Broadcasting Network', 23 Feb 2016, <https://www.youtube.com/watch?v=kdA4ru5Z1aI>
2. This point is supported by research carried out by the Pew Centre, which found that those without a college degree backed Trump 52%-44%. See Alec Tyson and Shiva Maniam, 'Behind Trump's Victory: Divisions by Race, Gender, Education', *Pew Research Center*, 9 November 2016, <https://pewrsr.ch/2IrtQex>. For a good summary of these issues see David Runciman, 'How the Educational Gap is Tearing Politics Apart', *The Guardian*, 5 October 2016, <https://bit.ly/2dIYjmz>
3. Rick Wallach, in conversation with Dianne Luce, has shown that the actual Sunset Limited was a transcontinental Amtrak train running from Orlando to Los Angeles. At the time of writing, this Sunset Limited still runs from New Orleans to Los Angeles three days a week. See Dianne C. Luce, 'Cormac McCarthy's *The Sunset Limited*: Dialogue of Life and Death (A Review of the Chicago Production)', *The Cormac McCarthy Journal* 6 (2008): 14.
4. See McCarthy, *The Sunset Limited* (London: Picador, 2011), 3 and 143. Hereafter *SL*.
5. It is worth noting the rich symbolic register of the play's title. That a sunset is limited implies ambiguity. It also points to the essential incompleteness of Black and White. Furthermore, the term 'limited' denotes the incomplete, the imperfect, the partial. The sun is the totality of a higher power, which is demarcated by the limitations of the different perspectives of Black and White. The play's title can also refer to a very concrete material thing – a very specific, named train. The train refers to death and the finitude of the human condition, as it is the method by which White seeks to end his life. Furthermore, there is an economic and financial symbolism at work. 'The Sunset Limited' could be the name of a company, incorporating financial and materialistic elements.

Sunset implies twilight. However, it is the twilight that is limited, as if the sun is the circle of the Dao bisected into its different parts. While the train is a very concrete and material thing, McCarthy, in keeping with his preoccupation with framing the human condition as a mixture of spirituality and materialism, also makes a spiritual reading plausible. The title can thus be read as evoking the Yin-Yang symbolism of Daoism, as found in Lao Tzu's *Tao Te Ching*. The Black and White resonance is indicated through the dark swirl of yin and the light swirl of yang. Both swirls have a dot of the other colour which affirms how Black and White inhabit each other. In *The Sunset Limited*, Black and White both contain seeds of their opposites. It is thus important that we see Black and White not as total opposites but as being relative to each other. However, some caution should be exercised in over-extending the Yin-Yang symbolism. Daoism is premised on living in harmony with reality. The two violent acts which overhang the play, White's suicide and Black's attempted murder, delimit the possibility of reading *The Sunset Limited* as a simple affirmation of cosmic harmony. See Lao Tzu, *Tao Te Ching: A Book about the Way and the Power of the Way*, trans. J. P. Seaton and U. K. Le Guin (Boulder: Shambala Publications), 1998.

6. The film version of *The Sunset Limited* has a black-and-white tiled floor redolent of a chessboard. *The Sunset Limited*, directed by Tommy Lee Jones (2011; Burbank, CA: Warner Home Video 2012), DVD.
7. McCarthy, *SL*, 105.
8. *Paideia* is a deeply resonant Greek term. It can mean 'civilisation', 'culture', 'development', 'tradition', 'literature' or 'education'.
9. Martin Heidegger, *The Essence of Truth: On Plato's Cave Allegory and Theaetetus*, trans. Ted Sadler (New York: Continuum, 2002), 82.
10. In the closing stage direction, Black undoes the chains to the door of the apartment (141).
11. Heidegger is clear that we cannot understand education as the mere transmission of information. There is a clear rejection of the idea that the mind is a *tabula rasa*, into which can be inscribed relevant lessons. The rejection of the human as a blank slate chimes with Heidegger's understanding of the historical nature of *Dasein*. If the human being is historical, this presupposes humans constantly move from a past to a present and on to a future, which cannot be equivalent to the passive reception of sensory information. Authentic education transforms our historical development. Thus, for Heidegger, education is not only *Bildung* or character-formation, it also requires historical development. See Heidegger, *The Essence of Truth*, 83. It is also worth noting that Heidegger sees a problem in Plato's pedagogy about the setting of standards. The urge to think of education as correct, or as a true measure, precipitates the understanding of the human being as a mere repository of educational content. Heidegger's interpretation of Plato recognises the ambiguous nature of Plato's contribution to education. On one

hand, Heidegger's Plato sees the transformational necessity of questioning and ignorance and knowledge, but on the other, Plato contains the seeds of a dry technologised education, or what is known pejoratively as 'rote learning'.

12. While many of Plato's dialogues express the desire for a common purpose, one of the most explicit examples of this can be found in Plato's *Gorgias*, where he confronts the ruthlessly cynical Callicles. Plato, *Gorgias*, trans. Robin Waterfield (Oxford: Oxford University Press, 2008), 102–5.

13. Plato, *Republic*, trans. Desmond Lee (Harmondsworth: Penguin, 2003), 237–40.

14. Plato, *Protagoras and Meno*, trans. W. K. C. Gutherie (Harmondsworth: Penguin, 1956), 140.

15. There are centuries of scholarship on what Plato means by the forms. I am not interested in these studies for the purposes of this analysis. While these commentaries are endlessly fascinating, I am only interested here in the pedagogical dimension of Plato's metaphysics. The most significant classical synthesis of Plato's work on education, to which I will refer herein, is by Werner Jaeger, *Paideia: The Ideals of Greek Culture*, vol. 2, *In Search of the Divine Centre*, trans. Gilbert Highhet (Oxford: Blackwell, 1947).

16. McCarthy, *SL*, 141 and 137.

17. The idea of the good relates to Plato's conception of form, or as it is also known, his theory of ideas. The good, or excellence, is *areté* which is not necessarily something that can be absolutely defined or thought just in terms of a correct standard. The idea is the orientation or disposition towards which all things move. Education is the process whereby we incorporate all that is good in the cosmos. Achieving this is not at all easy for Plato and requires enormous self-discipline: self-discipline to such a degree that it might not be possible for many mortals. However, the good is still a standard which we desire and towards which we aim.

18. McCarthy, *SL*, 5, 65, 70.

19. *The Sunset Limited* is not as pessimistic as *The Road*, which was published in the same year. In *The Road* the father-mentor teaches his child just enough to carry him towards a bleak future. As is so often the case in McCarthy, children are avatars of possibility. *The Sunset Limited*'s lack of children underlines the impossibility of redemption. Of course, the question of children strikes to the core of the question of *paideia*. The common understanding of the *paideia* refers to its Ancient Greek origin, where the term refers to education, rearing and the socialisation of children.

20. McCarthy, *SL*, 107.

21. This is not to say that theological or atheistic readings of *The Sunset Limited* are irrelevant. Such readings are perfectly legitimate and can be brilliantly helpful in elucidating the theological and atheistic traits

of both Black and White. The point is simply that one must be cautious and not biased towards either the religious or the atheistic characteristics of Black and White. My argument is that this play is valuable not because of who we sympathise with, but because of the way it stages a dialectical synthesis of these different positions. For a good example of a subtle theological reading see Mary Brewer, 'The light is all around you, cept you dont see nothin but shadow': Narratives of Religion and Race in *The Stonemason* and *The Sunset Limited*', *The Cormac McCarthy Journal* 12, no.1 (2014): 39–54. For an excellent account of Beckett's existential atheism see Lydia Cooper, '"A Howling Void": Beckett's Influence in Cormac McCarthy's *The Sunset Limited*', *The Cormac McCarthy Journal* 10, no.1 (2012): 1–15.

22. McCarthy, *SL*, 140.
23. Ibid. 40.
24. Ibid. 62.
25. Ibid.
26. Ibid.
27. Ibid. 63.
28. Robert Wyllie notes that Black exhibits a very strange universalism, one deviating from traditional Christianity, where: 'whatever truth is wrote in these pages [of the Bible] is wrote in the human heart'. Robert Wyllie, 'Kierkegaard Talking Down Schopenhauer: *The Sunset Limited* as a Philosophical Dialogue', *The Cormac McCarthy Journal* 14, no.2 (2016): 195.
29. McCarthy, *SL*, 67.
30. Ibid. 137.
31. Again, see Robert Wyllie for a good account of White's Schopenhauerian characteristics.
32. McCarthy, *SL*, 120.
33. Ibid. 25.
34. Ibid.
35. Ibid. 137.
36. Ibid. 137–8.
37. Ibid. 136.
38. Ibid. 90.
39. Ibid. 17.
40. Ibid.
41. Ibid. 78.
42. Ibid. 95.
43. Ibid. 27.
44. Ibid. 26, 82.
45. The *maieutic* relates to Socrates's role as the 'midwife' of knowledge. Education is the painful process of giving birth to our latent dispositions to know the truth. The necessity of Philosophy as a discipline is that it helps ensure that we can reproduce forms of life which are not just

based on ourselves, that is, based on a narcissistic re-appropriation of ourselves. *Eros* is the impulse of our bodies and desires to be 'immortal'. The closest we come to attaining such a state is a makeshift reproduction of ourselves in our offspring. Generally, Plato saw that if this desire for immortal life or lasting reputation were to be channelled into ambition it would have malign consequences. Plato resists the Sophists, since their form of education was directed towards reproducing techniques which allowed people to attain and maintain political glory. What remains of their mortal life is the stamp they put on the history of their times, the making of their own names. For Plato, what is of the utmost significance is that all that is meaningful is dependent on the begetting of oneself, the desire to perpetuate oneself through creation and love. Love and work, passion and labour are what become most important.

46. The obvious absences of women, homosexuals, lesbians and transgender people preclude suggestion that the play represents the totality of human experience. As a play, however, the text can be more flexible in performance. For example, with special permission from McCarthy, a staging of the play took place in June 2019 in Key West, Florida which cast women in the lead roles. See 'Actresses pull a gender flip on *The Sunset Limited*', *Florida Weekly: Key West Edition*, 30 May 2019, <https://keywest.floridaweekly.com/articles/actresses-pull-a-gender-flip-on-the-sunset-limited/> [accessed 1 July 2019]

47. Jaeger, *Paideia: The Ideals of Greek Culture*, vol. 2, 178.

48. Ibid. 178.

49. Dianne Luce, in her reading of *Child of God* in *Reading the World: Cormac McCarthy's Tennessee Period*, provides a careful delineation of the Platonic influences on McCarthy. Luce argues that while the work of Plato and McCarthy are not synonymous, McCarthy is motivated by the same spirit of searching for value and meaning. For Luce, at least in the earlier novels, McCarthy does not share Plato's affirmation of an afterlife, unification with the divine or reincarnation. Luce's broader point is that McCarthy's Platonism is tempered by his interest in existentialism and American transcendentalism. Dianne Luce, *Reading the World: Cormac McCarthy's Tennessee Period*, (Columbia, SC: University of South Carolina Press, 2010), 158–9.

50. Plato, *Symposium*, trans. Christopher Gill (London: Penguin, 2003), 23–4.

51. McCarthy, *SL*, 85.

52. This characterisation of the unexamined life is drawn directly from Rebecca Goldstein's account of the transformation from the Homeric tradition of heroism to the philosophical tradition, or the movement from *kleos* to the examined life. See Rebecca Goldstein, *Plato at the Googleplex* (London: Atlantic Books, 2014), 254.

53. McCarthy, *SL*, 96.

54. Ibid. 100–1.

Chapter 5

Anti-Matters: Mortal Ethics in *The Road*

To say McCarthy's writing is describable as a form of tempered Platonism, as I did in the previous chapter, requires further elaboration. *The Road*, published in the same year as Chapter 4's *The Sunset Limited*, thus becomes a key text for helping to expand and develop my overall thesis that McCarthy provides a unique literary fusion of materialism and metaphysics. *The Road* is specifically important because the novel provides a clear example of how the material and metaphysical entwine in an idiosyncratic way in McCarthy's writing. In *The Road* we find McCarthy's appreciation of how physical and material processes, writ large in the thermodynamic collapse of the material universe, function as a metaphysical horizon for the novel's protagonists. While such an understanding of metaphysics might not align with the conventional or classical understanding of metaphysics, where metaphysics is the 'science' of reality as such, or the 'science' of the first causes of things, McCarthy's writing, I will argue, is premised on such a bold proposition.

In *The Road*, we find McCarthy's physics of the damned most dramatically expressed. While there have been valuable theological, metaphysical and materialist readings of *The Road*, it is important to say that neither the materialist nor theological ultimately suffices for apprehending just what McCarthy has philosophically accomplished with *The Road*.[1] I argue therefore that welding the materialist elements of the novel with the novel's more clearly theological and spiritual elements – whilst not reducing one to the other – is essential for articulating the difficult philosophical 'between' in McCarthy's thought. This fusion, in turn, offers a mortal ethics which I argue has distinct consequences for understanding philosophical concepts of memory, community and McCarthy's effort to construct universal forms of being together.

McCarthy's *The Road* presents a perverse 'anti-metaphysics' which emerges from the consequences of the material destruction of the world. This is not to say that McCarthy may be called solely a materialist or a metaphysician, but is rather to argue that his work exists in a hinterland between. Hence, it is necessary to show how traditional metaphysical questions about the nature of justice, the soul and values meld with the brutally indifferent reality of the material universe. This, I argue, is the key to understanding both *The Road* specifically and McCarthy's philosophical concerns more generally. Firstly, I will attempt to explain how *The Road* works to confront this material logic. Secondly, I will develop McCarthy's material logic through examples from the novel. Finally, I will specify how questions of materialism show the ways in which the novel stages questions of memory and community. *The Road* is particularly instructive for examining these themes. The novel's staging of the material destruction of the world, the brutal consequences this presents for the protagonists, and their forlorn fumbling for ethical values, provides an exemplar for articulating McCarthy's philosophical concerns.

As I have noted from the outset, the role of philosophy in the work of Cormac McCarthy has been examined in a variety of academic contexts. For several decades this scholarship, naturally interdisciplinary, has revolved around issues concerning existentialism, theological and religious questions, post-structural readings of power, and often Nietzschean interpretations which see McCarthy's work as shorthand for the search for transcendent meaning in a meaningless world. Much philosophical work on McCarthy characterises his reflections as a direct response to philosophical and political themes such as the post-theological, neoliberalism, late capitalism, deindustrialisation, violence, jurisprudence and mortality.[2] If I am correct that placing McCarthy's work in a philosophical context allows a richer account of his literature, then it is necessary to show how McCarthy's literature provides its own unique response to very traditional philosophical questions of ethics, ontology, epistemology and aesthetics.

It is important to realise that just as McCarthy is resistant to literary classification, this also holds for classification of his work into the various branches of philosophy. McCarthy's literature works at the intersection of traditional philosophical categories. For instance, in this chapter, I will look at how McCarthy evokes and subverts metaphysical questions about the nature of the material universe in order to make specific claims about the nature of ethics and mortality. The value of my approach is that it allows a novel way to understand McCarthy's ethical concerns. While scholars such as David

Holloway and Alberto Siani have already proposed that McCarthy's literature is geared towards undermining the centrality of human beings and our values, with a view towards placing humans in the wider context of society, nature, environment and the material and economic production of the world we inhabit, my analysis allows a distinct account of how McCarthy's representation of the material world informs his ethical and ontological vision of humans as ethical beings.[3] However, in the final analysis, *The Road*'s anti-metaphysics is in fact a more radical fusion of materialism and metaphysics, where characters are entangled in a cold cosmology, struggling to construct ethics in the face of the ultimate thermodynamic collapse of the universe. *The Road* is philosophically interesting because it continues McCarthy's commitment to understanding the human as caught up in the wider processes of the world, the lawlessness and indifference of nature and the ways in which such lawlessness affects the human community. This quest for understanding is most palpable in the bleak world stripped of all civility which we find in *The Road*.

The physics of the damned

How is it possible to configure materialism in *The Road*? Basically, materialism is the philosophical thesis wherein all manifestations of life are subordinate to processes involved in the organisation of matter. The different philosophical registers of materialism include material monism, which is the philosophical proposition that all things can be reduced to one substance, such as matter; there is also historical materialism in the Marxist sense, where the progression of history is determinable by material relations of economics and production. In addition – and a key theme in *The Road* – is the question of consumer materialism, where humans are defined through the consumption of material commodities. In his 2006 appearance on *The Oprah Winfrey Show*, McCarthy clearly expresses his indifference to consumer materialism. The common denominator of the different materialisms is that all explanation must be a direct result of physical interactions. Vital or spiritual accounts are not possible. In other interpretations, materialism can offer a more sophisticated account of the world than simple reductionism. Philosophers of science call this physicalism, where material processes are complex rather than simple, including quarks, forces, dark matter, space-time and thermodynamics. This physicalism is perhaps more relevant to McCarthy, since he is neither a reductionist nor a spiritualist and he does have a literary and philosophical purchase. From Plato onwards, the material world is tangled, twisted and subterranean, a shadow of the real.

How, then, is *The Road* a novel about materialism, when its setting is unambiguously the aftermath of the material destruction of the world? The answer is complicated. The world the father and son inhabit is certainly material, made up of stuff, denuded of any vital or spiritual force. The biosphere in the novel is saturated in ash; the apocalyptic landscape is a by-product of materialism. However, this is certainly a type of material monism at work. The world of the novel is reduced to one indistinguishable substance. In *The Road*, material things are becoming indistinct. There are no longer distinct objects with distinct form. Plants, trees, roads, coins, buildings are all faced with the prospect of becoming a homogenous material whole, where no object is individuated. Spinoza sees such indistinction as the foundation for a form of pantheism, where all bodies are not different objects, but different configurations of one substance: God or nature.[4] However, I will argue here that this interpretation is not possible within the anti-metaphysics presented in *The Road*. The uniform ash which attaches itself to all objects, persistently sticking to all things including the air itself, only reveals further forms of elemental matter and is no benign spiritual substance which can offer salvation to the characters or even the universe itself.

McCarthy, rather than erecting a theological cosmology, presents in *The Road* an inverted cosmology. Here there is no longer a world of substantial things and such things have no guarantee of a spiritual foundation. Instead, things are presented as sinking into a uniform void. The aesthetic of *The Road* that emerges through the material destruction of the world is fascistic; wanton material destruction reveals uniformity and homogeneity. The world in which the father and son dwell revels in a mix of destruction and homogeneity; communities in the novel are closed orgiastic blood cults and innumerable survivors exist in cannibal camps, becoming indistinguishable from each other. In this novel more than any other, McCarthy tackles head-on the power of nothingness and destruction, as they formally manifest in uniformity. The father worries: 'everything depended on reaching the coast, yet waking in the night he knew that all of this was empty and had no substance to it'.[5] This is a world in which: 'The frailty of everything [is] revealed at last.'[6]

At the core of all things there is, as Maurice Blanchot would have it, a mute and anonymous void. *The Road* is an exemplar of Blanchot's theory of literature. Here, language and the literary text operate without ownership and are 'addressed to no one, which has no centre, and which reveals nothing'.[7] To put it in terms more relevant to McCarthy's fiction, the personal, collective and objective movement of all life propels itself towards death. For Blanchot, when all things become nothing or absolute death, it becomes impossible to discern purpose or significance. In *The Road*, the creation of value and purpose is only valuable to the extent that we negate the nothingness that accompanies our existence. This evacuation of substance illuminates McCarthy's anti-metaphysics most acutely. McCarthy certainly thinks there is human participation in something larger than ourselves. However, that something greater is the material negation of the universe.

In scientific terms, we can hypothesise how this metaphysical horizon maps onto the second law of thermodynamics, where entropy, the measure of disorder inherent in any system, increases.[8] Basically, all systems, anything that exists, including the universe, progressively devolves into a state of disorder. The more the energy in the universe is spread out, the harder it is to use energy in the construction of systems and life. To understand McCarthy, it is necessary to see humans as in some way participating in this type of interminable destruction. However, we must retain caution regarding the aptness of using thermodynamics as a literary metaphor. This is because thermodynamics easily conflates with gothic metaphors of the beauty of decay and degeneration. The reason thermodynamics is richer metaphorically is because it gives expression to how systems decay and construct themselves. The way systems conserve energy and structure, despite entropy, is a suitable metaphor relevant to *The Road*, since this is a novel that valorises neither the theological spirit of life, nor the nihilism of absolute death, but instead attempts to understand the complicity of materiality and its dissolution. Indeed, the struggles of the father and son exist at the threshold of life and death, thus giving *The Road* a unique philosophical aesthetic in its own right – one neither conventionally metaphysical nor reductively materialist.

More specifically, the intermingling of matter and metaphysics is evident in the disintegration of objects in the novel. Take for example McCarthy's description of a swamp:

A dead swamp. Dead trees standing out of the grey water trailing grey and relic hagmoss. The silky spills of ash against the curbing. He stood leaning on the gritty concrete rail. Perhaps in the world's destruction it would be possible at last to see how it was made. Oceans, mountains. The ponderous counterspectacle of things ceasing to be. The sweeping waste, hydroptic and coldly secular. The silence.[9]

Despite the spectacle of cosmic devastation, the obvious anti-creationism, we still glimpse the skeletal and formal structure of the world. All systems susceptible to the loss of energy are simultaneously systems that maintain a relative identity over time. Even at the level of absolute destruction, just before everything sinks into the void, existence itself offers a 'counterspectacle'. In the world's destruction, things that cease to be have their own life. Therefore, McCarthy cannot be stringently categorised as either a materialist or a spiritualist; he is not on the side of immanence or transcendence. If theologically we might say that we participate in something larger than ourselves – in energy, or in the cosmos – then for McCarthy, what we participate in is the inherent violence of a universe living on borrowed time:

> He'd had this feeling before, beyond the numbness and the dull despair. The world shrinking down about a raw core of parsible entities. The names of things slowly following those things into oblivion. Colors. The names of birds. Things to eat. Finally the names of things one believed to be true. More fragile than he would have thought. How much was gone already. The sacred idiom shorn of its referents and so of its reality. Drawing down like something trying to preserve heat. In time to wink out forever.[10]

McCarthy thus offers a fundamentally tragic and pessimistic ontology.[11] Reality itself is neutral, inhospitable and cold; the material universe offers no meaning or purpose. 'Truth has no temperature', as Malkina suggests in McCarthy's *The Counsellor*.[12] It is not just that the universe is indifferent; there is also a negativity attached to all things. We see this in *Suttree*, in *Outer Dark*, in *Blood Meridian*, and it is represented by Chigurh in *No Country for Old Men*. In *Suttree*, this perverse material logic is evident when Suttree, following Harrogate, descends into an anti-Cathedral beneath Knoxville. This 'material negativity' persists throughout McCarthy's work, haunting all characters, objects and structures. Existence has no theological origin, only the possibility of systems and structures persisting in resistance to the impending material negation of the cosmos. As Markus Wierschem suggests:

> [T]he full extent of McCarthy's syncretic vision is revealed in condensed form: the fall of the planet, the decline of civilization, and the loss of meaning are inseparable from each other. In the aesthetics of *The Road*, notions of thermodynamic, cultural and informational entropy form a programmatic whole with its apocalyptic and secular dimensions.[13]

The broader dissolution of the universe is intractable and can only be mitigated at best. Suttree is just one of McCarthy's characters who finds a way to coexist with this.

The ethical force of *The Road* develops through the way in which father and son can sustain ethical possibility despite their predicament and the brutal reality of the cosmos. This resistance to the theological origin of the universe incorporates all forms of spiritualism. Spiritual materialisms and versions of pantheisms such as, for example, the pantheism of Spinoza, are entangled with theological ideas of eternity, or the idea that all things are derived from one eternal substance. Conventional theologies, as well as pantheistic ones, are ultimately without time, without becoming. As the boy grasps early in *The Road*: 'Ever is a long time. But the boy knew what he knew. That ever is no time at all.'[14] In eternity, nothing can happen or come to be as there is no temporal life, no violence and no contradiction. The boy is a symbol of temporal and mortal life, exposed to violence and risk, standing in stark opposition to an eternity where nothing is possible.

Additionally, the avatar of complete hopelessness in the novel is the mother. The mother desires eternal peace as the only rational route to salvation: 'my only hope is for eternal nothingness and I hope it with all my heart'.[15] The mother, exhibiting a brutally rational theology, sees the inevitable presence and the absolute death of eternity as the best of all possible worlds and the best possible outcome for all. Conversely, the boy and his father act respectively as symbols of the future and the past. The ability of the father and the son to survive within a precarious world, for the father to turn the past into the future through his son and for the son to take up the possibility of the future despite the incessant dissolution which inhabits all things and structures, gives the novel its distinct ethical outlook. *The Road* acknowledges the complicity of life and death, as well as the material structure and decay within the ethical struggles of the central protagonists of the novel.

While there is certainly a sense that humans are caught up in wider material processes, we must not be tempted to replace this with spiritualism of any sort, as this would diminish the dramatic potency of the text, as well as diminishing *The Road*'s unique attempt to articulate a mortal ethics outside strictly metaphysical or materialist frameworks.[16] For the aesthetic staging of the novel, the material world of things sinks into a uniform material void. McCarthy resists a strict material reductionism, as much as he resists conventional theological explanations of the universe. This resistance is decisive for articulating the unique ethical focus of the novel and for his attempt to think through ethical affirmation despite the material absurdity of the universe. As such, *The Road* presents the aftermath of materialism; the material universe is decaying and the world of *The Road* is the apogee of nihilism, with an absolute void manifested openly in a world without distinction. Philosophically, *The Road* thus endorses neither a conventional theology nor crude materialism.[17] *The Road*'s philosophical power emerges from elaborating how humans can have resistance, transformation, possibility, creation, a future and hope alongside and despite the material negation of the universe.

One might object that the anti-metaphysical reading I am proposing veers too much towards the godless. However, the point is that McCarthy is offering neither a conventional theology nor a crude atheism. It is fair to say that *The Road* frequently uses sacramental language, particularly in relation to the aura of the boy. For example, the boy is likened to a golden chalice: 'good enough to house a god'. His father is convinced that he is 'appointed by God' to care for the child.[18] From the outset the recurring symbol of fire is present, with the boy considered as equivalent to a lit candle. The boy is a 'tiny paradise'.[19] Most obviously, the boy is considered equivalent to the Eucharist as a messianic Host watching a flake of snow fall, expiring 'like the last host of christendom'.[20] The novel ends with an image of a fish, which could be read as a Christian symbol.[21]

However, while sacramental language is used, it would be a non-sequitur to suggest that such sacramental imagery endorses a theological desire to transcend material life, or that the values which emerge from the struggle for mortal survival are redundant simply because there is sacramental imagery in the novel.[22] The function of religious terminology in *The Road* operates to make the empty material universe more palpable. McCarthy uses sacramental language to make a clear ethical point. The boy is a symbol of inherent goodness. However, this goodness is brittle and fragile, even if inherent. It is premised on the contingency of the future and the material struggles of the protagonists. By the conclusion of *The Road* it is clear that the boy, like all the others, is not spiritually elevated nor immune from very real material needs. The boy must face the prospect of starvation and its attendant spiritual and moral degradation once the scavenging of ever-dwindling resources and canned goods expires. The world cannot be redeemed. This is underlined in the final words of the novel:

Once there were brook trout in the streams in the mountains. You could see them standing in the amber current where the white edges of their fins wimpled softly in the flow. They smelled of moss in your hand.

Polished and muscular and torsional. On their back were vermiculate patterns that were maps of the world in its becoming. Maps and mazes. Of a thing which could not be put back. Not be made right again. In the deep glens where they lived all things were older than man and they hummed of mystery.[23]

The order of the cosmos is broken and irreparable, and the possibility of reaching a redeemed state is firmly precluded. Thus, all the sacramental images in *The Road* are entwined with notions of expiration and death.[24] At the opening of the novel we see the father wake: 'He pushed away the plastic tarpaulin and raised himself in the stinking robes and blankets and looked toward the east for any light but there was none.'[25] This could easily be read as a reference to the Magi, and yet it is clear that the messianic is entwined with the profane, as no redemption is present. It is wholly necessary for the ethical consistency of the novel that sacramental iconography is entwined with images of dissolution and decay. The mingling of structures and dissolution gives the novel its distinct perspective on mortal ethics and is thus exceptionally important for the moral fulcrum of the novel, as we cannot literally take the child to be a Host, since what separates the father and the boy from others is that they do not eat anybody in any circumstances. After all, in communion, the divine Host is literally the divine-made-mortal flesh which is to be incorporated via ingestion.

Perhaps a more obvious example of the dissolution of the sacramental is the use of tabernacles in the novel. The boy is represented as a tabernacle. Tabernacles are usually ornate, bejewelled and considered as sacred and inviolable places where the Host is kept. As such, this would suggest the boy is drawing on some immortal spirit. However, the tabernacle as an image, even within a Biblical context, is not necessarily devoted to evoking an immortal spirit. The tabernacle was a tent, or a meeting place; in short, it was a precarious and moveable structure in the wilderness providing temporary respite from the wasteland. In addition, the tabernacle is also a nautical term.[26] The father 'raise[s] his weeping eyes and see[s] him standing there in the road looking back at him from some unimaginable future, glowing in that waste like a tabernacle'.[27] The tabernacle as a structure is the future itself: it is a metaphor for the future, for a navigation that is fragile rather than inviolable, and it is as susceptible to material decay as anything else in the universe. The sacramental is evident in *The Road* only to the extent that the sacramental is elemental and therefore of a deeper, more profound wisdom.

How then is McCarthy's anti-metaphysics manifest in the novel? The process of indistinction is reflected in the formal presentation of *The Road*, particularly evident in the placelessness of the text. As much as there is no time or future in the text, there is also no sense of space, that is, a space distinct and localised. Certainly, the setting is somewhere in the South-Eastern United States, but mostly the action is non-descript, anchorless and without location. Or as the father suggests: 'Everything uncoupled from its shoring. Unsupported in the ashen.'[28] World and place are largely indistinct, the setting mute and anonymous:

> The blind dogs of the sun in their running. The crushing black vacuum of the universe. And somewhere two hunted animals trembling like ground-foxes in their cover. Borrowed time and borrowed world and borrowed eyes with which to sorrow it.[29]

This quotation reveals an anti-metaphysics of the heat-death of the universe. The universe itself runs, but it runs on borrowed time. The ethical dimension of the novel takes shape against this backdrop, where the struggle of life and the ability to endure are only meaningful in direct confrontation with the crushing black vacuum of the universe. What further consequences can we draw from this anti-metaphysics? There are three main points where the consequences become apparent: memory, community and structure.

The dissolution of memory

McCarthy's anti-metaphysics is evident in attempts to assert the psychological coherence of memory. Material destruction and negativity are entwined with the psychological coherence and self-identity of characters. As the father looks at a forest fire, he commends the injunction to remember, as a form of prayer. There is something pathetically defiant about the father's nostalgic desire to retrieve past archives and conventions. The father draws succour from memory: 'Make a list. Recite a litany. Remember.'[30] In addition, the father attests to the desire to arrest the flow of memory, to make time stop, to construct fortified images immune to the brutal world in which he exists. For example, he remembers his wife at the theatre: 'She held his hand in her lap and he could feel the tops of her stockings through the thin stuff of her summer dress. Freeze this frame. Now call down your dark and your cold and be damned.'[31]

The father positively constructs memory; the struggle to remember and to reinforce the past is simultaneous with his struggle to be ethical. The preservation of cultural memory, customs and inherited tradition is all a father without a future can do to teach a child values in the face of cold reality, offering relief from his perpetual realism and pragmatism: 'You forget what you want to remember and you remember what you want to forget.'[32] He looks forward retroactively: 'This is the day to shape the days upon.'[33] Past images allow the father to regenerate; there is something inherently conservative about his retrieval of the past in the face of material chaos. However, the father is also dimly aware that his memory is not absolute. He sees that 'each memory recalled must do some violence to its origin. As in a party game. Say the word and pass it on. So be sparing. What you alter in remembering has yet a reality, known or not.'[34] The father's partial insight is very telling, as the brute reality of his situation impinges on his desire to revel in a lost past, or a quasi-eternity insusceptible to the destruction of the universe. Memory and the yearning for the psychological coherence of an individual mind over time is just as susceptible to the relentless negativity of the world as anything else. The truth is indifferent to the father's desire for his past to conform to the future. The reality of the material world ensures every memory is entwined with its own dissolution.

The father most of all represents the struggle to connect with other humans. The urgent pressures of survival mitigate his attempt to construct an enduring legacy between past, present and future. For example, the father finds it threatening when the boy asks 'him questions about the world that was for him not even a memory. There is no past.'[35] Without a past, there is also no future. There are:

> No lists of things to be done. The day providential to itself. The hour. There is no later. This is later. All things of grace and beauty such that one holds them to one's heart have a common provenance in pain. Their birth in grief and ashes.[36]

The difficulty for the father stems from his realisation of a world where only survival matters: all that is palpable is the now and the immediate task-by-task effort to find food, shelter and clothing. This is why he leaves the picture of his wife on the road. He is conflicted about the value of maintaining a sense of the past, enchanted with a nostalgia for a past life, but fraught with his inability to retain that life as he 'tried to keep their lives in some way but he didnt know how'.[37]

The very material of memory is infected with the broader global and cosmological collapse of the universe. The father's struggle to focus on the immediate present, accompanied by the temptation to surrender to an idealised version of the past, is ever present in the novel. For example, the desire to arrest the past is evident when the father returns to his family home, finding marks where Christmas cards hung from a mantelpiece. These small marks in the material world illustrate the father's desire to arrest the passage of time, ensuring a coherency of his sense of self; figuratively, his memory of home is pinned in place. The son's resistance to enter the old family home expresses his reluctance to luxuriate in lost memories, but also that he sees possibility rather than a simple past, or hopeless present. What the father fails to see is the boy's own form of pragmatism. This pragmatism manifests in the boy's moral armature; the boy is always other-focused and forward-looking. The boy's ethical disposition is maintained not just in his capacity to discern others, but when he discerns the inherent risk of encountering other people and their various possibilities. The material world continues on, survives, imprinting its remains without reifying them. Certainly, the father accepts the reality of violence, but this is purely with a view to protecting the micro-community of father and son. What distinguishes the boy's elevated ethical status is his effort to construct some meaningful future encompassing others, despite the inherent violence and negativity of the universe.

The boy also accepts the ruthless reality of ethical materialism. This is because the material world provides the imprint of pain and cruelty. It is because of the ruthless material negativity of the universe that we are ethical. The father struggles with his son's ethical awareness, seeing such moral perceptiveness as an impediment to the instrumental realities of survival. However, the boy's superior moral vision emerges from the tragic acceptance of violence at the core of all things, from the acceptance of the inescapable fact that any attempt to construct security, community and civilisation is irredeemably precarious and subject to the broader dissolution of the world. Only violence, contestation and struggle can help discern the ethical illumination of the future, rather than the pragmatic realism of the father. In a 1992 interview with Richard Woodward, McCarthy argues precisely this point, stating that the primary peace of human perfection is not desirable.[38]

The desire of the father to see in his son a vestige of divine perfection is necessary for confronting the material needs of a violent world. It provides his motivation to prolong his life as a survivor and not to commit suicide as the child's mother did. However, the father exemplifies the logic that McCarthy outlines in the Woodward interview, in that his nostalgic desire for perfection and peace is inherently connected to the empty universe. The boy represents an ethical alternative. He has a capacity to discern others, the future, consequences, to discern risk and danger, other people and their possibilities.[39] The boy's intransigence to indulging in the past is irreversible. For the boy the material world continues on, it survives, human imprints remain and endure, possibility is very real. The boy chastises the father for leaving the thief where he was.

> I wasn't going to kill him, he said. But the boy didn't answer. They rolled themselves in the blankets and lay there in the dark . . . He could tell by his breathing that the boy was awake and after a while the boy said: But we did kill him.[40]

The boy's acute moral perception means that he understands that the thief is as good as dead. The boy must deepen his moral vision, which encompasses the future, incorporating consequences and outcomes as well as possibility. This vision is elevated above the father's urgent need to deal with immediate threat in the present. Here the boy's ethics gives expression to the temporal span of mortal life, both in terms of how fraught it is and in relation to the fact that human endurance is entwined with material vulnerability, which itself is the very condition of ethical life.

The father resists McCarthy's anti-metaphysics in *The Road*. His effort to construct fortified images within memory is radically susceptible to dispersal. The realisation that 'each memory recalled must do some violence to its origin' undermines the father's patriarchal urge to conserve, to maintain the past, to restore order, to protect his ward.[41] Ultimately, in this context, McCarthy delivers an anti-conservative message: one cannot satisfactorily retrieve the past; there is no golden age and any attempt to construct memory, to fortify it, to make it immune from contamination, is automatically negated. The father acknowledges as much when he sees the boy as alien. The reason it is essential that the father is differentiated from the boy, like all fathers, is that the son comes from a future world, one that is as alien and monstrous as another planet. The moral force of the boy emerges precisely because he is not of the present and ultimately not of the father's lost world:

> A being from a planet that no longer existed. The tales of which were suspect. He could not construct for the child's pleasure the world he'd

lost without constructing the loss as well and he thought perhaps the child had known this better than he.[42]

In terms of the relation of memory to matter, the boy demonstrates that the future is as much a part of the present as the past is. Memory cannot revel in a lost past, in an immaterial psychological recollection, but to be real, memory is dependent on the reality of past and prospective material traces.

McCarthy draws a contrast between the father and son existing at a fraught nexus of past, present and future, and the mute eternal void towards which the world sinks. The novel presents an ethics of legacy and survival, asking how we can materially improve the world where we are, with a view to improving the material conditions of humans. The ethical injunction the boy represents is the simple demand to help people. He transfigures the father's pragmatism, shifting focus from the brute and immediate pragmatism of survival towards thinking of different ways to help improve the material conditions of other people, irrespective of their pragmatic use. The boy's tenacious refrain to 'carry the fire' is an attempt to give his father's pragmatism a future.

As the false prophet Ely suggests in the novel, even the Gods are lost without memory or legacy.[43] All things, even divinity itself, are subject to the material negativity present in the cosmos. Ely is an excellent example of the anti-metaphysical logic of the text. This spiritually impoverished and 'threadbare Buddha' joins a long list of ambiguous soothsayers in McCarthy's fiction.[44] Ely is the anti-prophet that is apt for the dying universe in which the characters reside. Ely revels in absolute nihilism:

> Where men cant live gods fare no better. It's better to be alone. So I hope that's not true what you said because to be on the road with the last god would be a terrible thing so I hope it's not true. Things will be better when everybody's gone.[45]

Such messianic nihilism sees humans as the ultimate aberration; the universe is simply better off without us. But if we probe deeper, we see this is because of our desire to elevate ourselves above the material world in the vain hope of transcending the material destruction at the core of all things. Ely claims he predicted the apocalypse: 'I knew this was coming [. . .] People were always getting ready for tomorrow. I didnt believe in that. Tomorrow wasn't getting ready for them. It didn't even know they were there.'[46] For Ely, there is disjunction between humans' rational and controlled expectations of a future state of affairs based on past memories and the chaotic reality which is simultaneously unfolding. Ely represents the rejection of the forlorn effort that future outcomes can be subordinate to the present; humanity's attempt to own the future, to plan, to implement projects, to affirm past certainty in the predictability of events, exposes a fundamental human vanity in the face of a chaotic and indifferent universe.

As such, Ely sees the denial of the inherent destructibility of the world and future events as central to the very destructive tendencies that lead humans to think they can transcend time and truth. As Ely suggests, the Gods only have power where humans exist. The desire to transmute our vain desire for order into the eternal – and with it, immortal life – separates humans from the desire to care for the future of the world itself and for the future of others. For this reason, the function of Ely should be read in a more sympathetic light than other commentators suggest.[47] Ely sees the comic side of death; death is left on the road, with no one left to kill and with death's days numbered. Here we are left with a world of pure death. Without death there are no humans, and without humans there is no sense of possibility.[48] The tragedy and comedy of *The Road* resides in the dearth of human connection and Ely's symbolic function explains the ultimate absurdity and folly of humanity's inability to connect not just with immediate peers, but with humans of the past and future.

To understand the ethical dimension of the novel, it is crucial to understand the interrelation of legacy and survival. As with many of McCarthy's other works, most overtly *Suttree, The Gardener's Son, The Stonemason, The Border Trilogy* and *No Country for Old Men*, a dominant theme is generational dysfunction. A recurring theme for McCarthy is the capacity for humans to negotiate enduring human values across a fraught temporal span. More specifically, in *The Road* this generational dysfunction is manifested through the parents and the child. The mother represents a lost present, the father the brute instrumentalist survival of tradition and the past, and the child represents possibility and the future. These characters inhabit a lost universe where past, present and future have no continuity or duration in the face of the relentless material negativity of the post-apocalyptic world.

The ambiguity of the father is that he is struggling to see the point of engaging in the desperate scramble for survival, to such a degree that he loses sight of the idea of possibility, of activity that can be enriching and transformative, of creating a future world worthy of his son. This is never more evident than when he struggles between his memory of the past and his material present. The ethical implication of the father's struggle with memory is that there is a different relation to memory necessary for constructing an ethical response to the world. McCarthy shows that we ought not to aim for the needless conservation of memory, but instead need to look for what makes memory endure, rather than succumbing to the nostalgic desire to conserve the past and attempting to impose something that we can 'shape the days upon'.[49] The tragedy of the father is the trauma of losing the temporal arc of human life. The value of memory is premised on the ability not to retain a past that never was, but to see that what is of value is only valuable insofar as it can be lost: 'He'd not have thought the value of the smallest thing predicated on a world to come. It surprised him. That the space which these things occupied was an expectation.'[50]

The ethical import of memory is intertwined with testimony in *The Road* and testimony is a form of promise that stories can continue to the future, that they will remain 'the good guys'. Memory, as Henri Bergson shows, requires continuity to work; otherwise one could not discriminate between the past and the present. As Bergson designates it, memory is a form of duration.[51] Memory is as real as the stories which allow memory to continue to the future. It is necessary that there is a minimal structure in a memory to support continuity and endurance in the face of the relentless negation of the flux of experience. Hence, we see the father's reticence and difficulty in telling stories of good guys and bad guys.

The anti-metaphysics of the novel embellishes the action with the combination of structure and dissolution, and this is also evident in the psychological coherence of the characters. Any memory not open to duration, to the present, to the future, cannot become intimate with the reality of pain, suffering and loss. The painful struggle for the persistence of memory in *The Road*, the sense that the past is premised on the future existing, requires the intertwining of memory with promise. Hence narration is decisive in the novel. Stories of good guys and bad guys are defiant acts of creation. Injecting narrative into survival is an indefatigable form of creation in the face of a universe where all is dying. The mixture of life and death, of future and past, of creation and destruction intermingle in *The Road*. This mixture is necessary for the ethical stakes of the novel, as it negates the anti-metaphysical void at the core of the novel. Life is intimate with death, yet life draws fraught succour from the universe around it.

The dissolution of community

Another element of McCarthy's anti-metaphysics is his representation of structure and community. The question of fortification and shelter is ever present, working in tandem with the novel's reflection on the desirability of community.[52] When father and son find a bunker full of supplies, McCarthy's anti-metaphysics is fully in evidence. The structure, although self-contained, fortified, a tiny survivalist bourgeois paradise, is clearly susceptible to violation since it did not offer protection to its creators. Any sense of fortification, of a structure that can shelter a group together, is premised on its own dissolution. For a brief period, the boy and the father find respite in a tiny mausoleum of forgotten consumer choices. However, one cannot consume one's way out of the apocalypse. Thus, any attempt at constructing a fortified structure remains essentially precarious. Any commitment to the formation of substance or structure is as subject to destruction as the material universe itself. Nevertheless, an ambiguous dignity does emerge in committing to forming structures physically, communally, even psychologically, that are resilient and tenacious to the extent that they confront, challenge, construct and create in opposition to the dissolution of the material universe. While ostensibly the father and son are usually alone, everywhere there are traces of others: roads, gas stations, toy trucks, tracks in the tar, a can of Coca-Cola, a trailer full of cadavers. In line with the father's inherent suspicion of all possible encounters, he remains wary and resistant to the temptation which groups and structures offer. They remind him of the imminent possibility of meeting others and the dangers attendant to any encounter.[53]

Communal structures as represented in *The Road* conform to the material logic developed in this essay. The suspicion of 'gathering' can be understood in relation to what Blanchot considers as an unworking of identity. *The Road* is one of the great American anti-novels, drenched in destruction and negation, foreclosing easy resolution. The richness of the novel's character, plot, imagery, themes, emerges from the anonymous nothingness pervading the text. This is particularly evident with regard to the formation of communal structures. For Blanchot, 'Every being's substance is contested without respite by every other being. [. . .] The truth of a community is its own incompletion, insufficiency and interruption.'[54] *The Road* performs an emptying of community with a view to expressing a more universal depiction of human life. All protagonists in the novel do not know where to belong, socially or personally; people have forgotten how to co-exist. Any attempt to draw succour from communal gathering is only ever temporary. The ability to form a community, a group for mutual security, or even a cannibal militia, is automatically considered suspect. McCarthy's broader point is that the assertion of an absolute, consecrated community is impossible to instantiate from its inception.

Why might a rejection of community be a good thing? It is because there is a universalism in *The Road* which resists community. Alongside the mute placelessness of the novel, attempts to form community are considered suspect. We see the orgiastic fusion of the blood cults, where groupings and communities enslave prisoners, collections of roaming cannibals perpetuating enclosed communities with enforced abortions. Groups are seen to be dangerous, violent and untrustworthy, formed only for allegiances of defence and fortification. For example, when the father is fatally injured towards the end of the novel, his assailants desert each other. The final community offering aid to the boy is temporary; the boy treats with scepticism the matriarch's religious overtures to talk to God. The matriarch affirms a theological eternity common to all humans which transcends time and space, imposing on the boy the idea of a 'breath of God', passing from 'man to man through all of time'.[55] However, the boy prefers to talk to 'his father and he did talk to him and he didnt forget'.[56] There is a form of faith in the novel; however, this is not faith in a theological eternity, but a faith in mortal survival.

The stakes of the rejection of community are necessary for configuring the ethical function of *The Road*. This is because *The Road* articulates a suspicion of types of communal life with a view to articulating a more universal form of being together, one where all humans have a sense of both inheritance and promise. Blanchot's logic here applies to *The Road*: the truth of community is paradoxically its weakness, its incompletion and insufficiency. Notwithstanding the micro-community of the father and son, the novel is generally hostile to the idea of humans being together. However, the comforts and solace of community are only viable as far as they acknowledge the broader anti-metaphysics of the novel. McCarthy offers a form of universalism, one that paradoxically requires undermining community. McCarthy is seeking to find a more fundamental type of being together, one that transcends local determinations of identity. Determinations of community are not eternal but historically specific, valuable only when a community is tentative, and only to the extent that human goodness materially sustains humans in the face of a menacing future. There is no orgiastic fusion possible as we find in the blood cults of the novel; the cults form to perpetuate death, figuratively worshipping the new god of eternal death and negation.

The community of two which characterises the father and the son must also dissolve. Formally, for the ethical force of the novel it is necessary that the father dies. Their micro-community must dissolve in order that the promise of the future can endure. The dissolution of this micro-community is essential, permitting the mixing of life and death in the boy, who survives, remembers and lives on with the memory of his dead father. McCarthy's depiction of mortal ethics in the novel comes to fruition in the closing scenes of *The Road*, where we see a minimal reconciliation of the temporal dimensions necessary for ethical life. The present, the future and now the past coexist in the boy. Faith in mortal survival permeates the novel rather than faith in the nihilism of eternity. Any form of continuity is premised on loss and mourning. Therefore, it would be unwise to read the boy joining a family at the end of the novel as McCarthy's unambiguous affirmation of the family unit. This is one community among many, haunted and vulnerable to the anonymous negativity that the novel performs.

Throughout the novel McCarthy presents an anti-cartography, a geography of a world without borders. Thus, any markers of location are resolutely dissolved, encapsulated by the hollow and mocking shipwreck *Pájaro de Esperanza* receding back into the world on the border of land and ocean. Indeed, symbols of navigation, that is, objects which make people, places and the world visible and distinct, become redundant: the broken map, the sextant, the binoculars. This is ambiguous; now that the world is indistinct, we finally live in a borderless world and ought to be free from the regressive proclivities of nativism, chauvinism and nationalism. However, this is not the case. Borders and divisions may have kept us civil, but of course they are the same borders that led to, or at least did not prevent, the cataclysm which precipitates the novel. This is seen when the father chastises the boy for worrying about everything: 'You're not the one who has to worry about everything. The boy said something but he couldnt understand him. What? He said. He looked up, his wet and grimy face, Yes I am, he said. I am the one.'[57] This is the boy acknowledging his future role: the burden is on him to 'carry the fire' towards the future. The boy is one insofar as he is many. 'Fire' is an elemental metaphor 'for the practice of civility and ethics'.[58] This means that in addition to surviving he must take up the burden of the 'fire' and attempt the impossible task of warranting the virtuous survival of the human species.[59]

It is important to be cautious here. It is impossible to demarcate *The Road*'s characters entirely from the global nihilism they inhabit.

This is because all characters are susceptible to the material negativity upon which the form, content and narration of the novel are based. However, there is a minimal sense that humans can differentiate themselves from the cosmic nihilism and violence ever present in McCarthy's work. While the father and the boy are ostensibly alone, the possibility remains of a different type of belonging. McCarthy endorses a form of universalism; everyone's possibility is the father and son's possibility. The father and son are exemplars of the attempt to construct a meaningful endurance between past, present and future in the face of the material negativity of the universe. Their struggle is everybody's struggle and cannot be restricted to specific communities. This is precisely what is required to carry the burden of humanity into the future. This universal experience differentiates them from those who revel in the material destruction implicit to all things.

Conclusion: mortal ethics

There is an unambiguous material ethics on display in *The Road*. While McCarthy is not offering a naïve materialist reductionism, there is a sense that human endeavour is caught up in the wider material processes of the world, which in *The Road* is the material decay of the world itself. In a direct reversal of a theological cosmos, the characters of the novel participate in the broader material dissolution of the universe. The consequences of this strange anti-metaphysics allow us to grasp more clearly the philosophical, ethical and political imaginary of *The Road*. This is particularly evident in relation to questions of structure, memory and the suspicion of community. *The Road* attempts to overcome the generational dysfunction of past, present and future in an effort to reconcile human destruction with possibility. The father must die for the boy to gain wisdom and faith in mortal forms of survival. What survives is neither the Gods nor the eternal, but the material stories of ourselves, stories of how to help others in actual, real and physical ways. The resistance to luxuriating in memory and the past allows community to be overcome, to reveal something generically human. Therefore, *The Road* depicts a radical difference between those entrenched in cults and communities and those who are refugees, those without borders, those without walls. The attempt to form fortification, whether in community, belonging or psychological coherence, is embedded in wider material processes; efforts to construct any form of resilience can only draw physical support from the confines of the material and existent world. Here,

The Road expresses a desire for the universal: that which transcends belonging and community offers more resilience to human values than any community that immunises itself to the implacable material absurdity of the universe. And when it comes to moral absurdity, no work articulates this more than *No Country for Old Men*, to which this book now turns.

Notes

1. For a perceptive account of how McCarthy uses gnostic philosophy and theology see Daugherty, 'Gravers False and True: *Blood Meridian* as Gnostic Tragedy', 159–74. For the definitive explorations of the question of Gnosticism in McCarthy, see Dianne C. Luce, *Reading the World: Cormac McCarthy's Tennessee Period* and Petra Mundik, *A Bloody and Barbarous God: The Metaphysics of Cormac McCarthy* (Albuquerque: University of New Mexico Press, 2016).

2. A good example of how McCarthy is interpreted within a postmodern framework is available in Linda Woodson, 'McCarthy's Heroes and the Will to Truth', as well as Philip A. Snyder and Delys W. Snyder, 'Modernism, Postmodernism, and Language: McCarthy's Style', both of which appear in *The Cambridge Companion to Cormac McCarthy*, ed. Steven Frye (Cambridge: Cambridge University Press, 2013) 15–26, 27–38. Here we can also note other post-Nietzschean readings, such as the one proposed by Shane Schimpf in the Introduction to his *Reader's Guide to* Blood Meridian (Seattle: Bon Mot, 2008). Schimpf's observations are valuable for understanding the philosophical implications of McCarthy's work; as I noted in the Introduction, it is necessary to see not so much that McCarthy makes positive claims about the existence or non-existence of God, but rather that he is trying to think through the consequences of Nietzsche's proposition of what the universe amounts to after the death of God.

3. Another philosophical trajectory worth nothing is the attempt to understand McCarthy in Marxist terms, or as a literary author who is attempting to think through the consequences of the neoliberal political and economic order. The principal work here is David Holloway's *The Late Modernism of Cormac McCarthy* (Westport, CT: Greenwood Press, 2002). Another exceptionally valuable recent contribution to this strand of McCarthy studies is Raymond Malewitz, *The Practice of Misuse*. Malewitz stringently argues that McCarthy's *No Country for Old Men* offers a direct repudiation of the rugged consumerism of neoliberalism. So, while there has been some work that tries to understand the philosophical strains within McCarthy's work, it is clear that much of this work is geared towards understanding McCarthy under specific critical optics such as Marxist, religious, post-structural, Nietzschean

or existential, and that consequently, there has not been an attempt to understand the totality of McCarthy's philosophical reflections, nor the distinct manner his fiction operates on at the intersection of literature and philosophy. A welcome addition to this debate is Chris Eagle's edited collection, *Philosophical Approaches to Cormac McCarthy: Beyond Reckoning* (2017), particularly Alberto Siani's Nagelian reading of McCarthy, which is important because it attempts to discern a core philosophical logic at the heart of McCarthy's philosophical reflections. See Siani, 'Nowhere Between River and Road: A Nagelian Reading of *Suttree* and *The Road*', in *Philosophical Approaches to Cormac McCarthy: Beyond Reckoning*, ed. Chris Eagle (London: Routledge, 2017), 202–20.

4. I would argue that it is not possible to say McCarthy's work can strictly be defined as a pantheist theology, since pantheism must be premised on the perfect unity of cosmos, and McCarthy's worldview tends to steer away from perfection. Of course, this does not preclude examining the ontological status of nature in his work. For a valuable account of the metaphysics of nature in McCarthy, see Julius Greve, '"Another kind of clay": On *Blood Meridian*'s Okenian Philosophy of Nature', *The Cormac McCarthy Journal* 13, no.1 (2015): 27–53.

5. Cormac McCarthy, *The Road* (London: Picador, 2006), 29.

6. Ibid. 28.

7. Blanchot, *The Space of Literature*, 26.

8. For a rich description of thermodynamics as metaphor see Markus Wierschem, 'The Other End of *The Road*: Re-Reading McCarthy in Light of Thermodynamics and Information Theory', *The Cormac McCarthy Journal* 11, no.1 (2013): 1–22. See also Wierschem's 'At a Crossroads of Life and Death: The Apocalyptic Journey(s) of Cormac McCarthy's Fiction', in *The Journey of Life in American Literature*, ed. Peter Freese (Heidelberg: Winter, 2015), 159–85.

9. McCarthy, *The Road*, 293.

10. Ibid.

11. For an excellent account of how *The Road* represents an optimistic argument for a new type of fiction, one surpassing postmodern interpretations of McCarthy, see Ashley Kunsa, 'Maps of the World in Its Becoming: Post-Apocalyptic Naming in Cormac McCarthy's *The Road*', *Journal of Modern Literature* 33, no.1 (Fall 2009): 57–74.

12. McCarthy, *The Counsellor* (London: Picador, 2013), 21.

13. Wierschem, 'At a Crossroads', 179.

14. McCarthy, *The Road*, 28.

15. Ibid. 58–9.

16. It should be again noted that McCarthy is not offering a vulgar form of atheism. It would be erroneous to suggest that McCarthy is offering an atheism of the variety promulgated by, say, Richard Dawkins, Sam Harris or Christopher Hitchens.

17. Erik Wielenberg offers a good account of the ambiguities of a theological reading of *The Road*, suggesting that 'the existence of God remains ambiguous throughout the novel'. See 'God, Morality and Meaning in Cormac McCarthy's *The Road*', *The Cormac McCarthy Journal* 8, no.1 (Fall 2010): 1.
18. McCarthy, *The Road*, 78–80.
19. Ibid. 159.
20. Ibid. 15.
21. Joseph Allen suggests that McCarthy subscribes to a form of Christian existentialism. See Joseph Allen, 'The Quest for God in *The Road*', in *The Cambridge Companion to Cormac McCarthy*, ed. Steven Frye (Cambridge: Cambridge University Press, 2013), 142–3. This is not wholly inaccurate, expressing well the fraught intersection of non-belief and faith which we find in *The Road*. However, as I have argued here, it is necessary to develop a philosophical register which does justice to the way McCarthy has vastly different metaphysical commitments than either Christianity or existentialism on their own terms.
22. I agree with Matthew Potts, who argues that ultimately McCarthy is not expressly a Christian novelist. However, it is certainly the case that McCarthy invokes Christian sacrament and imagery to make palpable the value of human life in the lived and practical world. As Potts suggests, McCarthy does not overreach for 'systems of metaphysical meaning' (4). Instead, sacramental imagery offers succour, respite and temporary shelter against the unpalatable universe in which McCarthy's protagonists exist. See Matthew Potts, *Cormac McCarthy and the Signs of Sacrament: Literature, Theology, and the Moral of Stories* (London: Bloomsbury, 2015), 70.
23. McCarthy, *The Road*, 306.
24. Throughout *The Road* the dissolution of objects is ever present and this dissolution is represented through the insertion of contradiction and juxtaposition. In many instances, this amounts to a direct reversal of common symbolism. For example, we see a collapsing of mortal and immortal symbols when we see a single grey snowflake 'expire' on the man's palm 'like the last host of christendom' (McCarthy, *The Road*, 15). For an excellent summary of symbolic juxtaposition see Yuliya A. Tsutserova, 'Seeing Nothing', in *Philosophical Approaches to Cormac McCarthy: Beyond Reckoning*, ed. Chris Eagle (London: Routledge, 2017), 195.
25. McCarthy, *The Road*, 1.
26. In nautical terms, the tabernacle is the object which mounts the mast to the deck.
27. McCarthy, *The Road*, 293.
28. Ibid. 10.
29. Ibid. 138.
30. Ibid. 31.

31. Ibid. 18.

32. Ibid. 11.

33. Ibid. 12.

34. Ibid. 139.

35. Ibid. 55.

36. Ibid. 55–6.

37. Ibid. 56.

38. McCarthy, in his interview with Woodward, rejects the notion of harmony and peace as worthy aspirations: 'I think the notion that the species can be improved in some way, that everyone could live in harmony, is a really dangerous idea. Those who are afflicted with this notion are the first ones to give up their souls, their freedom. Your desire that it be that way will enslave you and make your life vacuous.' See Richard B. Woodward, 'Cormac McCarthy's Venomous Fiction', 29.

39. For an excellent analysis of sight as metaphor in *The Road* see Eric Pudney, 'Christianity and Cormac McCarthy's *The Road*'. Pudney, of all the critical readers of *The Road*, comes closest to expressing the contradictions and struggles of life in an empty universe. He writes: 'Throughout the novel, atheism is associated with despair, hopelessness and death, and Christianity with the rare moments of hope. In the final analysis, *The Road* can also be understood as a challenge to the atheistic view of the universe, and this challenge is one that any atheist ought to take seriously.' See Eric Pudney, 'Christianity and Cormac McCarthy's *The Road*', *English Studies* 96, no.3 (March 2015): 309. Pudney is surely right about this. However, this logic also must extend to Christian readings of the novel. As I have argued previously in this chapter, the simple opposition of atheism and Christianity doesn't fully do justice to what McCarthy is trying to achieve in *The Road*, since it is necessary to reconfigure both strands.

40. McCarthy, *The Road*, 278.

41. Ibid. 139.

42. Ibid. 163.

43. Ibid. 178–83.

44. Ibid. 179.

45. Ibid. 183.

46. Ibid. 178–9.

47. For example, Benjamin Mangrum calls Ely a 'dark prophet', unable to perceive the boy as an 'affirmation not of God but of the continuation of humanity'. See Benjamin Mangrum, 'Accounting for *The Road*: Tragedy, Courage, and Cavell's Acknowledgement', *Philosophy and Literature* 37, no.2 (2013): 285. Similarly, Stefan Skrimshire sees the limitation of Ely in the incapacity to discern 'the realisation that, in the very act of their survival, something unshakeable of the trace of God (in the book it moves from 'word' to 'breath' to 'dream', in that order) is incarnate.' See Stefan Skrimshire, '"There is no God, and we

are his Prophets": Deconstructing Redemption in Cormac McCarthy's *The Road*', *Journal for Cultural Research* 15, no.1 (January 2011): 7. Lydia Cooper also suggests that Ely is the voice of 'the catastrophic loss of faith in the human endeavour'. See Lydia Cooper, 'Cormac McCarthy's *The Road* as Apocalyptic Grail Narrative', *Studies in the Novel* 43, no.2 (Summer 2011): 223.

48. McCarthy, *The Road*, 184.
49. Ibid. 12.
50. Ibid. 199.
51. Henri Bergson, *Time and Free Will*, trans. F.L. Pogson (New York: Dover, 2001), 126–8.
52. For example, in *The Road*, buildings, mansions, the father's family home, gas stations, highways are in a process of disintegration. This anti-architecture reveals what Martin Heidegger calls world-withdrawal, or the idea that the lived world and possibilities of any building recede into the material world. See Martin Heidegger, *Poetry, Language, Thought*, trans. Albert Hofstader (New York: Harper and Row, 2001), 40.
53. McCarthy, *The Road*, 48.
54. Blanchot, *The Unavowable Community*, 5 and 9.
55. McCarthy, *The Road*, 306.
56. Ibid.
57. Ibid. 277.
58. Cooper, 'Cormac McCarthy's *The Road* as Apocalyptic Grail Narrative', 234.
59. Cooper provides an excellent analysis of the way in which the symbolism of fire and water stands in for questions of inheritance, and the way 'inheritance and the future is entwined with survival and the continuation of the human race'. Cooper, 227.

Chapter 6

Saving Sheriff Bell: Derrida, McCarthy and the Opening of Mercantile Ethics in *No Country for Old Men*

If *Blood Meridian* shows McCarthy at his most fatalistic, struggling to extricate his characters from an implacable moral nihilism, then his later novel *No Country for Old Men* marks a return to this theme. In the non-confrontation of Sheriff Bell and Chigurh, McCarthy revisits the theme of a morally compromised protagonist confronting a superior immoral force. What is philosophically interesting about *No Country for Old Men* is that McCarthy becomes less ambiguous about how to be ethical, despite the most adverse of foes. I aim to show in this chapter how McCarthy offers a nuanced account of ethical relations and ethical deliberation beyond the seemingly unavoidable reality of nihilism in *No Country for Old Men*. I argue that rather than categorising McCarthy's novel as a paean to a lost conservatism, there is a subtler philosophical reading available. Utilising Jacques Derrida's account of ethical responsibility, I show that while on the surface the novel presents a putative conservative ethics, with Bell lamenting the prevailing state of social laws and yearning for the simplicity of natural justice, a deeper ethical interpretation is possible. I argue that while Chigurh represents the logical conclusion of a world where morals are consistent with predictable and mechanical laws of nature, the actual moral fulcrum of the novel dwells in the deepening wisdom of Bell in the face of Chigurh's mechanisation and naturalisation of ethics. McCarthy's philosophical and ethical insight in *No Country for Old Men* specifically emerges from Sheriff Bell's struggles to exist beyond simple expressions of good and evil as he faces the psychopath Chigurh's relentless rationalism. I will conclude that McCarthy philosophically demonstrates the density and flawed nature of ethical decision-making, one that requires civil disobedience at the heart of the law.

In McCarthy's *No Country for Old Men*, Bell blames the moral barbarism of his age on a 'breakdown in mercantile ethics'.[1] This enigmatic phrase belies a simple ethical logic: the just is connected to a traditional view of the marketplace; if one does good things, one may expect a just reward. Exchange dictates moral certainty. The status of mercantile ethics is present across the different versions of McCarthy's *No Country for Old Men*. In the draft archival material at the Wittliff Collections we discover that *No Country for Old Men* began as a screenplay which McCarthy later adapted into novel form, which itself was readapted by the Coen Brothers for the screen. Here we can begin to see the formation of the brooding and morally reflective Bell:

> I aint really a pessimistic man, <Don,> but you tell what there is on the horizon to indicate that this thing is going to turn around. I dont see it. The power to do ill is much greater than the power to do good Its just naturally easier to break something than to build something. We're losin it little by little. Things that used to be considered disgraceful get to be not so bad and then after a while they're okay.[2]

This quotation provides evidence of a continuity of character across different iterations of *No Country for Old Men*. McCarthy makes Bell a powerless figure, limited to face-to-face values in a context of the communal exchange of an honour-based society. Sheriff Bell is only dimly able to perceive broader technological and economic forces undermining how he thinks the world is and ought to be. When Sheriff Bell faces Anton Chigurh, he is confronted with an entirely different moral logic, one which empties his character of conservative dispositions and ethical habits. All that was important to Bell is eroded and he is left struggling to conceptualise an alternative ethics. The strength of McCarthy's insight into ethical life lies in illuminating what happens to a conservative character when they must carry on making ethical valuations after their foundations are ripped asunder.[3] McCarthy's philosophical and ethical insight in *No Country for Old Men* is Nietzschean, showing Bell struggling to exist beyond good and evil.

This chapter also offers a novel account of how McCarthy conceives of ethical questions and decisions. McCarthy, I argue, offers acute insight into the tragic nature of decisions, where values emerge in conjunction with an inevitably violent world. To support this argument, I use the work of Jacques Derrida on ethical decision-making. Derrida's work is valuable because it shows that ethical decisions are more than autonomous and isolated. Derrida helps us understand *No Country for Old Men*, particularly by giving context to decision-making at the intersection of a contested past and future, and the tension between regulated and unpredictable codes of behaviour. The moral force of *No Country for Old Men* emerges in the breakdown in similarity between Bell and Chigurh. While Bell and Chigurh are both avatars of certainty, it is Bell who is confronted with an existential crisis of values, while Chigurh has the certainty of a God.[4] Bell's uncertainties reveal a more profound moral wisdom than it initially appears. This allows us to see Bell – and the novel itself – as being open to a reading that takes on Derrida's alternative ethical trajectory, one that is open, contingent and exposed to radical uncertainty.

My reading requires a reframing of the critical consensus around the character of Chigurh. In opposition to existing accounts of Chigurh as a chaotic figure, I argue that this dominant character should not be understood as a harbinger of chaos but instead as a purveyor of order and certainty. Chigurh is a rationalist and a mechanist, dedicated to calculable and programmatic decisions. Chigurh functions as a foil to the deepening ethical development of Sheriff Bell. The more Bell becomes uncertain, the more Chigurh clings irrationally to entrenched rationalism. This reading is important, as it allows us to resist the temptation to see how the backdrop to the novel – the drugs war of the American southwest – is not reducible, nor can it be combatted by the simple 'mercantile ethics' for which Bell yearns. The unendurable suffering and violence that McCarthy is at pains to reveal as the by-product of the illegal drugs war stands in stark contrast to the rational, corporate efficiency of the illegal drugs trade. The drugs war is an idealist, immaterial site of mercantile exchange, which obscures violence, suffering and the brutal historical reality of the narcotic trade. Chigurh represents the slick efficiency and natural inevitability of corporate exchange. Bell, on the other hand, begins with a lament for the cosy circularity and face-to-face reciprocity of mercantile ethics, but moves to a position which recognises the utter contingency of the world and the ethical priorities which emerge when faced with more vicious forms of capital exchange.

This chapter's analysis builds in a significant way on existing McCarthy scholarship. Many influential McCarthy critics have rejected a naïve conservative reading of McCarthy. For example, Raymond Malewitz in *The Practice of Misuse* argues forcefully that *No*

Country for Old Men presents an implicit critique of the rugged consumerism of neoliberalism. For Malewitz, the 'rugged individualism'
of the mythic American West transforms into a 'rugged consumerism', where self-reliance is no longer materially grounded, but instead
amounts to a merely commercial performance of a lost authentic
self-reliance.[5] The characters tragically inhabit a de-historicised
world, unable to see that such a world leads to 'conceptual imprisonment'.[6] In addition, David Holloway in *The Late Modernism of
Cormac McCarthy* has argued that McCarthy's work makes manifest
attempts to de-historicise ethical, political and economic exchange.
While *No Country for Old Men* succeeded Holloway's work, his
analysis remains salient since the characters of the novel inhabit a
de-historicised world, unable to illuminate any ethical alternative to
the automatised circularity of capitalist production. Therefore, it is
necessary to see this text as one of the strongest within McCarthy's
oeuvre for dealing with philosophical problems pertaining to ethical
decision-making.

Bell represents McCarthy's attempt, albeit a pessimistic one, to
think an ethical alternative to the seemingly inescapable certainty of
capitalist exchange. Building on the above scholarship, this chapter
will develop a historically and materially based ethics. This is crucial both for understanding McCarthy's novel and for understanding the ethical and philosophical stakes of his work more generally.
What is important to grasp is that the novel stages a move beyond
the closed circularity of the 'mercantile ethics' of Chigurh towards
a more nuanced theory of ethics based on the deepening moral
uncertainty of Bell, as he begins to grasp the concrete and historical
consequences of the rampant capitalism of the illegal drugs wars.
The austere and rational violence Chigurh represents is not desirable for McCarthy, but is always possible and thus ethical decisions
for McCarthy inevitably remain entwined with a necessary confrontation with violence. In the last analysis, I argue that McCarthy's
ethical vision is not wholly conservative, even if Bell himself is definitively conservative in outlook. Real ethical deliberation takes hold
once one transgresses any moral shibboleths that constitute one's
character, as represented by Moss and Bell; deeper ethical comprehension becomes possible when, paradoxically, the contingency of
one's communal ethics becomes visible. The virtue of Sheriff Bell is
precisely that he does not remain entrenched in existing social mores.
No Country for Old Men articulates something generically human,
an ethics that necessarily transcends cherished values, identity and
communal belonging.

Derrida, McCarthy and the paradox of decision

Derrida's reading of the ethical decision, principally in *The Gift of Death* and his essay 'Force of Law', offers an instructive account of ethical decisions. Derrida explains the conditions of an ethical decision – that is, what must be the case for an ethical decision to be ethical in the first place. The ethical decision is radically split; a decision cannot guarantee the ultimate success or failure of its intended outcomes. If a decision is to be ethical from its inception, it must be structurally contingent. This means that any ethical decision is open to corruption or perversion from the outset. If this were not the case, then the ethical decision could not become responsive to the particularity of ethical situations. This is also why, for Derrida, an ethical decision in pursuit of justice remains incalculable, since the good can never decisively upend the bad.[7] Bell and Moss reflect this logic in *No Country for Old Men*, as a just decision can always be usurped by other possible outcomes.

For Derrida, the: 'idea of justice is always very close to the bad, even to the worst for it can always be re-appropriated by the most perverse calculation'.[8] The law, as represented in the novel by Bell and following Derrida's logic, is structurally obliged to incessantly reconsider itself in terms of how it is previously calculated.[9] As I will go on to show, Chigurh is a figure of the law, of the calculable, of a rational accounting, where everything is counted and determined in advance. He is risk-averse to the excesses of capitalism and the risks of the pursuit of unchecked profit: 'The prospect of outsized profits leads people to exaggerate their own capabilities.'[10] Chigurh is a figure of unambiguous control; his ethical decisions are configured towards ensuring the past is the same as the present and is the same as the future. Bell, despite his obvious conservatism, represents the domain of the incalculable. As Derrida suggests, all ethical decisions are haunted by a temporal duration, haunted by the past and by future communities: an ethical decision cannot be reduced to the purely present. What is valuable about Derrida's reading of the ethical decision is that it helps show the transition from the law to justice, as manifested through the development of Bell's character.

Bell begins as a figure of law and authority; the origin of that authority is a fictional sham for Bell by the end. Due to his non-confrontation with Chigurh, he moves towards becoming a figure of justice as Derrida understands it. The achievement of Bell is that he reaches a more profound ethical knowledge, one that sees justice as a form of promise. For Bell, ethical decisions must retain a sense of possibility, whereas for Chigurh, future and past are only ever a reproduction of the present. As Derrida says: 'The Future loses the openness, the coming of the other (who comes) without which there is no justice; and the future can always reproduce the present, announce itself or present itself as a future present in the modified form of the present.'[11]

Chigurh endorses what Derrida calls the calculable; his ethics are methodical, instrumental and systematic. Chigurh encapsulates Derrida's logic of the calculable, where an ethical decision is valuable only if instrumental, only if reproducing a predetermined programme. For example, when murdering Carla Jean, Chigurh says: 'You can say things could have turned out differently. That they could have been some other way. But what does that mean? They are not some other way.'[12] What distinguishes Chigurh is that he is unethical precisely because he has a rational, preordained code. When Derrida examines the status of responsibility, he argues that the structure of a responsible decision is not calculable. If a responsible decision were to be prearranged in advance, then it is simply not ethical. The philosophical point is elementary; ethical decisions need to be about more than themselves if they are to relate to others and the world. As Chigurh's decision is not ethical when he murders Carla Jean, there is no rational reason for him to 'second say the world'.[13]

An authentic ethical decision is therefore not easy to come by. The opposite is true for Chigurh, whose principles are exceptionally easy to enact. What stops us drawing equivalence between the weird rational relativism of Chigurh and Bell's ethical uncertainty is that Bell remains a figure who is unable to take for granted any of the values he inhabits; he undergoes what Derrida calls 'the test and ordeal of the undecidable'.[14] Bell, confronting his cowardice in the war, the sheer luck he perceives in marrying Loretta and the fear which facing Chigurh represents, is certainly a conservative, but one at the intersection of the calculable and the incalculable. This demonstrates McCarthy's nuanced philosophical understanding of what an ethical decision requires, and matches the inevitable degree of undecidability which Derrida asserts haunts all decision: 'A decision that would not go through the test or ordeal of the undecidable would not be a free decision; it would be the programmable application or the continuous unfolding of a calculable process.'[15] The rules that so enamour Chigurh are specifically those which Bell transgresses in his vacillation between the calculable and the incalculable. McCarthy demonstrates through the characters of Moss and Bell that while rules and regulations certainly exist, they only become ethical once they stop being rule-bound. What disturbs Bell the lawman throughout the novel is the inadequacy of the law for justice, or as Derrida puts it:

> At no moment, it seems, can a decision be said to be presently and fully just: either it has not yet been made according to a rule, and nothing allows one to call it just, or it has already followed a rule – whether given, received, confirmed, preserved or reinvented – which, in its turn, nothing guarantees absolutely.[16]

If there is a necessary sacrifice of rules as a precondition for ethical life, then Bell corresponds to Derrida's logic.

In *The Gift of Death* Derrida, commenting on Søren Kierkegaard's *Fear and Trembling*, argues that it is precisely because a responsible decision is inflected with uncertainty from beginning to end that it is ethical in the first place. The example Derrida gives is Kierkegaard's reading of the Biblical story of Abraham. For Kierkegaard, Abraham represents the sacrifice of the ethical world for the affirmation of the religious and transcendent, or, in Kierkegaardian terms, the shift from the ethical and universal sphere of existence to the leap to the religious sphere of existence. Derrida agrees with Kierkegaard to a point; the story of Abraham reveals the structural necessity of sacrifice and disobedience for ethical decision-making. To be ethical, the moral rules, traditions and customs one inhabits become contingent in order for a real ethical decision to take place. Put simply, civil disobedience is essential for ethical decision-making.

The story of Abraham has such resonance because it demonstrates the necessity of violence for ethics. Derrida is not prescribing violence – he is arguing that violence and sacrifice are inherent to ethical decisions. As such, all the moral rules upon which we count, with which we calculate, are sacrificed in the lived experience of ethical dilemmas. While Derrida sees Kierkegaard's account of Abraham as valuable, he questions Kierkegaard's transition from the ethical and universal sphere to a religious one.[17] For Kierkegaard, the radical abyss presented by the Biblical story allows reconciliation with faith, and this faith invariably leads to recompense, namely the return of Isaac. As such, God can be counted on to save Isaac. Derrida famously suggests that the deeper wisdom in the Bible story reveals that ethics is radically paradoxical rather than religious. Ethical paradoxes are universal not religious where *'tout autre est tout autre'*– every other is wholly other.[18] As Adam Kelly shows, for Derrida the power of the Biblical story resides in seeing Abraham as the 'exemplary everyman, faced with the choice between incompatible demands'.[19]

Thus, ethical decisions must take place without the solace and comfort of one's communal belonging. A responsible decision only takes place when one's loyalty to one's community is undermined. Considering this, the covenant between father and son we witness at the end of the novel, where Bell dreams of his father's promise, represents Bell's haunting by the persistence and survival of human resilience in the proximity of relentless violence. Bell finds that behind all our pretensions, our value judgements and moral codes, lies uncertainty, but an uncertainty bound to survival (*survivance*), promise and affirmation. For Derrida, such survival is 'an originary concept that constitutes the very structure of what we call existence, *Dasein*, if you will. We are structurally survivors, marked by this structure of the trace and of the testament.'[20] For Derrida, any notion of: 'responsibility, of decision, or of duty are condemned *a priori* to paradox, scandal and aporia. Paradox, scandal and aporia are themselves nothing other than sacrifice, the revelation of conceptual thinking at its limit, at its death and finitude.'[21] Crucially, Bell's ethical quandaries reveal a fundamental paradox: our ethical decision introduces both an irretrievable violence into ethical life, as well as affirmation and tenacity. As Derrida shows, an ethical decision cannot be mere convenience nor can it be programmatic. Ty Hawkins suggests that *No Country for Old Men* subverts mythological frontiersman types, as well as American identity more generally. I think this is right; Hawkins captures the sense in which *No Country for Old Men* is a valuable literary and philosophical resource, as defined by the novel's unique ability to represent that which is both 'subversive *and* affirmative'.[22] As Hawkins further notes, a driving impetus of McCarthy's ethical thinking is continual friction, where '[t]his friction leads [to] a simultaneous demand for and negation of Justice'.[23] In opposition to such a view stands Anton Chigurh.

Anton Chigurh and the calculable order of decision

How can we interpret the enigmatic Chigurh as an ethical decision-maker? Hawkins provides the most insightful observation on this matter. Using Žižek's conception of the transcendent subject, Hawkins argues that Chigurh stands as an antithesis to the possibility of Sheriff Bell emptying out and transcending his own subjectivity.[24] On the surface, Chigurh is a calculating, merciless and relentless psychopath. He is an archetypal Angel of Death, destabilising Bell's very local sense of justice and fairness. McCarthy defines Chigurh preternaturally. He is real, existing alongside this world, yet wholly not of it. He is 'a true and living prophet of destruction', a man who 'by his own admission has no soul'.[25] Within the novel's wider geo-political context, Chigurh is the *telos* of the American drugs war, a by-product of ruthless profiteering and the hedonistic instrumentalism of drug cartels and their consumers. Despite his fellow hitman, Carson Wells, suggesting that he: 'has principles. Principles that even transcend money or drugs', his aesthetic remains dark and nihilistic.[26] Chigurh devotes himself to the creative power of negation, exalting in the deterministic concatenations of cause and effect.

Conventionally, scholarly wisdom emphasises that Chigurh is an agent of fortune and chaos, dispensing life and death on a mere flip of a coin, to which Sheriff Bell is a sober and measured contrast. Chigurh is often regarded as an incarnation of chaos theory, a Mephistophelian reminder of the power of chaos over order, his coin toss a cosmic conduit for 'material chaos'.[27] For Richard B. Woodward, Chigurh is a byword for moral disorder and: 'A symbol of the terrifying randomness that in the author's view governs the universe.'[28] However, rather than characterising Chigurh as an agent of pure chance and destruction, I argue that he represents order. He is more representative of a hyper-rationalism and ruthless efficiency than an anarchic moral vacuum. In this way, he corresponds firmly to what Derrida calls the 'calculable'. Chigurh represents a moral absence especially because of his commitment to the calculable, to order and to determinism, not despite it, whereas Bell is best described as the figure who must go through the necessary human trial of what Derrida calls 'impossible' and competing ethical demands. It is Chigurh's moral hyper-rationalism that leads Bell to re-evaluate his longstanding beliefs and gain a more enriched sense of ethics by the end of the novel.

The most obvious symbol of Chigurh's instrumentalism is his means of dispatching his victims. His weapon of choice is a captive bolt-pistol or cattle stun-gun, dispensing instantaneous death. A cattle gun is used in industrial meat production, providing an easy and efficient way to kill animals. The cattle gun operates on several symbolic registers. Firstly, it acts as a punctuation mark, separating the act of death from what comes before and after. In *No Country for Old Men* McCarthy describes its action as being accompanied by a 'pneumatic hiss and click'.[29] Already, Chigurh diminishes the possibility that his victims' decisions might involve a negotiation between past and future; his inhumanness discards any narrative span belonging to the victims. He is indifferent to the possibility that humans can live their past, present and future, preferring instead to reduce them to the immediate present. Secondly, the cattle gun has a brute physicality, forcing a direct equivalence between human and animal worlds. For Chigurh, people cannot elevate themselves above the determinism of the mechanical world. Thirdly, the cattle gun reveals the clear rationality and logic of his murders; Chigurh is devoted to mechanised death. The cattle gun is a means to an end, a fitting instrumental weapon reducing all ethical possibilities to an instantaneous now. Finally, and most importantly, the cattle gun displays Chigurh's philosophical voluntarism.[30] In philosophical terms, Chigurh is what would be called a naïve realist. He thinks the world is as he perceives it and his perception equates with deterministic organisation of physical matter.[31] Chigurh's decisions are only ever reflections of causal precedents that determine each act. He remains indifferent to the real risk that human beings face when making ethical decisions.

McCarthy shows that Chigurh is unethical because he diminishes victims of their incalculability, that is, the existential fact that human events have promise or may experience themselves otherwise. His mechanistic moral code is without what Derrida sees as the uncertainty of the decision, as an ethical decision necessarily disrupts 'both the freedom and the will of every subject – surprise in a word the very subjectivity of the subject'.[32] Chigurh's moral code is unethical because it attempts to avoid unpredictability in favour of absolute determination. As Carla Jean pleads for her life towards the end of the novel, she tells Chigurh, 'You don't have to. You don't. You don't', but for Chigurh there can be no other way.[33] The only thing that can truly offer salvation to humans is choice; a choice that coincides with the way the world has mechanically come to be at that moment – hence the coin toss. Within Chigurh's perverse logic, he requires humans to endorse the mechanical reality of choice: a choice that affirms things can be no other way. The choice of a coin toss which Chigurh offers his victims is a mechanised and determined choice; it is not a human choice, one that involves uncertainty with a view of possible consequences. Chigurh's logic cannot be discerned by Carla Jean and from her perspective, Chigurh will be responsible for her murder: 'You make it like it was the coin. But you're the one.'[34]

Carla Jean cannot disentangle herself from the chain of choices and consequences that brought Chigurh to her home. Choice, for Carla Jean, in a very human way, entails surviving with the uncertainty of its consequences, as well as the possibility that things might be otherwise. Chigurh reverses this procedure, as for him certainty and instrumentality govern all choice; in the most rational way possible, choice is an adornment of the determinism of the mechanical world. Chigurh says as much. Prior to murdering Wells, he argues: 'I wanted to see if I could extricate myself through an act of will. Because I believe that one can. That such a thing is possible. But it was a foolish thing to do. A vain thing to do.'[35] Interrogating his own voluntarism, Chigurh clearly determines that an act of will cannot elevate one beyond the brute physics of the material world. As such, Chigurh is the truly conservative and nihilistic figure of the novel, not Sheriff Bell. For Chigurh, the choices we take, the attempts to change our lives or the world for the better, are always predestined to fail. The choice Chigurh offers is not a meaningful choice – it is aimed at conserving the way things are and undermining any possibility that an ethical decision might promise progress. In this way, Chigurh is the true conservative cynic, a loathsome fatalist that represents the nihilistic levelling of all possible ethical alternatives.

Chigurh's character, rather than being cast as a chaotic figure, should thus be considered as radically rational. Every effect follows a predetermined cause; every means is an instrument to some end. What distinguishes the dysfunctional rationality of Chigurh's moral code is his inability to discriminate between objects in the world and human decisions or values. For McCarthy, Chigurh manifests himself through his control of and engagement with the physical world, and this world is an instrument to be manipulated to his will. This physicalism is why he cannot distinguish the life of a human from that of a thing. The vanity of humans for Chigurh is that we think choice can save us, making us exceptional and separate from the rest of the world. This is underlined in his altercation with the shopkeeper, where he proposes: 'Anything can be an instrument . . . Small things. Things you wouldnt even notice.'[36]

The obvious symbol of Chigurh's commitment to determinism over ethics is the coin he uses to offer his victims an alternative. The coin Chigurh uses prior to dispensing victims represents a culmination of calculable determination. The coin is a cosmic conduit of order, control and the acceptance of the physical determinism of nature. Therefore, a coin is apt for Chigurh, as it is evacuated of any symbolic value and is merely interchangeable with the rest of the physical world. Interestingly, Chigurh tells the shopkeeper not to put the coin in his pocket, as he would not be able to tell the difference between it and other coins:

> He picked the coin from his wrist and handed it across.
> What do I want with that?
> Take it. It's your lucky coin.

I dont need it.
Yes you do. Take it.
The man took the coin. I got to close now, he said.
Don't put it in your pocket.
Sir?
Don't put it in your pocket.
Where do you want me to put it?
Dont put it in your pocket. You wont know which one it is.[37]

At first glance, this might seem as if he is telling the shopkeeper that this specific coin is special and exceptional and ought to be treasured, having more value than other coins. However, the coin that Chigurh uses does not denote fortune or luck, but rather probability, interminable cost/benefit analysis, the elimination of contingency and risk from decisions, and a sovereign certitude over the hazardous reality of life. It is Chigurh's decision to invest the coin with power and value and it remains his decision whether the shopkeeper lives or dies. There is nothing uncertain about it. The coin toss confirms Chigurh's preternatural superiority as the most invulnerable man in the world, someone who does not see the coin as an agent of chaos or luck, but of the control of the order inherent in all things. As Wells is reminded: 'Somewhere in the world is the most invincible man. Just as somewhere is the most vulnerable [. . .] That's a belief that you have? No. It's called statistics.'[38]

A coin, just as much as Chigurh, represents the abolition of the lived history of his victims. The coin toss Chigurh offers his victims is a reduction of the narrative and developmental arc of ethical decision-making. The coin crystallises all past and future moments in the chain of cause and effect, cohering in a mechanical now-point, no different to any other moment in history. The coin is thus not a symbol of disorder and chaos, but precisely the opposite. For Chigurh, the truth of the world resides in the ability to separate the act from the thing: 'You see the problem. To separate the act from the thing. As if the parts of some moment in history might be interchangeable with some other moment.'[39] Any object within the world can be subject to an 'accounting'. Chigurh's code is on the side of the object, rather than the existential act, with humans being indistinguishable from other objects. Chigurh's fatalism emerges from his unquestioning acceptance of the way the world is and his scientific adherence to the obdurate determinism of nature. His victims are as interchangeable as money, reduced to the isolated and discrete moment of a coin toss. What is most tragic about this logic is that his victims become disconnected from the arc of their temporal life and every-day decisions, becoming concentrated in a single now-point. Chigurh denudes victims of their imminent possibilities, their lost past, as well as any meaningful present: 'I'm talking about your life. In which now everything can be seen at once.'[40]

Chigurh's voluntarism is fascistic; his destructive powers are short-hand for conventional homogeneity, rather than contingency and chaos. Combining destruction and uniformity underlines Chigurh's weird confluence of choice and determinism. Put through the lens of Derrida's account of ethics, Chigurh represents the precise opposite of what an ethical decision is. If an ethical decision requires both promise and uncertainty, then Chigurh wilfully reduces the future and past to the present of a single moment. If an ethical decision is to be ethical, it must take place at the intersection of the past, present and future. Chigurh nullifies any sense that an ethical decision can develop. He cannot elevate himself above the ebb and flow of history. Notably, Chigurh never wears a seatbelt, as he is a master of fate and fortune. However, Chigurh ultimately discovers that he is as subject to chance events as anybody when a car accidently hits him at an intersection.[41] In summary, we can discern McCarthy's distinct philosophical position on the status of ethical decisions. Chigurh's moral code emerges from the reduction of the human to the brute physicality of the world. Any ethical decision is only an expression of the mechanical *logos* of the causes and effects of the material world. Chigurh is a calculating machine presenting an absolute ethical nega-tion that reduces the human being to a mere mechanical present.

Llewellyn Moss and the tragedy of renewal

The novel itself is set in 1980, a threshold year, a punctuation mark between past and future, where America is still experiencing gen-erational tension between the old and young in the aftermath of the Vietnam War.[42] Ronald Reagan's election as president represents an uneasy accommodation between a modernising capitalism and a nostalgic return to the Mythic West. Moss and Bell are veterans of two different wars and McCarthy elaborates their generational disconnection. The decisions of characters serve to isolate them from others; they are immiserated due to their separation from the collec-tive fate and historical possibility of generational struggles. Jay Ellis astutely shows how the form of the novel expresses fraught dialogue between past, present and future.[43] The different narratives represent stories of a 'young man' and an 'old man', of disconnected worlds existing apprehensively alongside each other. Consolidating Ellis's analysis, the novel works as a negotiation of generational anxieties. The novel is understood best as a staging of the elongated experience of both Bell and Moss in tandem. The three central protagonists, within their own context, represent the past (Bell), the future (Moss/ Carla Jean/Hitchhiker) and the present (Chigurh). The tragedy of the novel resides in the inability of central characters to comprehend how their decisions are part of a shared tradition, as well as a shared future – except for Chigurh, for whom every choice remains tied to a determined present.

Moss's character is remarkably typical of the traditional cowboy. He is a rugged individual, independent and self-sustaining, at ease with the borderless desert. He adheres to a chivalric code of honour, as demonstrated by his return to the scene where he leaves a man dying. Moss is also a liminal figure; he exists inside and outside the law. He is loyal and caring, yet also a maverick who transgresses the law of the jungle, as well as the law of the State, by stealing money from a drug deal gone wrong. The tragedy of his character is simple. Moss commits the cardinal sin of American mercantile ethics: he tries to get something for nothing.

The function of Moss in this scene is exceptionally important. As a liminal figure, Moss is torn between different ethical possibilities. On the one hand, he is a symbol of the type of ethical decision-making that Derrida outlines. On the other, stealing the money entangles Moss within the inevitable cycle of exchange and violence that characterises the drugs trade. After stealing the money, Moss's decision to return to the scene where he has left the cartel member dying can be decisively read alongside Derrida's understanding of the ethical decision. Moss's guilt and his subsequent decision to perform an act of kindness inevitably put his own life at risk, placing him in the impossible situation of rectifying his theft of the money. McCarthy injects the narrative of Moss with the type of uncertainty, risk and contingency necessary for the taking place of an authentic ethical decision as Derrida outlines it.

Unfortunately, for Moss it is too late: his fate is already preordained for the fatal encounter with Chigurh. Moss represents a version of Bell, tempted by the false promise of the unlimited rewards and exchange of the drugs trade. As with Chigurh, Moss acts as a foil for illuminating Bell's moral development and functionally, within the novel, he serves to illuminate the ethical uncertainty that Bell is slowly exposed to as the novel unfolds. Moss tragically oscillates between Bell and the world of Chigurh. The dominating decision

Moss takes is of course to take the money. Moss makes a mistake and must live uncertainly with the consequences. Strikingly, the decision to take the money enters Moss into the circularity of exchange and thus overlaps with Chigurh's moral aesthetic. Moss's decision crystallises into something exceptional and immune from the movement of history as well as other people: 'His whole life was sitting there in front of him. Day after day from dawn til dark until he was dead. All of it cooked down into forty pounds of paper in a satchel.'[44] The point is clear: Moss is tempted by security and certainty; life can simply crystallise into a single choice. This choice is salvation, a radical decision that illuminates all the things that have gone and are to come. Moss says to himself: 'You have to take this seriously. You can't treat it like luck.'[45] For him, this is not fate; it cannot be any other way.

This is a fatal error, as Moss is imposing meaning upon an event that is senseless. At any rate, his initial voluntarism is moot, as later in the novel we see a tracking device in the satchel of money. McCarthy presents Moss as tragically human. He makes a mistake, he experiences guilt and he tries to rectify his initial mistake by returning to the dying man with water. Again, Derrida's analysis of the ethical decision is relevant. The idea that seduces Moss is that he can wilfully choose and transform his existence, so that his previous and future selves become irrelevant. As Derrida shows, the freedom of the ethical decision is something anxious and tortured, which befits Moss's decision to return to help the cartel member. The ethical force of the novel is evident in Bell – and to a lesser extent Moss – since ethical possibility becomes more visible when communal consensus is exposed to uncertainty and violence. An ethical decision must require the following of a rule, in the sense that a decision is right and lawful, but on the other hand, an ethical choice also needs to be re-evaluated in newer contexts. This is not the case for Chigurh though, since if one judges an ethical decision as strictly adhering to a determinate code, then one becomes what Derrida calls a 'calculating machine'.[46]

The enigma of the law requires it to be transgressed and conserved at the same time. Tragically, at the point where Moss steals the money from the cartel, he cannot discern that ethical decisions are both regulated and unregulated, both inside and outside the law at the same time. Moss's tragic decision to take the money is an attempt to elevate his decision above the interplay of rule and sacrifice, in a doomed attempt at absolute self-creation. The choice of theft is designed to generate infinite possibilities and the further choices money can offer to Moss.[47] While Moss and Bell waver between the predictable and the unpredictable, this is not the case for Chigurh. Moss's tragedy is that he does not have a future. What differentiates Moss from Chigurh is that absolute choice cannot wholly tempt Moss, nor can his later realisation that one cannot remake one's life *ex nihilo*.

Moss's initial seduction by the possibilities afforded by money is tempered by his kindness, and a grim reality where: 'Everybody's huntin me.'[48] In a philosophical discussion with the Hitchhiker, Moss fully realises the consequences of his initial decision. He rejects the thinking that one arrives at one's current position in an act of self-creation which transcends history. He rejects the idea 'that you got there without taking anything with you'.[49] His hitchhiker is going to California, the American paragon of ambition, renewal, escape and regeneration. In philosophical terms, Moss repudiates the idea of *tabula rasa* or the possibility of completely 'startin over'.[50] Any renewal of the self is entangled with the historical genesis and sacrifices of one's character:

> It's not about knowin where you are. It's about thinkin you got there without takin anything with you. Your notions about startin over. Or anybody's. You don't start over. That's what it's about. Ever step you take is forever. You cant make it go away. None of it . . . You think when you wake up in the morning yesterday don't count. But yesterday is all that does count. What else is there? Your life is made out of the days it's made out of. Nothin else.[51]

Once Moss realises the true nature of decision, he dies. In Moss's conversation with Chigurh on the telephone, the call that ultimately condemns Carla Jean to death, Moss realises not just the meaninglessness of his initial choice, but the fact that any choice will not save either him or Carla Jean from Chigurh's distorted rationalism. Moss, while injured, allows himself one last feeble defiant outburst: 'I'm goin to bring you something all right, Moss said. I've decided to make you a special project of mine.'[52]

McCarthy distinguishes Moss from Chigurh by showing the inevitable erosion of Moss's autonomy; Moss's character develops in the novel from a rugged individual to one utterly dependent on others, such as Wells, the Hitchhiker, the boys who sell him clothes, or the fellow veteran who allows him back over the border. Moss comes to see that the free choice he grabbed with rampant opportunism in the desert offers a corrupted version of human freedom, one bringing misery in its aftermath. Choice cannot save Moss. McCarthy uses Moss to show that a choice is only ethical once it is not wholly individual. The only character wholly self-determining is Chigurh, whereas Moss only attains a paltry degree of self-determination, a self-determination painfully mitigated by the wider context of a more developed and profounder dependence on others, as well as the world in general. But is it possible to extend this combination of determination and dependency, to a figure as supposedly conservative and recalcitrant as Bell?

Sheriff Bell and ethical sacrifice

Bell comes closer to ethical decision-making because he undergoes an ordeal of renunciation, an inescapable sacrifice and renunciation of those things he holds dear: ethical belonging; the Myths of the American West; the values and manners he constantly reiterates throughout the novel. It is only because his convictions and traditions are exposed to a violent uncertainty that his ethical deliberations are more insightful. Stephen Tatum envisages a similar context, and a helpful critique of the limitations of mercantile ethics, in his incisive exploration of *No Country for Old Men* in relation to the *narcocorrido*. For Tatum, despite Bell's inchoate protestations about the loss of 'mercantile ethics', manners and customs, the ethical foundation of the novel emerges from the deepening wisdom Bell accumulates from facing down the uncertainties he is exposed to through the illegal narcotics trade. In the unpublished screenplay version of *No Country for Old Men*, there is further evidence to consolidate Tatum's reading. One version of the screenplay has a much happier ending than the published novel. In the screenplay, Bell and Moss come to an arrangement regarding the purloined money, with Bell arranging for the money to be redistributed to the people of his county towards the establishment of a medical centre. While this conclusion is radically different to that of the published novel, it shows that from the outset of the telling of this story, McCarthy intends it that Bell is open to ethical transformation, reconfiguring his attachment to mercantile ethics, even if in original screenplay drafts, the move is from mercantile exchange to a more redistributive deployment of the stolen money.[53] In the published novel, Bell's internal narration conflicts with the reality of the external world; Bell's cognitive world itself is subject to uncertainty, with Bell attempting to impose stability on the chaos of the world.[54] What is significant in Tatum's reading, for my analysis, is that it shows that Bell's virtue is solely defined by a recalcitrant mindset whose sole purpose is a return to the nostalgic lost past of mercantile ethics. This is because embedded within the formal organisation of the novel is the contingency of Bell's moral psychology, or as Tatum argues: 'Bell's abiding narrative desire is to produce a narrative explanation that will make disjunctive things and events in space and time cohere.'[55] This desire is never satiated within *No Country for Old Men*, since with Chigurh, Bell confronts the absolute irrationality of certainty, which creates a 'cognitive paralysis' in which Bell must acknowledge his own finitude.[56]

Bell is a typical McCarthy character; he is a cowboy out of time. As with characters in *The Border Trilogy*, Bell fails to cope with modernisation, perceiving time-honoured values waning in the face of wanton violence. At the outset, Bell is obstinate in lamenting the diminishment of a Golden Age and rendered useless in the face of the intractable ruthlessness of Chigurh. As with other McCarthy characters such as the kid, Suttree or Culla, Bell is radically flawed, haunted by his cowardice in the Second World War and the manufactured heroism he is feted with on his return. Like Moss, he is a veteran of war, as well as a threshold figure existing in the world of past and present, but at home in neither. As the name 'Bell' suggests, he is both fixed and out of time, a punctuating character at the end of a period, crystallised in a present moment between a time that is gone and a time to come, an alarm and a warning of a lost future. Bell sees his world transfigured in an irretrievable way. As befitting his conservatism, Bell is rooted in the past, resistant to change and thus unable to imagine an alternative future. Bell is proud of the fact that he was sheriff at the same time as his grandfather. He takes pride in generational continuity; he yearns for the immutable, whilst valuing the coincidence of the past and present.[57] Elsewhere, Bell describes 'truth'. 'It dont move about from place to place and it dont change from time to time. You cant corrupt it any more than you can salt salt. You cant corrupt it because that's what it is.'[58] Truth is something elemental and irreducible, clearly more eminent than the narrative and stories which Bell considers trivial. There are deeper truths than the vicissitudes of human affairs and any change happening to human beings is secondary to the primary truth of the past. Here Bell is drawn as an arch-conservative:

> But I think it goes deeper than that. It is community and it is respect, of course, but the dead have more claims on you than you might want to admit or you even might know about and them claims can be very strong indeed. Very strong indeed.[59]

It does seem as though the simplicity of Bell's values aligns with some of McCarthy's own view of ethics. Garry Wallace reports, in his encounter with McCarthy, that McCarthy endorses the simplicity of ethics, where one learns all one needs to know by the time one graduates from kindergarten, such as, 'To tell the truth. Not to hit each other. To be fair.'[60] That McCarthy is willing to expose his own views to the frightening moral vacuum of Chigurh testifies to his interest in putting to the test these personal views on the acquisition of ethical values. The ethical force of the novel depends on Bell's inherent conservatism being exposed to risk and uncertainty.

While on the surface Bell makes a strong claim to the truth of tradition, this is undermined through his persistent ignorance. One of his most oft-repeated refrains throughout the book is 'I don't know'. The value of McCarthy's story arc is the extent to which Bell manages to surpass his rootedness in the past. The ethical insight McCarthy achieves in the novel emerges through the opening of the conservative mind. Bell's philosophical enlightenment emerges from the non-confrontation with Chigurh, who makes manifest the fallibility of his conservatism. Bell's ethical development materialises when his certainty about the deeper order of the universe is undermined. Chigurh injects a radical uncertainty into his existence, forcing him to re-evaluate the structure of his existing values. This is what distinguishes Bell from Chigurh and what makes Chigurh psychopathic. Chigurh is a solipsist who accepts his subjective view of the universe as objective, whereas Bell's subjective view of the universe exists alongside doubts about the objective nature of the world. Bell's character is ultimately Socratic, where ignorance is essential to the constitution of truth. For example, Wells offers a damning appraisal of Bell's limited knowledge: 'He's a redneck sheriff in a hick town in a hick county. In a hick state.'[61] The contrast between the slick, knowing Wells and the supposedly backward and ignorant Bell foregrounds Bell's deepening wisdom that ethical knowledge irretrievably coexists with violence and uncertainty. As we saw with Derrida's reading of Abraham, ethical life becomes more visible when contested and open to the sacrifice of pre-existing customs.

Notwithstanding Chigurh, many of the central characters in *No Country for Old Men* begin in a state of knowing and proceed to states of unknowing. This dynamic can be seen in Bell's conversation with Carla Jean, where he extols and explains the virtues of a youthful marriage, in which account the decision to marry his wife remains steadfast, immune to 'ever dumb thing I ever done'.[62] Carla Jean challenges this sentiment, suggesting 'Nineteen is old enough to know that if you have got somethin that means the world to you it's all that more likely it'll get took away.'[63] Bell responds that he is no stranger to this idea. The ethical dimension of these sentiments reveals that what is purposeful and meaningful is dependent on the potential threat of their removal; meaning and purpose are inextricably tied to loss. The ethical and philosophical purpose of Bell's character reveals the split nature of the ethical decision. Bell's ultimate decision not to confront Chigurh reveals to him a sense of connection between past, present and future, with Bell struggling to come to terms with the reality that ethics is precarious and fragile, with a very weak guarantee of value.

Bell reveals the extent to which conservative characters have the capacity to overcome their own dull rationality and realise that things exist beyond family, locale and community. What is valuable can only be sustained in the face of contingency. As Bell acknowledges: 'We dedicate ourselves anew daily. Somethin like that. I think I'm goin to commence dedicatin myself twice daily. It might come to three fore it's over.'[64] Therefore, an ethical decision does not subscribe to immutable truths independent of humans. Nor must we argue that Bell subscribes to the liberal choice of an autonomous self. Instead, ethical decisions are precarious, demanding sustenance and application. Dedication can only draw sustenance from that which is uncertain, and those things that are worth sticking to are not immune from challenge, indecision and ambiguity. Bell becomes conscious that ethical choice is not about ownership of choice. As Lydia Cooper puts it, what Bell realises through the experience of violence is that the only ethical identity worth having emerges through 'unrelenting commitment to being in relationship with other people'.[65]

The nuance of Bell's character arises from the extent to which his conservatism is negated. As the novel progresses, many supposed lynchpins of his conservatism are found to be on hollow ground. His war heroism is a sham to the extent that he thinks he stole his own life.[66] Any guarantee of salvation is spurned in the face of the superior enemy that is Chigurh; he loses belief in an American Golden age; the Second World War creates traumas and generational strife between 'rednecks' and GI's intellectualised by the GI Bill.[67] It could be argued that Bell's anxieties represent a banal type of conservatism, namely a profound scepticism about human nature. But this misrecognises the extent to which Bell's character is stripped of his identity as the novel progresses. As well as the fact that he does not deem himself worthy of his community, he is stripped of his assurance of how others perceive him. It is not simply the case that America had a

Golden Age when mercantile ethics were flourishing and now things have turned foul. Chigurh instigates a radical stripping of Bell's subjectivity to the extent that Bell's folksiness is dimly transcended and opened to the universal dilemmas of human decisions.

In what could be taken as a critical broadside against liberal America, Bell makes an argument against cultural relativism: 'anybody that cant tell the difference between rapin and murderin people and chewin gum has a whole lot bigger of a problem than what I've got'.[68] This is undeniably framed in conservative terms, but the rejection of rape and murder is not restricted to conservatism. The nostalgic assumption that things were just simply better in the past is impossible and radically negated. In Bell's inchoate way, he recognises a universal appeal beyond the narrow logic of family, loyalty and community. He is trying to find some fundamentals which transcend particular historical periods and connect different generations in a common humanity. The generational dysfunction brought about by the GI Bill, as well as by the Sixties more generally, means that culture is more fractious and Bell is trying to heal the rifts between the past, present and future. In one of the most telling scenes in the book, Bell argues with a woman at a university who is pro-choice:

> I dont like the way this country is headed. I want my granddaughter to be able to have an abortion. And I said well mam I dont think you got any worries about the way the country is headed. The way I see it goin I dont have much doubt but what she'll be able to have an abortion. I'm going to say that not only will she be able to have an abortion, she'll be able to have you put to sleep. Which pretty much ended the conversation.[69]

This denotes obvious conservative anxiety about cultures of death. Early in the novel, Bell is alarmed at the cheapening of life, reflecting on a child being thrown in a waste disposal. However, we need to read the above extract in a subtler way, which sees both the mother and Bell exposed to – and needing to transcend – each other's moral certainties. Abortion ought not to be literally read as Bell's personal objection to abortion. It should instead be understood as an indicator of generational disharmony, of the disjoining of the future from the present, as well as the necessarily unpredictable ordeal that is required to transcend the polarisation of American culture wars. Given that Bell and Loretta have lost a child, abortion represents a more fundamental philosophical point. It is not about the ethics of abortion *per se*, but can rather be read as a metaphor for lost potential and futurity.[70] The unsubtle equivalence Bell draws between euthanasia and abortion is not about the ethics of these issues but expresses a fear on Bell's part about the intimate relation between rational choice and death.

No Country for Old Men peters out, intentionally. Formally, the novel is *High Noon* without the shoot-out. Bell is wholly unresolved, attempting to deepen his character with an investigation of Mammon. This signifies a deepening of his character, one which allows him to surpass his engrained conservatism and attempt to see the economic conditions of a fallen world. The philosophical difference between Chigurh and Bell rests on McCarthy embedding a chronic fallibility within Bell's knowledge. Paradoxically, Bell's ignorance of the real world allows him to grasp something fundamental: the radical contingency of human existence. In the last analysis, Bell becomes Nietzschean, confronting the inevitable breakdown in 'mercantile ethics that leaves people settin out in the desert dead in their vehicles and by then it is too late'.[71] Bell realises that the moral code he has inhabited all his life is sacrificed to a rabid capitalism and a cultural narcotisation induced by the illegal drugs trade. By the end of the novel, Bell has a more enriched sense of ethical decision-making, realising that ethics requires a deeper logic than the rational certainties of reward and payment, or the idea that morality is something that can be predetermined, or accounted for as a balanced economic exchange. Bell sees how 'we're bein bought with our own money'.[72] This is in direct opposition to Chigurh, whose 'accounting is scrupulous'.[73] Bell's ethical epistemology is one divested of self-reliance, as well as the humiliating destabilisation he is dealt by his failure to defeat Chigurh. By the end of the novel Bell has entered a state of Socratic wisdom, where his ethical refrain is one of uncertainty:

> Money that can buy whole countries. It done has. Can it buy this one? I don't think so. But it will put you in bed with people you ought not to be there with. It's not even a law enforcement problem I doubt that it ever was. There's always been narcotics. But people dont just up and decide to dope theirselves for no reason. By the millions. I dont have no answer about that. In particular I don't have no answer to take heart from.[74]

Bell reaches terminal and abject defeat after confronting economic forces beyond his capacity to comprehend. He demonstrates the position that ethical life is more valuable when exposed to loss. It is precisely because decisions take place at the intersection of past, present and future, and precisely because, as Derrida has shown, the truest ethical decision demands the desertion of one's cultural affiliation and loyalty, that ethical wisdom comes to take place. Bell sees beyond the calculable exchange of mercantile ethics, remaining a survivor who has not earned his trauma.

What type of choice does *No Country for Old Men* reveal as an ethical decision? It is important to note that the ethical choice McCarthy has his characters live through is not consumerist choice. Such choices are easy, such as choosing between the different options on a McDonald's menu. The type of choice McCarthy philosophically presents in *No Country for Old Men* is not the supposed liberation of consumer choice. This is very clear from Bell's chastisement of those who consume drugs from the drugs wars, for clearly playing their part in perpetuating suffering. Ethical decisions, as Derrida shows, are not easy; they are difficult and require a profound sacrifice of the 'law of the home (*oikos*), of the hearth, of what is one's own or proper, of the private, of the love and affection of one's kin'.[75] Consumerist choice does not offer any meaningful connection with tradition or its sacrifice, nor does it offer any aspiration towards a different future. Such choice is not liberation, but an imprisonment in the hedonism of the now. Consumption is only an ethical choice tied to the present and remains ahistorical, effortlessly luxuriating in the pleasures of the senses without recognition of tradition, value and future aspiration. Bell offers us a different type of choice, an existential one, one in which our ethical decisions are cognisant of the world they are embedded in, whilst understanding the demands and burden of our own limitations. Ultimately, Moss tragically cannot carry on to the future, leaving Bell offering a complex alternative to Chigurh. Chigurh is ultimately a feeble existentialist, who reduces all decisions to a rational self-authenticating choice that can be determined and controlled.[76] However, the irony is that by the close of the novel, the conservative Bell has the deeper understanding of existentialism.

The end of the novel sees McCarthy align Bell with some opaque symbolism. As with *Suttree*, *No Country for Old Men* ends with water symbolism. Bell reflects on the significance of an ancient stone water trough:

> But this man had set down with a hammer and chisel and carved out a stone water trough to last ten thousand years. Why was that? What was it that he had faith in? It wasnt that nothin would change. Which is what you might think, I suppose. He had to know bettern that. I've thought about it a good deal. I thought about it after I left there with that house blown to pieces. I'm goin to say that water trough is there yet. It would of took something to move it, I can tell you that. So I think about him

settin there with his hammer and his chisel, maybe just a hour or two
after supper, I dont know. And I have to say that the only thing I can
think of is that there was some sort of promise in his heart.[77]

Specifically, Bell asks what type of decision it takes to carve a well
out of rock with a chisel. A few things occur here. Firstly, stone and
rock express Bell's appreciation for achieving something fundamental and durable. Secondly, Bell admires something deeper than the
instrumental function of the water trough. He admires the capacity
for continuity that the water trough offers, the sustenance it gives
across the span of generations. Thirdly, while this desire for continuity could be read as a conservative nostalgia, it is more accurate to see that any reification of the past is undermined by Bell's
suggestion that the original maker of the trough was too wise to
think that 'nothin would change'.[78] Finally, the wisdom Bell takes
from this elemental symbol is that any type of faith, like that of the
trough maker, is not faith in an immutable truth which transcends
history, but a faith that sustains itself alongside the finite uncertainties of history. As such, Bell is Nietzschean by the end of the novel,
realising that the sincerest ethical decision is one that can only wilfully be steadfast in the face of the struggles of history. One can
resort to the rabid and mechanistic rationalism of Chigurh, or one
can struggle to elevate oneself alongside the brute material world
as Bell tries to do.

Conclusion

No Country for Old Men begins and ends with a promise, a promise
full of certainty and inevitability. The promise in the opening pages
is Bell's witness to death and condemnation: 'I sent one boy to the
gas chamber at Huntsville. One and only one. My arrest and my
testimony.'[79] Here Bell's decision is coldly nihilistic and instrumentalist, condemning a murdering boy to death. By the final pages of the
novel, he dreams of a covenant with his father: 'And in the dream
I know that he was goin on ahead and he was fixin to make a fire
somewhere out there in all that dark and all that cold and I know
that whenever I got there he would be there. And then I woke up.'[80]
The dream of his father is significant because it shows Bell simultaneously relying on an interpretation of the past along with an open
futurity. The dream stands for a covenant of the past, present and
future. By the close of the novel, the spark of fire in the wasteland, in

the context of a father and son, as with *The Road*, shows that moral wisdom requires the intimacy of truth, ethics and uncertainty; the dream signifies the impossible and infinitely demanding task of finding a common humanity beyond the moral certainties of different generations. With water and fire, birth and death, McCarthy shows ethical life enriched with ambiguity.

The importance of *No Country for Old Men* for understanding the ethical and philosophical stakes of McCarthy's novels cannot be overstated. The rationalism and borderline totalitarianism of Chigurh's certainty illuminates the burdensome recognition by Bell of human frailties and uncertainties, and with this recognition comes the ability to understand the struggles and suffering of fellow humans in their anxious attempts to be builders of a common world. McCarthy is self-consciously offering a different type of materialism, an elemental one, which differs radically from the certainty and hyper-rationalism of Chigurh's mechanistic materialism. McCarthy offers the gloomy and fraught ethical decision-making of Bell as a palliative to Chigurh's schizoid binary of free will and determinism. Chigurh's instrumentalism and efficiency point to the 'easiness' of his decisions; Bell's ethical illumination is onerous. The difference between Bell and Moss against Chigurh is that their existence is deeply enmeshed in the concrete and material world; they have an ability to reflect and deliberate on their decisions, their outcomes and the lived consequences of their actions, for better or for worse. This type of ethical deliberation is impossible for Chigurh, as his immaterial rationalism dictates no meaning or purpose which can be attached to such reflections.

What McCarthy demonstrates philosophically is the density and flawed nature of ethical decision-making. An ethical decision requires the complication of the moral habits, loyalties and cultural affiliations which embed one in a moral community. An authentic ethical decision necessitates that humans survive and carry on with the burden of their choices and consequences. In this way, *No Country for Old Men* typifies McCarthy's unworking of the Emersonian individualism that plays such a decisive role in the formation of American identity. The decisions of Sheriff Bell articulate a temporal ethics, one defined by endurance in the face of loss, as well as the inherent necessity of civil disobedience at the heart of the law in this lawmaker. The ethical achievement of Bell, despite his cowardice and ignorance, is the integration of loss into his ethical vision in the face of the relentless moral vacuum which Chigurh represents.

Notes

1. Cormac McCarthy, *No Country for Old Men* (London: Picador, 2005), 304.
2. McCarthy, *Cormac McCarthy Papers (1964–2007)*, Box 79: Folder 1, 100. Generally, McCarthy's screenplays tend to be the least devoted of his texts to explicit examination of philosophical themes. For example, the original screenplay drafts of *No Country for Old Men* do not contain excessive philosophical material beyond the themes which I am also discussing in the published novel here. The same can be said for McCarthy's *The Counsellor*, which contains only a handful of interesting observations about psychological character motivation concerning the ethical consequences of guilt and transgression, as well as some ambling monologues on life and death. The philosophical elements of the screenplays are more tacit than in McCarthy's other writings. One exception is McCarthy's screenplay for the 1977 PBS broadcast *The Gardener's Son*, which does contain some obvious philosophical themes such as the status of technology for humans, the functioning of patriarchy, violence, mortal survival, and scepticism of moral instrumentalism. Specifically, these philosophical themes emerge in the character of the Timekeeper, who looms large over the action. For example, 'Time-Keeper: They aint the thing. Old papers or pitchers. You copy something down don't mean you have it. You just have the record. Times past are fugitive. They caint be kept in no box.' McCarthy, *The Gardener's Son* (New York: Harper Collins, 1996), 3. The most relevant philosophical theme of *The Gardener's Son*, which corroborates the argument of this chapter, is McCarthy's concern to chronicle the losers and winners of radical shifts in society's economic arrangements, as best represented in the ghost of Mr Gregg, who illustrates the shift from agricultural exchange to the industrial capitalism of Graniteville's mill. For the most thorough account of the journeys and adaptations of McCarthy's screenplays, and *The Gardener's Son* itself, see Peebles, *Cormac McCarthy and Performance*, 15–40.
3. There is some critical speculation that McCarthy's work has become progressively more conservative. *No Country for Old Men* is supposedly representative of this trend. For example, F. H. Buckley places the novel in *National Review*'s ten great conservative novels, citing the novel's scepticism of human perfectibility, its view of a flawed humanity and the resolution these find in grace. For a good summary of McCarthy's purported conservatism, see Linda Woodson, 'Materiality, Moral Responsibility, and Determinism in *No Country for Old Men*', in *From Novel to Film: No Country for Old Men*, ed. Lynnea C. King, Rick Wallach and Jim Welsh (Toronto: Scarecrow Press, 2009), 8. For a persuasive and vigorous critique of McCarthy's purported conservatism see David Cremean, 'For Whom Bell Tolls: Cormac McCarthy's Sheriff Bell

as Spiritual Hero', in *From Novel to Film: No Country for Old Men*, ed. Lynnea C. King, Rick Wallach and Jim Welsh (Toronto: Scarecrow Press, 2009), 1–12.

4. In the archival drafts of *No Country for Old Men* Chigurh directly states, 'I like to model myself on a god.' McCarthy, *Cormac McCarthy Papers (1964–2007)*, Box 80: Folder 7, 101.

5. Malewitz, *The Practice of Misuse*, 158–64.

6. Ibid. 178.

7. Jacques Derrida, 'Force of Law: The Mystical Foundation of Authority', In *Acts of Religion*, trans. Mary Quaintance, ed. Gil Anidjar (London: Routledge, 2002), 257.

8. Ibid.

9. Ibid. 251.

10. McCarthy, *No Country*, 253.

11. Derrida, 'Force of Law', 256.

12. McCarthy, *No Country*, 260.

13. Ibid. 260.

14. Derrida, 'Force of Law', 252.

15. Ibid.

16. Ibid. 253.

17. Derrida, *Learning to Live Finally: The Last Interview*, trans. Pascale-Ann Brault and Michael Naas (Hoboken: Melville House Publishing, 2007), 51.

18. Derrida, *The Gift of Death; And, Literature in Secret*, trans. David Wills (Chicago: University of Chicago Press, 2008), 84–8.

19. Adam Kelly, *American Fiction in Transition: Observer-Hero Narrative, the 1990s, and Postmodernism* (London: Bloomsbury, 2013), 34.

20. Derrida, *Learning to Live Finally*, 51.

21. Derrida, *The Gift of Death*, 69.

22. Hawkins, *Cormac McCarthy's Philosophy*, 22.

23. Ibid. 63.

24. Ibid. 96.

25. McCarthy, *No Country*, 3–4.

26. Ibid. 153.

27. Chigurh is commonly considered a figure of chaos. Benjamin Mangrum cites Chigurh as representative of a deterministic order of material chaos. See Benjamin Mangrum, 'Democracy, Justice and Tragedy in Cormac McCarthy's *No Country for Old Men*', *Religion and Literature* 43, no.3 (Autumn 2011): 117. For Lydia Cooper, Chigurh is: 'an arbitrary wreaker-of-havoc like Native American tricksters'. See Lydia Cooper, '"He's a Psychopathic Killer, but So What?": Folklore and Morality in Cormac McCarthy's *No Country for Old Men*', *Papers on Language and Literature* 45, no.1 (Winter 2009): 49. John Cant sees Chigurh as a figure of 'implacable chaos'. See John Cant, 'The Silent Sheriff: *No Country for Old Men* – A Comparison of Novel and Film',

in *Intertextual and Interdisciplinary Approaches to Cormac McCarthy*, ed. Nicholas Monk (London: Routledge, 2012), 95. Dennis Cuthcins characterises Chigurh as a synthesis of fate and determinism. See Dennis Cutchins, 'Grace and Moss's End in *No Country for Old Men*', in *From Novel to Film: No Country for Old Men*, ed. Lynnea C. King, Rick Wallach and Jim Welsh (Toronto: Scarecrow Press, 2009), 158. Steven Frye notes the role of chaos theory as a principal motivator for Chigurh. However, Frye offers a subtle deviation, acknowledging the symbiosis of order and chance: 'From his point of view, consistent with chaos theory, an irreducibly complex matrix of cause and effect has brought them both to the present moment, and though chance governs the fall of the coin, it is a chance mitigated by all the intricate consequential moments that precede it. Even the portentous fortune in the toss is circumscribed by time and previous events.' See Frye, *Understanding Cormac McCarthy*, 162.

28. Woodward, 'Bernard Madoff and Anton Chigurh'.
29. McCarthy, *No Country*, 7.
30. Voluntarism argues that acts of will transcend intellect, embodiment and emotions.
31. Naïve realism, often a pejorative term in philosophy, claims that we perceive objects via our senses as they really are, via the experience of physical laws such as cause and effect, matter, size and shape.
32. Derrida, *The Politics of Friendship*, trans. George Collins (London: Verso, 2005), 68.
33. McCarthy, *No Country*, 257–8.
34. Ibid. 258.
35. Ibid. 174–5.
36. Ibid. 57.
37. Ibid.
38. Ibid. 141.
39. Ibid. 57.
40. Ibid. 175.
41. Ibid. 260.
42. Moss, Wells, Bell and Chigurh are all ex-military. This book is about the Vietnam War fallout. For example, see Erika Spoden's 'Let There Be Blood: The Vein of Vietnam in *No Country for Old Men*' for a good account of how the novel raises questions of inter-generational conflict. In *The Cormac McCarthy Journal* 10, no.1 (2012): 76–92.
43. Ellis, *No Place for Home*, 32.
44. McCarthy, *No Country*, 17–18. McCarthy's novels are often concerned with the loss of history, or what David Holloway calls, following Frederic Jameson, in the context of *Blood Meridian*, the 'waning of history', where there is crisis in a 'living dialectical continuum of past, present and future'. Holloway, *The Late Modernism of Cormac McCarthy*, 58.

45. McCarthy, *No Country*, 23.
46. Derrida, 'Force of Law', 252.
47. For example, Moss briefly revels in consumerism, using bloodstained dollar bills to buy clothes and labels he likes, as well as using the money to bribe a wary taxi driver to take him to Mexico. McCarthy, *No Country*, 186–91.
48. McCarthy, *No Country*, 231.
49. Ibid. 227.
50. Ibid.
51. Ibid.
52. Ibid. 185.
53. For example, 'You want to think that people dont really change. That people are the same. But people do change'. McCarthy, *Cormac McCarthy Papers (1964–2007)*, Box 79: Folder 2, 101.
54. Stephen Tatum, '"Mercantile Ethics": *No Country for Old Men* and the Narcocorrido', in *Cormac McCarthy: All the Pretty Horses, No Country for Old Men, The Road*, ed. Sara Spurgeon (London: Bloomsbury, 2011), 80.
55. Ibid. 80.
56. Ibid. 93.
57. McCarthy, *No Country*, 90.
58. Ibid. 123.
59. Ibid. 124.
60. Wallace, *Meeting Cormac McCarthy Plus 9 Notable Essays of The Year*, 6.
61. McCarthy, *No Country*, 124.
62. Ibid. 133.
63. Ibid. 134.
64. Ibid. 168.
65. Cooper, '"He's a Psychopathic Killer, but So What?"', 52.
66. McCarthy, *No Country*, 278.
67. Ibid. 195.
68. Ibid. 196.
69. Ibid. 197.
70. Bell is taunted by an inmate on death row: 'Where do they find somebody like you? Have they got you in diapers yet? I shot that son of a bitch right between the eyes and drug him back to his car by the hair of the head and set the car on fire and burned him to grease.' McCarthy, *No Country*, 297. This obscene symbolic mix of birth and death confronts Bell with a cavalier disrespect for possibility.
71. Ibid. 304.
72. Ibid. 302.
73. Ibid. 259.
74. Ibid. 303.
75. Derrida, *The Gift of Death*, 95.

76. About the film adaptation, see Enda McCaffrey's 'Crimes of Passion, Freedom and a Clash of Sartrean Moralities' for a good account of how Chigurh represents a limited existentialism. Enda McCaffrey, 'Crimes of Passion, Freedom and a Clash of Sartrean Moralities in the Coen Brothers' *No Country for Old Men*', in *Existentialism and Contemporary Cinema: A Sartrean Perspective*, ed. Enda McCaffrey and Jean-Pierre Boulé (Oxford: Berghahn Books, 2014), 25–142.
77. McCarthy, *No Country*, 301.
78. Ibid. 307.
79. Ibid. 3.
80. Ibid. 309.

Chapter 7

A Maelstrom of Doing and Undoing: McCarthy's Political Imaginary

Throughout this book I have argued that Cormac McCarthy is one of literature's great unifiers. In the preceding chapters, I have shown that a continual preoccupation of McCarthy's novels and plays is his effort to meld seemingly contradictory philosophical positions. This is the case whether discussing matter and spirit, good and evil, nature and artifice, or law and lawlessness. In this chapter, I will argue that this trend continues in the political domain, specifically with respect to questions of order and chaos. I do not aim to ascribe a specific political ideology to McCarthy, or even to ascribe political intent to his various literary outputs; rather, I am more interested in explaining the form of political thinking that McCarthy's writing enables. In short, given the philosophical themes I have discussed to this point, I want to explore the political imaginary present in McCarthy's work. Specifically, I aim to argue that the crux of McCarthy's political imaginary revolves around unifying themes of order and chaos, which will in turn enable me to demonstrate how ostensibly disparate political oppositions – ruler and ruled, equality and liberty, hierarchy and egalitarianism, system and anarchy – are negotiated in a variety of McCarthy's texts.

Blood Meridian showed us that the state of nature is at war with itself, from a point of being neither innocent nor pure. But what, then, happens to the social contract – the binding agreements and contracts adopted between all humans to stave off the state of nature? Is civilisation too subject to infection with ineradicable violence? According to *Blood Meridian*, the answer is yes, but this does not automatically imply savagery. McCarthy, throughout his literature, remains faithful to the political ontology I outlined in Chapter 3 when analysing *Blood Meridian*. The intensity with which civility is defined by contest and antagonism does not necessarily entail atavism and, as I will argue, McCarthy offers a unique type of 'constructive disorder' that can be channelled productively and destructively. In short, I will argue that McCarthy's political imaginary is irreverent and anarchistic.

McCarthy's work demonstrates a persistent scepticism of agents of state, institutions and governance, whilst also respecting humans' deep resilience and capacity for forming autonomous communities. That these communities exist alongside, and sometimes despite, the regulatory processes of law and order, testifies to McCarthy's faith in the human ability to generate one's own sense of belonging and meaning. This is not to say that McCarthy offers a worked-out anarchist political theory, since his work is not written in the register of political philosophy. Regardless of the fact that McCarthy himself has been notoriously obstinate in withholding his own political opinions and that he may very well be wilfully apolitical, his work can still reveal the political effects of ruling and being ruled.[1] Having examined the Blanchotian element of *Suttree* in Chapter 2, where I argued that McCarthy's literary form deliberately resists literary classification, I now extend this point to the political dimension, even if McCarthy's novels are strictly non-ideological. To suggest that McCarthy's literature is liberal, conservative, socialist or environmentalist would be entirely to miss the point of how McCarthy conceives of the function of literature, as well as the functioning of political power. It is more the case that McCarthy's literature, while not ideologically coherent, offers a distinctive account of human political nature.

I will begin by examining the work of the most significant scholars who have commented on the explicitly political dimension of McCarthy's books. Here, it will be especially necessary to recall Dianne Luce's analysis of the Tennessee Valley Authority (TVA) in the formation of McCarthy's earliest work, most specifically *The Orchard Keeper*. Luce's work is significant because McCarthy's representation of the TVA provides clues to patterns of political themes that McCarthy retains from his earliest career to his most recent writing. In *The Orchard Keeper* we can identify a working out of political themes concerning the function and limits of government intervention, association and liberty. Subsequently, I will proceed to a section where I draw comparisons between the political themes of Alexis de Tocqueville's *Democracy in America* and those of McCarthy. A comparison with Tocqueville will be important for two reasons. Firstly, Tocqueville's account of democracy offers a useful interpretive framework to help us understand how McCarthy

views humans' political nature. Tocqueville is one of the few political theorists who sees radical contingency as being crucial for the
functioning of democracy. For Tocqueville, democracy is a dynamic
phenomenon which is constantly made and unmade. What distinguishes democracy for Tocqueville is that it is defined by process and
activity, not through the implementation of detached or abstract
theoretical blueprints for how society or the social contract works.

Secondly, Tocqueville shows how active political contradictions,
such as equality and liberty, are essential for the functioning of
democracy. This chimes with McCarthy's political imaginary, which
functions analogously with some Tocquevillian themes, specifically
where we find matters of dissent and solidarity, home and alienation,
anti-authoritarianism and communal consensus. In the final section of this chapter, I will turn to what I call McCarthy's anarchistic
spirit. Here I will make the case that McCarthy, while not a political
anarchist, stages distinctly anarchistic themes. Principally, this will
require showing how McCarthy rejects formal regulations and hierarchical organisation in favour of offering a literary representation
of types of colloquial consensus and mutualism which precede formal institutional and state processes.

New World, New Deal, New Order

The most important literary treatments of the political character of
McCarthy's literature can be found in David Holloway's assessment
of *The Road* and Dianne Luce's monograph *Reading the World*:
Cormac McCarthy's Tennessee Period.[2] These texts are significant
in different ways. Holloway directly tackles McCarthy's potential
conservatism, while Luce describes McCarthy's relationship with
the Tennessee Valley Authority (TVA). Luce's analysis is notewor-
thy because it sets the parameters for understanding the extent and
limits of McCarthy's views on the role of state intervention and, in
doing so, helps to frame the enduring traits distinguishing McCarthy's work, such as the clash between nature and civilisation, culture
and technology, rule and disorder.

Holloway, following Raymond Williams, argues that *The Road*
is a distinctly post-9/11 novel, existing within a 'structure of feeling' dictated by the prevailing mood of the United States's post-9/11
neo-conservative state hegemony. Holloway's idea is that the defining ambience of the post-9/11 world order and the attendant War on
Terror make possible *The Road*'s political aesthetic. Holloway very

effectively argues that both *The Road* and *No Country for Old Men* revolve around a constellation of classic neo-conservative themes including, but not limited to, history as a traumatic cycle of crisis and catastrophe; never-ending impending threat; entropic nihilism; critiques of permissive liberalism and egalitarianism; amorality and relativism; opposition of moral absolutes and ruthless pragmatism. These traits infuse McCarthy's later novels with an ambience of pervasive threat and melancholy.[3] Holloway cautions against the temptation of liberal readers to see the novels, especially *The Road*, as a confirmation of their own political sensibilities, while making clear that *The Road* remains an open text, rich and variegated in its capacity for multiple readings, political and otherwise. For Holloway, *The Road* can be viewed as a left-wing critique of consumer capitalism, an ecological fable, or a critique of American exceptionalism.[4] While Holloway does not say it directly, one cannot but get the sense from his interpretation that *The Road* normalises and fetishises the catastrophes of the post-9/11 world, whilst only obliquely offering alternatives to the oppressive historical mood from whence it emerges.

Prima facie Holloway is correct: the political timbre of McCarthy's post-9/11 work directly reflects conservative political philosophy. It would be foolish to suggest otherwise, or to suggest that McCarthy's literature enthusiastically occupies any alternate political ideology such as liberalism or socialism. However, it would still be a grave injustice to the complexity of McCarthy's literature were one to suggest that it is ideologically conservative from its inception. It is a testament to McCarthy's literary talent that his writing transcends political classification or affiliation. Although Holloway's analysis is primarily restricted to McCarthy's later novels and their period, his analysis could easily be extended to all McCarthy's other works, which invariably contain a suffocating tone of apocalypticism, trauma, declinism and concerns over moral permissiveness. Indeed, there is not a single novel of McCarthy's that does not exhibit any of these qualities. This presents a number of possibilities for interpreting the political dimension of McCarthy's work.

On the one hand, one could simply argue that McCarthy was neo-conservative all along and that his novels of the early 'noughties' are a culmination of conservative impulses implicit from the beginning of his published work. On the other hand, however, one could say that McCarthy's continuing interest in these themes suggests a more perennial philosophy, a philosophy attempting to transcend the vagaries of historical determination. This last sense would still be plainly Burkian rather than neo-conservative, committing

McCarthy to championing the enduring features of humanity and human societies that exist through the ages. Neither of these options, while interesting, is ultimately satisfactory, since it is very difficult to argue that McCarthy fully embraces conservative political philosophy, if only for the simple reason that his work resists ideological classification. For every Sheriff Bell of *No Country for Old Men* lamenting a callous, modern Hobbesian world, there is the boy in *The Road*, whose indefatigable goodness and faith in the future persists despite the adverse circumstances he encounters. For all the elegies to the lost world of the mythic cowboy portrayed in *The Border Trilogy*, we also have the countless kindnesses, kinship and mutual aid that Billy Parham receives on his travels. Put simply, McCarthy's novels are more concerned with exploring a very human political nature, rather than any desirable political arrangements adopted for the ordering of society. Tentatively, at this point, it would be more fitting to suggest that McCarthy holds neither the tragic pessimism of a Thomas Hobbes nor the vigorous optimism of a Jean-Jacques Rousseau, but instead occupies a wholly different political register.

Luce's work can substantially help to map out the political sensibility evident in McCarthy's literature. Luce, in *Reading the World*, provides the definitive account of how the TVA influences McCarthy. To understand the political thinking present in McCarthy's writing, it is essential to come to terms with the role of the TVA in the formation of his early literature. The TVA itself was approved by the United States Congress in 1933 as part of President Franklin D. Roosevelt's New Deal economic plan. It was initiated to alleviate the effects of the Great Depression by providing government assistance and relief for the Tennessee Valley through government provision of navigation, regional planning, manufacturing fertiliser, hydroelectricity, flood quality control and economic and industrial development. The TVA also forms the specific backdrop to McCarthy's first novel, *The Orchard Keeper*.

Luce shows how the consequences of the TVA itself were revolutionary in scope for the denizens of the Tennessee Valley. According to Luce, the economic benefits of the TVA were far-reaching, providing employment and financial assistance, especially for young people completing high school who were without job prospects. In addition, the TVA offered social welfare programmes, agricultural development, electrification of farms and the construction of dams to reduce flooding. However, this centrally planned federal initiative also met with some scepticism and resistance. Perceived as an unaccountable external force transforming the lives of Valley residents, TVA programmes could be implemented without local or state supervision.[5] This dubiousness was more than just unreflective NIMBY-ism or kneejerk anti-utopianism.

TVA programmes had pernicious consequences because, as Luce points out, in many instances the engineering choices made in the construction of hydroelectric dams destroyed farmlands, homes, livelihoods and the community networks of hundreds of families.[6] The technocratic New Deal's drive to maximise efficiency in electrical output led to internal migration, evictions and cultural alienation. Furthermore, the administration's top-down approach created an abrupt displacement of traditional values, most pointedly through the flooding of thousands of graves in small communities.[7] McCarthy's political thinking begins, particularly in *The Orchard Keeper*, by articulating how humans confront both the dilemmas and the unintended consequences precipitated by material progress and technological innovation. Notwithstanding the significant fact that McCarthy's father was an attorney processing the condemning of properties for the TVA, the characters of McCarthy's earlier novels live in the world that was created by the TVA. Luce points out, for example, how in *The Orchard Keeper* a social worker is perceived as talking 'like a God-damned yankee'.[8] This distaste for a benevolent yet overweening government agent channels the contested political legacy of the TVA, with the social worker symbolising the impersonal and detached processes of governmental bureaucracy. It is within this contested political legacy of the TVA that we can begin to see the shape of McCarthy's consideration of human political nature emerge.

The TVA's presence in *The Orchard Keeper* provides a specific example of how political considerations inflect McCarthy's literature. McCarthy's scepticism of the TVA, as evinced in *The Orchard Keeper*'s setting, reveals an intense concern for the metaphysical transformation wrought on the inhabitants of the Tennessee Valley. The primary negative consequences of the quasi-utopian New Deal for the Tennessee Valley were borne of economic instrumentalism – an instrumentalism which controlled and managed nature, as well as sacrificed the lives and culture of individuals on the altar of economic function. Principally, this inflection is present in the ways in which McCarthy's characters coordinate their lived responses to classic political binaries of progress and reaction, material prosperity and self-reliant frugality, tradition and innovation, ecology and technological development, government intervention and personal liberty. As such, McCarthy's literature attempts to collapse and transcend all these antagonistic dichotomies.

What differentiates *The Orchard Keeper* as a novel is that it is neither bucolic nor techno-utopian. This is important to note, as it demonstrates that McCarthy is less interested in ideological coherence than in aesthetic and metaphysical questions about the working of political life. McCarthy's characters are by-products of political ideologies rather than avatars for them. Furthermore, as much as the titular orchard is 'kept', what is really kept in Arthur Ownby's pit is the cadaver of the murdered Kenneth Rattner, indicating a corruption that excludes the possibility of both Edenic harmony and technological salvation. While nothing is more Biblical than murder in paradise, it still does not necessarily follow that McCarthy laments the loss of a harmonious utopia and nor does he offer full-throated support to the forces of material progress. McCarthy's literature is more subtle than this, attempting to render the lived complexities and realities of contemporary political life without ideological commitment. This is particularly the case where we see McCarthy's early work unite the antagonistic strains of technology and pastoralism. *The Orchard Keeper* pleads for an understanding of political humans as living in a world of technocratic utopian management as well as its fallout. While one gets a clear sense that McCarthy's sympathies firmly lie with the suffering inhabitants of the Tennessee Valley, this sympathy is not bolstered by outright castigation of industry and technology, or by a valorisation of an innocent nature.

In fact, McCarthy's syntheses of varying trends of modern political life reveal that he is more Aristotelian in his depiction of human political nature. The common denominator of the social contracts advanced by Hobbes and Rousseau is that natural freedom requires the imposition of restrictions upon individuals in order to establish a social contract which ensures the freedom to found the laws that bind humans in common self-interest. In contrast, modern political theorists – Hobbes, Locke, Rousseau, Spinoza – suggest that political freedom has its natural origins in the state of nature, where free humans consent to the contracts and regulations binding their society, which elevates them above the natural caprice. For McCarthy, the establishment of any social contract remains infected by the state of nature itself. Thus, Aristotle offers a better starting point for thinking about the political in McCarthy.

For Aristotle, the human is a political animal.[9] Human freedom is found in political life itself and in whatever relations and activities mediate rulers and ruled. Aristotle, at least in his metaphysical depiction of political life, shows the truth: politics is how it is done; it is the activities defining political life which are necessarily neither moral, appealing nor attractive and can lead to a variety of political configurations. McCarthy also has a more classically metaphysical understanding of politics, where humans are viewed as struggling for freedom, subject to luck and circumstance as well as negotiating artifice and nature, order and disorder, progress and regression.

We can identify McCarthy's peculiar vision of the contingency of our political nature through his symbolic strategy of using precarious dwellings throughout his work, a strategy which begins in *The Orchard Keeper*. The persistence of precarious dwellings throughout McCarthy's writing reveals his concern with how the state of nature is entangled with human construction and artifice. By extension, this demonstrates his view of human political life as a commixture of nature and structure. Fragile architectural structures highlight a salient feature of his political thinking. If one were to offer a shorthand description of McCarthy's political metaphysics, one could describe the political norm as precarious survival amid unstable structural formations. We can find examples of these unstable accommodations strewn across his literature, where buildings are shorthand for the precarity of civilisation itself and, by extension, of the functioning of governance. Political autonomy and community formation are portrayed as essentially unstable, co-existing in an uneasy alliance with nature. Liminal marks of insubstantial architectural civility are a common feature of innumerable examples of McCarthy's depictions of abodes. This is the case with Suttree's houseboat, Lester Ballard's cave in *Child of God*, the various temporary accommodations that father and son occupy in *The Road*, the multiple encampments of *Blood Meridian*, and beneath the underpass where the homeless Billy Parham finally takes shelter in *Cities of the Plain*. All of these resting-places furnish direct examples of the delicate accommodation of nature and culture.

The pattern of unstable dwellings begins in *The Orchard Keeper*. Here, for example, we have the rickety and perilous Green Fly Inn located on the edge of a precipice, nailed to a tree, whose porch collapses. By the close of the novel we find John Rattner observing his family home returning to nature, where McCarthy asserts a fraught coalescence of nature and culture, biology and technique, all prefigured in the opening pages of the novel by the wrought-iron fence that 'growed all through the tree'.[10] As Luce suggests, 'the tree contains and distorts the fence to the same extent that the fence penetrates and distorts the tree'.[11]

While McCarthy certainly holds a scepticism of unchecked technological expansion, he does not necessarily reject technological implements that co-exist with the natural world. This is as much the case in *The Stonemason* as it is in the epilogue to *Blood Meridian*, with civility and chaos indelibly entwined. Neither the state of nature nor the civilising power of technology and material acquisition holds ascendancy. The political thinking defining McCarthy's work defies categorisation, since confirmation of any specific rule of law, regulatory process or sovereign social contract is not immune to nature, nor is nature immune to material progress or the civility generated by political systems. Therefore, McCarthy is not easily assigned political labels such as 'liberal' or 'conservative', or any other political ideology for that matter. This is necessarily the case, since McCarthy's literature collapses the binary of nature and culture, and with it any separation of human civilisation and the state of nature. This strategy demands an effort on the reader's part to articulate and attend to different forms of how the political emerges in his literature. The rule of law, the prerequisite for the foundation of any political constellation or social contract, remains as shaky as The Green Fly Inn, with McCarthy expressing the paradoxical idea that the anomic is as fundamental as law and order itself. In this way, the philosophical dimension of McCarthy's work continues in the vein I have being arguing throughout this book. In terms of political philosophy, more specifically, McCarthy can again be demonstrated as drawing together chaos and disorder, law and lawlessness, nature and culture, sovereignty and subjection, artifice and wilderness.

In the overall arc of McCarthy's career, *The Orchard Keeper* starts the process of blending artifice and the state of nature which culminates in *The Road*. Like *The Road*, *The Orchard Keeper* offers neither salvation nor obliteration, redemption nor demise. Hence, McCarthy's vision of political life is neither a brutal Hobbesian natural egalitarianism, where all pursue selfish ends equally, nor a naïve romantic Rousseauianism, where nomadic existence is considered superior to the ill-effects of civilisation. As *The Road*, *The Border Trilogy* and *Blood Meridian* bear witness, nomadic existence cannot guarantee political salvation. However, the common denominator of all of McCarthy's more sympathetic characters is their ability to persist, survive, gather and regenerate their values despite the brutal conditions they inhabit, whether this is the kid in *Blood Meridian*, Culla and Rinthy in *Outer Dark*, or the boy in *The Road*.

While it is fair to say that McCarthy is distinctly sceptical of utopian efforts to remodel, remake or manufacture nature into a form of earthly paradise, it should also be noted that he is equally sceptical of forms of thought which argue that humans have lapsed from a harmonious pastoral plenitude. Here, it is worth repeating McCarthy's oft-quoted 1992 comments when interviewed by Richard Woodward for the *New York Times Magazine*:

> 'There's no such thing as life without bloodshed' . . . I think the notion that the species can be improved in some way, that everyone could live in harmony, is a really dangerous idea. Those who are afflicted with this notion are the first ones to give up their souls, their freedom. Your desire that it be that way will enslave you and make your life vacuous.[12]

What could apparently be taken as a basic conservative rejection of political idealism and utopian projects also contains an implicit rejection of the idealism of any conservative nostalgia for erstwhile social harmony. The other term worth attending to in the above quotation is 'enslave'. If political individuals become motivated by external or abstract ideals or ideas, their freedom is emptied; they become enslaved to abstract ideas rather than focusing on how reality itself coheres. The problem, however, is that if we accept 'bloodshed' as an inevitable part of human experience then violence, as we see in *Blood Meridian*, becomes fundamental to any act we engage in, political or otherwise. Therefore, in McCarthy's version of the state of nature, a certain violence is entwined with any act of human production or destruction and vice versa. Contingency is what we are, and we are better placed if we acknowledge this reality before engaging in any abstract efforts to establish law, civility or individual rights. McCarthy is suggesting that we ought to understand human nature before we engage in any effort to inaugurate states and laws prescribing human behaviour. And so the question remains, if McCarthy's political imaginary is neither Hobbesian nor Rousseauian, then what if anything is McCarthy's relevance to political philosophy?

McCarthy, Tocqueville and democracy in America

Rather than speak in terms of Hobbes or Rousseau, it is more useful to suggest that there is a Tocquevillian political ethos present in McCarthy's body of work. This is because Alexis de Tocqueville encapsulates some of the political and philosophical contradictions which I argue are present in McCarthy's work. Moreover, Tocqueville's own work embodies precisely the resistance to ideological classification that we find in McCarthy.[13] Tocqueville has received scant, if any, critical attention in terms of understanding McCarthy. However, his sprawling text *Democracy in America* offers political observations and critical insights about democratic practices and American identity which are of enormous value for understanding the political components of McCarthy's fiction.[14] While I do not aim to suggest that McCarthy aligns necessarily with Tocqueville's political preferences, it is relevant to elaborate on how some of Tocqueville's observations about American political life help us to understand the political reflections implicit to McCarthy's prose.

The most obvious reason why Tocqueville is relevant to understanding McCarthy's work is that Tocqueville wrote in a later period in the chronology of political philosophy, so his ideas therefore are more historically proximate to McCarthy's own political milieu. Tocqueville made the observations on which he based *Democracy in America* in 1831, when the American democratic experiment was relatively young, if decisively maturing. While indebted to writers in the history of political thought – Hobbes, Rousseau and Montesquieu – Tocqueville was unencumbered by the philosophical expressions of the state of nature found in political theory. Tocqueville based his understanding of democratic political philosophy on concrete and factual observations of one of history's first grand-scale democratic experiments. *Democracy in America* is a remarkable work in ambition: because of its depth and range it functions at the intersection of journalism, anthropology, history, sociology, travelogue, political pathologies and political philosophy.

On the surface, McCarthy would not seem a natural ally for Tocqueville. Tocqueville suggested that the dominant trait of the United States is its ahistoricality. Given that the United States was in its relative infancy when Tocqueville was observing and writing about it, this positing of ahistoricality is based on his observation that American democracy arises from an ancestral amnesia where: 'each man forgets his ancestors, but it hides his descendants from him and separates him from his contemporaries'.[15] This is certainly one place where we can say that McCarthy is not Tocquevillian. McCarthy is fascinated with how the long history of humanity illuminates the present and foreshadows the future – as I have evidenced in my appraisal of McCarthy's philosophical arguments for the continuing relevance of our evolutionary antecedents – where the ancient and the primeval coexist with humans' ongoing linguistic and technological development. Moreover, McCarthy is continually at pains to show how a forgetting, individually and collectively, of an enigmatic covenant of the past, present and future removes the possibility of any form of purposive meaning.

While Tocqueville noted the ahistoricality of American democracy, this view was tempered by his belief in the necessity of the continual refashioning of American democracy. The vitality of America stems from affirming process over identity; it is a country constantly engaged in the making of itself and its history. For Tocqueville, the dearth of historical meaning in American democracy is not necessarily a bad thing, since it bequeaths the populace with some necessary contradictions. While fraught on an individual level, that democracy is the constant process of being made and unmade is utterly essential for the proper functioning of the political sphere. As such, the American democratic spirit, the pursuit of a more perfect constitutional union, does imply a repudiation of the historical, since dogged individual self-determination, under a guiding ethos of 'equality of opportunity', requires one's historical origins to remain secondary to the capacity for self-reinvention. If self-invention is necessary, one ought not to be, and is not, strictly bound to one's own history. It follows that the overall body politic must be essentially weak and fallible rather than fixed or over-determined by past political mechanisms. Meaning is there to be achieved by an effort of will. For Tocqueville, in the political world: 'political principles, laws, and human institutions seem malleable, things that can be turned and combined at will [. . .] everything is agitated, contested, uncertain'.[16] Thus, the fundamental weakness of democratic institutions is essential to American political identity. The absence of a centre delimits sovereign centralisation and hierarchy. According to Tocqueville, by partitioning federal authority through a constitutional separation of powers, the effect is that power remains weak and indirect. This should not be mistaken for anarchy or disorder, but on the contrary should be viewed as a 'love of order and of legality'.[17]

Tocqueville's necessary contingency at the heart of government and democratic institutions evokes McCarthy's metaphysical proposition seen in the Woodward interview. If violence and contest are the central tenets of reality for McCarthy, it follows that McCarthy is a democratic writer in a Tocquevillian vein, as the political constitution of the American body politic reflects the contingent nature of reality itself. The political register of McCarthy's writing thus corresponds to what I described, when analysing *The Sunset Limited*, as a type of 'mitigated Platonism'. Democracy is not indexed to an external idea or reality which is impervious to historical power relations. McCarthy, while not necessarily endorsing this or that class or party of participatory or representative democracy, or even the desirability of democracy itself, can still be argued to be a type of democratic realist. He is a writer who aims to represent the unblemished consequences of the contested *demos* as it transpires.[18] The reality which American democracy generates is not ideal and neither is it to be idolised or fetishised. For Tocqueville, as much as for McCarthy, democratic reality, whether oppressive or emancipatory, is always considered fabricated: there to be made, manufactured and produced, and consequently unfinished. In literary terms, this has a cacophonous effect, giving voice to benign and malign voices, recognising the inevitability of power, rhetoric and political seduction as much as a tolerance of the multiple traditions constituting the *demos*.

Elsewhere, Tocqueville determined that American democracy was defined by a fundamental contradiction: it was both optimistic and pessimistic simultaneously. Fatalism was, as it is usually understood, dismal, inert and pessimistic. For example, inherent to democracy is the possibility of a situation where:

> The vices of those who govern and the imbecility of the governed would not be slow to bring it to ruin; and the people, tired of its representatives and of themselves, would create freer institutions or soon return to stretching out at the feet of a single master.[19]

However, this fatalism is paired with a faith in progress, since Americans:

> All have a lively faith in human perfectibility; they judge that the diffusion of enlightenment will necessarily produce useful results, that ignorance will bring fatal effects; all consider society as a body in progress; humanity as a changing picture, in which nothing is or ought to be fixed forever, and they admit that what seems good to them today can be replaced tomorrow by the better that is still hidden.[20]

What is interesting about Tocqueville's descriptions is that the contradiction is functional. American optimism works because of American fatalism. Tocqueville's America is an optimistic democratic society; however, paradoxically, this optimism is entwined with a fraught pessimism. Because the foundation of the American body politic is built on equality of opportunity as well as the individual's pursuit of happiness, Americans in Tocqueville's account come to believe that prosperity, material acquisition and wellbeing are always within their grasp. But, because material wellbeing is directly correlated to the pleasures of their mortal bodies, they are condemned to agonise continually over any prospective loss of the pleasures they hold, or over not achieving the pleasures they perceive they merit. Pursuing individual material prosperity leads to honour and respectability, but beneath the veneer of respectable prosperity there exists a deeper malaise.[21] For Tocqueville, such are the costs of existing in a meritocracy in which prosperity is enchained to personal abilities in direct competition with all others:

> When the man who lives in democratic countries compares himself individually to all those who surround him, he feels with pride that he is the equal of each of them; but when he comes to view the sum of those like him and places himself at the side of this great body, he is immediately overwhelmed by his own insignificance and his weakness.[22]

With respect to McCarthy, Tocqueville offers a unique precursor to the chaotic democratic spirit present in McCarthy's literature.

McCarthy also, throughout his work, depicts the two sides of democratic fatalism. McCarthy's writing is obviously a by-product of a democratic state and one is constantly struck by the passive, pessimistic fatalism of the literary world and characters he creates. Even so, the upside of his characters' pursuit of either essential material wellbeing or riches continually affirms a survival of hope and possibility – most acutely in *Blood Meridian, The Road* and *No Country for Old Men* – even if such hope remains fretful, fidgety and wholly brittle. As with the unfolding of American democracy itself, the perpetual pursuit of psychological or social harmony offers no guarantees or resolution in the end. McCarthy's characters are invariably trapped in an anxious wait for the good news that never arrives due to the essential incompletion of the American project he portrays. The framing of democratic politics in McCarthy is necessarily bleak because American democracy, either as a nascent or a mature entity, is chaotic, imperfect, contentious, tumultuous and ultimately without hope. Thus, as so often with McCarthy, we can see a collapsing of oppositional thinking, in this case optimism and pessimism.

What makes McCarthy's writing interesting is that he is both optimistic and pessimistic. McCarthy, like Tocqueville, spotted the tension in democracies, where individuals hold a faith that things will stubbornly work themselves out in the end, and this faith coexists with the ever-present sense of impending threat that prosperity will be taken away. McCarthy does not so much refuse the idea of progress as refuse the idea that American democracy is necessarily self-correcting. In colloquial terms, you cannot have the good without the bad. McCarthy's democratic world entails that the general political mood of his fiction situates itself firmly within American political identity, providing a remarkable mix of failed idealism and stubborn pragmatism. Ultimately, what unites the characters of his *oeuvre* is the inevitability of failed idealism co-existing with a pragmatic hope for survival.

The political pathology in Tocqueville's version of democracy is present throughout McCarthy's work. McCarthy's novels, with the notable exception of democratic collapse represented in *The Road*, are uniformly situated within the era of American democracy.[23] If for Tocqueville, democracy invariably disturbs and unsettles the psychological self-description of individuals, then similarly, most of McCarthy's characters experience unsettled ways of feeling, cognising and behaving. As I have argued previously, this is particularly the case with Sheriff Bell's developing uncertainty and wisdom in *No Country for Old Men*; in Suttree's active rejection of prevailing customs and mores in *Suttree*; in the boy who transcends his father's pragmatism in *The Road*; in Lester Ballard and the perverse underbelly of the Tennessee social order, and with the kid grappling with the domineering influence of the Judge in *Blood Meridian* – all present the obverse underside of American optimism and exceptionalism.[24] Such as it is, McCarthy's characters are the creations of both democratic malaise and democratic accomplishment. This is necessarily the case, since American democracy exists to cultivate the optimistic self-determination of its citizenship. As Tocqueville proposes, 'From Maine to Florida, from Missouri to the Atlantic Ocean, they believe that the origin of all legitimate powers is in the people.'[25] McCarthy's characters stand or fall on the extent to which they can or cannot transcend themselves. They, too, are perpetually unfinished, in the process of making themselves, and are a consequence of the way democratic decisions subject them both to a life of uncertainty, but also to a life of possibility and renewal.

If there is a political imaginary in McCarthy's work it resides in coping with a contagion of breakdown, crisis and the mutability of power relations. McCarthy's democratic realism, in its simplest form, tries to understand democratic humans as they live and as they are produced. Given the radical contingency of character psychology that occupies his literature, we can add another trait that McCarthy shares with Tocqueville's account of American democracy: anti-authoritarianism. Put in the simplest terms, McCarthy's literature retains a rebellious, anarchic, even populist scorn for figures of institutional authority: police, social workers, lawyers, clergy and corporate functionaries. As I have argued in Chapter 6, Sheriff Bell offers a particularly sharp example of this: the tragedy of his character emerges from the gradual shedding of his conservative shibboleths. In his more Tocquevillian moments, the political ethos of McCarthy's writing vigorously pinpoints that authority and hierarchy is not natural, with McCarthy revelling in portraying misfits and anachronistic characters which embarrass and shame the pretensions of pompous and unfeeling authority. Thus, the tragedy and renewal of McCarthy's characters are shaped by an irresolution that amounts to a perverse egalitarianism, where all humans hold the possibility and denial of their salvation concurrently.

This weird egalitarianism shows why one cannot easily suggest that McCarthy's written work sits well with conventional conservative pieties. McCarthy continually represents the importance and equality of the forgotten, the lost, misfits and delinquents: those who lose out to historical shifts. That he keeps these voices alive serves to openly embarrass any pretensions that democracy is settled or residing in long traditions. McCarthy is perhaps therefore one of the most democratic of writers, as his work continually serves to stimulate enthusiasm for the possibility of social and political equality, even if that equality is bounded with the inevitable chaos and contingency of life. While it would be inaccurate to argue that McCarthy is a socialist or motivated specifically by, say, a Marxist critique of consumer capitalism, it is clearly the case that his characters engage in a perpetual material struggle for equal recognition. This is nowhere more evident than in *The Sunset Limited*, with the symmetrical struggle for mutual recognition we find in White and Black. However, because of the ineradicable contingency purveying all McCarthy's writing, and by extension his representation of American democracy itself, any struggle for equality is tragically inaccessible. And therefore, McCarthy exhibits the Tocquevillian paradox: American democracy is radically contingent and ordered; however, it is this very contingency that makes democracy possible. Also, if contingency implies that innumerable possibilities can come to pass, the end of democracy itself must be one of them, which is of course the thought-experiment that *The Road* entertains.

The fugue of impending threat that adorns practically all of McCarthy's writing thus must be read as undermining any inherent declinism, since ending, in the Tocquevillian sense, is entwined with a possibility of renewal. The rhetoric of declinism is usually distinguished by corruption, decay, nihilism and the weakness of political institutions, and this is certainly evident with McCarthy. Quite often, declinism accompanies a fascistic critique of intellectuals, ideas and economic instrumentalism over culture, spirit and vitality, where political institutions are in a state of irreversible decay.[26] While these themes are obvious in McCarthy, they are not paramount. Given that McCarthy's texts tend to gravitate inexorably towards the apocalypticism of *The Road*, clearly McCarthy thinks that the American democratic experiment, at best, is not robust enough to withstand whatever catastrophic event precipitates *The Road*, or at worst is in a *de facto* state of erosion to the point of self-annihilation. However, as I hope should be clear by now, *The Road* as ending, as decline, is not the end. The story actually shows that humans can muddle on in the face of enormous hardship. Thus, McCarthy unites the fatalism and optimism that Tocqueville sees at the core of American democracy. What is so interesting about McCarthy and why his literature resists political classification is that his representation of the relations between ruler and ruled show him at his most philosophical. The political inflection of his literature is fundamentally Socratic and McCarthy's political representation is a fly in the ointment of democratic self-assurance and smugness.

The political philosophy present in McCarthy's work is less libertarian conservatism and more democratic anarchism. As we saw in the way the TVA figures in McCarthy's work, we find a scepticism of authority and large-scale transformative projects as well as any faith in individuals and groups to self-govern successfully. McCarthy's democratic realism itself mirrors this logic in his representation of democratic life, with characters swaying between chaos and complacency, resentment, relief, hope and despair. The pursuit of enough material prosperity, as we saw with Llewelyn Moss, only offers an illusion of comfort as well as a complacent assumption that the political order is fundamentally sound. However, what McCarthy portrays throughout his literature is the underside of material progress, showing that American democracy 'works' through ever-present crises. It is not specific ideologies that fracture democracy; democracy must itself be fractured, weak and dispersed. Beneath the underlying stability of the democratic order lies a mélange of competing ideas, values and alternative 'truths'. In sum, the trauma that is always present in McCarthy's literature – Rinthy and Culla's base origin in *Outer Dark*, the apocalyptic disaster occasioning *The Road*, the original murder of *The Orchard Keeper*, the violence of *Blood Meridian* – is never just a singular traumatic event tied to individual character psychology, but instead reflects the broader manifestation of crises ever present in America's democratic experiment. However, as with the precarious structures in *The Orchard Keeper*, we should not take

McCarthy's writing of crises as a validation of wild, chaotic anarchy or authoritarian rule. Instead, the political philosophy that is detectable in McCarthy's writing endeavours to think the complications of structure and chaos, rule and misrule, law and anarchy.

While Tocqueville thought the never-ending impending threat and crises might not lead to anarchy, this cannot be said for McCarthy. Most probably, for Tocqueville, the eventual outcome of democratic fatalism would be inertia, lethargy and stagnation.[27] For McCarthy, the outcome foreshadowed in *The Orchard Keeper* is fulfilled in the anarchic savagery of *The Road* and American democracy's inability to cope with the novel's inaugural disaster. As with the other themes I have tackled throughout this work, the political function of McCarthy's literary imaginary blends the new and novel with the ancient and archaic. The chronology of McCarthy's narratives is preceded by an even longer story, one with deep roots in human evolution and the evolution of human societies. As we saw with *Blood Meridian*, humans' drive to civility, order and hierarchical rule is inseparable from popular demands for autonomy, self-organisation, mutual aid, voluntary association and even direct democracy. Hence, the conservative Sheriff Bell in *No Country for Old Men* vacillates between certainty and uncertainty, a representative of the state's power and frailty simultaneously. Bell's essential weakness and fallibility announces a broader desire for self-directed community and belonging. Bell is weak in the same sense that power is decentralised in America: power is elusive and ubiquitous, distant, yet somehow always to hand.

McCarthy and the gods of misrule

Tocqueville and McCarthy share a quiet disdain for both the representatives of a centralised state as well as concern over the uniformity engendered by democratic equality. Furthermore, Tocqueville's championing of the weakness of centralised governance finds a common ally in McCarthy's critique of the impersonal processes of bureaucratic centralism as well as its institutional representatives. More pointedly, for McCarthy, the looming inevitability of bureaucratic anonymity leads to an erosion of any possibility that citizenship might lead to a political transformation. On this ground, it becomes clearer that both writers retain some anarchistic concerns while not necessarily endorsing ideological anarchism *per se*. With McCarthy, this is obviously the case, since it is not at all evident that his texts provide a manifesto of the specific tenets of political anarchism such as a rejection of property rights, even if property, as we have seen, is contingent and fragile. Neither do we see explicit endorsement of anarchist shibboleths such as direct democracy, voluntary organisation, syndicalism, or an unquestioning devotion to statelessness as the primary guarantor of natural order and social unanimity.

While McCarthy does not present a theory for founding a viable anarchism, it is still possible to suggest that the political imaginary of his work retains an anarchistic spirit. Principally, this anarchistic spirit is evident in the anti-authoritarianism that we have already outlined with respect to the TVA. McCarthy's rejection of formal hierarchical organisations overlaps with Tocqueville's admiration for the association, vernacular cooperation and mutualism that precede formal centralised state regulation. While it would be an overstatement to suggest that McCarthy is root-and-branch Tocquevillian, he is Tocquevillian in some very important respects, one of which is the idea that the world is motivated by a crude egalitarian impulse. This impulse is one where all who participate in political sovereignties generally, and largely in the historical settings of McCarthy's novels, are connected to deeper versions of themselves, where modern and contemporary political arrangements reach for forms of archaic gatherings.

In strictly philosophical terms, McCarthy is apolitical. Any political grouping and affiliation, any social contract established between ruler and ruled, is preceded in McCarthy's vision by a more vigorous anarchical truth, which is the human desire for community, association, belonging, mutual support and aid, even if only temporarily. Here we find a more resilient vision of human cooperation in McCarthy's work. His ever-present auguries of doom and crisis coexist with an enduring human desire to form political communities, indeed communities surviving and persisting regardless of the mediating influence of sovereign regulation. For example, *Suttree* is characterised by Cornelius Suttree's chaotic interactions with incarceration and law enforcement, not to mention his opposition to his father's advice that real life exists: 'in the law courts, in business, in government', while Suttree's life on the streets is: 'nothing but a dumbshow composed of the helpless and the impotent'.[28] Suttree embarks upon a life alongside social outcasts on the margins of society, where micro-communities are constructed in an ad-hoc fashion, highlighting McCarthy's understanding of humanity's political nature as desirous of, and in perpetual pursuit of, self-governance rather than government. In *The Border Trilogy*'s first novel, *All the Pretty Horses*, where John Grady receives a fair ruling from a benign judge who later acts as his confessor, we can corroborate how McCarthy thinks the human desire to belong to groups is fundamental, preceding any regulating function of courts and the law system.[29] As Katja Laug is correct to point out: 'John Grady's treatment in the courtroom is not only a rare moment of recognition across social strata, but also a moment McCarthy depicts an agent of the justice system, the judge, as benevolent and just.'[30] To these examples we can add *The Road*, where all indicators of governmental control and centralised authority, indeed any community formation, is absent. One could even draw an inference here that the lack of even a minimal form of governmental intervention shows the necessity of some political order to guarantee the basic securement of food, shelter and essential goods. So, if we are to ask ourselves what Cormac McCarthy's political project is, or to search for the coherent ideology he proposes, this would be misguided. It is better to ask how he understands humanity's political nature. His rejection of state and authority figures is not absolute, but still retains a rejection of the mediating regulatory processes of sovereign power and their unintended negative consequences, much more than the human capacity to gather and self-govern. The latter exists and predates any instantiation of sovereign control. The human yearning for autonomous self-rule is as old as humanity itself, and thus McCarthy remains archaically anarchic in disposition.

McCarthy's anarchistic disposition is founded on a metaphysical assumption about human nature and human relations. The foundation of sovereign rule and with it processes of regulation, inspection, quantification, appraisal and bureaucratic admonishment, are only ever secondary efforts to order and stave off the radical contingency at the heart of nature itself. It is not that such activities are necessarily immoral; it is just that the mediating power of processes and regulations only ever remain artificial, whereas human cooperation and mutual aid is spontaneous and immediate. This logic is clearly in evidence in McCarthy's 1994 play *The Stonemason*. Here McCarthy draws an explicit opposition between the craft of the stonemason Papaw and the formal rule-driven processes of industrial stonemasonry. Sovereign regulatory structures of accounting, inspection and balancing cannot furnish a ledger of the activity of labour itself. For Papaw: 'The man's labor that did the work is in the work. You caint make it go away.'[31] Papaw's grandson Ben consolidates this point:

> Because the world is made of stone the mason is prey to a great conceit and to whatever extent the look and the shape of the world is the work of the mason then that work exists outside of the claims of workers and landholders alike.[32]

Stone retains history and possibility; it bespeaks pragmatism and the pursuit of the work itself as an end in itself. Rules, measurements and regulations are an abstraction from the activity of stone masoning.

In a draft unpublished stage direction, McCarthy reinforces this argument when describing Papaw:

> His statements are matter of fact, as if they were shared conclusions with sensible men, and yet he has told me things I've never heard from any living man. He reflects an appealing brand of pragmatism and his views are even worldly and yet his understanding of life is not a system that he has worked out, not a series of checks and balances or compromises or concessions. It is rather an exemplification of access to life itself. The way to live is not a construction. It is a known.[33]

Although not necessarily an evocation of the philosophical school that is American Pragmatism, McCarthy does present Papaw as a markedly New World figure, committed to doing rather than thinking, acting rather than reflecting. Reflection implies abstraction and hence a step back from the world itself. It is human activity, labour and interactions themselves which are pre-eminent for McCarthy. Any effort to codify, institutionalise or account for human craft forcefully imposes a prefabricated form on the order of things. Given the eminence, dignity and sympathetic portrayal of Papaw, we can only assume that his views reflect some of McCarthy's own, especially where human efforts to control and order have regrettable consequences. The political technologies we devise – bureaucratic, administrative, governmental, clerical – unwittingly obscure the primacy of necessity, community, work and humans cooperating to survive. Within McCarthy's political imaginary the doing itself, the appreciation of making and unmaking, is the most revolutionary thing possible:

> But not ashlar. Not cut stone. All trades have their origin in the domestic and their corruption in the state. Freestone masonry is the work of free men while sawing stone is the work of slaves and of course it is just those works of antiquity most admired in the history books that require nothing but time and slavery for their completion. It is a priestridden stonecraft, whether in Egypt or Peru. Or Louisville Kentucky. I'd read a great deal in the Old Testament before it occurred to me that it was a handbook for revolutionaries. That what it extols above all else is freedom.[34]

The political spirit McCarthy is valorising here is clearly anarchistic. Within the register of political philosophy, what is just, even sacred, is free production and fabrication regardless of any sovereign authority. Or as Ben puts it at the play's conclusion: 'To make the world. To make it again and again. Or make in the very maelstrom of its undoing.'[35] McCarthy is valorising the persistence and significance of informal, unsurveilled activities. These invisible acts and works are figurative battlegrounds affirming endless labour and activity, the perpetual work required to achieve some semblance of communal solidarity. However, efforts at group formation mask the perpetual violence at the heart of McCarthy's literary ontology. Efforts to form solidarity can be malign or wholesome. The inevitable sovereign effort to measure and contain activity results in a torrid, interminable tangle of contradiction and anxiety, which can be either a source of liberation and belonging, or of violence and social excision.

Still, resistance in the face of sovereign authority, clearly symbolised in Papaw's rejection of President Nixon's ceremonial invite, holds its own significance for McCarthy, offering succour in a tempest of pompous formality, inauthenticity and domination by channelling: 'where God and matter are locked in collaboration'.[36] McCarthy's anarchistic spirit opposes sovereign authority and ceremony with a celebration of active labour and the kinship, informal cooperation, practised coordination and the activity associated with it. These traits embody voluntary and spontaneous activity, as well as reciprocity without hierarchy. We should, however, remain careful. It is not the case that McCarthy is explicitly calling for the overthrow of the state. It is more the case that he is naming anarchic dispositions anterior to the inescapable regulating mechanisms of society. For McCarthy, such habits are in fact the very stuff of the quotidian and while they do not necessarily, either explicitly or implicitly, contest state, church or institution, they have their own authority. They are only accountable to the work and activity that is done on their own terms rather than to mediated supervisory procedures: 'The work is everything, and whatever is learned is learned in the doing.'[37] Such self-determined authority is a fundamental human experience, one that is ubiquitous, persisting and surviving irrespective of the existence of any authoritarian impulses of society.

As observed when comparing Tocqueville and McCarthy, what draws these seemingly disparate writers together is an acute sense of the sheer, turbulent contingency of democracy. Progress and renewal, either individually or collectively, depend vitally on extra-institutional misrule and disorder. McCarthy endorses a vernacular mutualism, where communities coalesce, associate and form in ad-hoc ways. McCarthy's protagonists frequently flee, or are forced

from, domestic order in order to seek out – or even fail to seek out –
alternative communities. This is the case with Kenneth Rattner in
The Orchard Keeper; with the forcible removal of Lester Ballard
from his family farm in *Child of God*; it is a perpetual preoccupation
of Suttree, especially in his abandoned efforts at pseudo-domesticity
with Joyce and Wanda; it is seen when Culla and Rinthy leave their
darkly Edenic incestual home. McCarthy's literature contains multiple such instances of groups self-organising, associating and forming temporary communal bonds. This is especially so in the novels
from the Tennessee period, as well as in *The Border Trilogy*, where
we find countless examples of subcultures of miscreants, rogues and
renegades, such as moonshiners, communities of alcoholism and the
destitute in Suttree's McAnally Flats, or the *campesinos* and revolu-
tionaries of Mexico in *The Border Trilogy*. All create: 'communities
of support and kindness in opposition to and rejection of main-
stream societal practices and standards'.[38] McCarthy's literary ontology precludes the arrival of any political utopia. For example, *Blood
Meridian* and *The Road* clearly pose versions of social amalgamation
for nefarious purposes. However ersatz groups are formed, whether
for riot, cruelty, disruption, or for compassionate purposes such as
providing aid, shelter, or sustenance, the common denominator is
the human instinct for founding communities in a world of shifting
borders unrestricted by technologies of governance. Only here can
McCarthy fulfil the broader purpose of his literature, which is to give
voice to the poor, the unheard and the forgotten.

As I have argued consistently, McCarthy's political ontology
should not be assumed to be an idyllic pastoralism or an innocent state
of nature. Instead, McCarthy's communities of outcasts are barely
communities at all, characterised as they are by lawbreaking, addic-
tion, drug cultures and informal activities which resist institutional
and governmental surveillance. McCarthy is no starry-eyed romantic. There is something more interesting taking place. The various
versions of community formation we find in McCarthy's literature,
whether criminal or otherwise, underscore a distinct species of voluntary collective action. That the poor, downtrodden and forgotten
are not recognised has its own aesthetic necessity; McCarthy is repre-
senting the unrepresentable. The 'deplorables' are not on institutional
or governmental radar, nor do they need to be. The success of their
association, it could be said, depends on their labours and organising,
on remaining shrouded from official assignation. And it is this ubiquitous experience that is powerful, as it relates to everybody: no class
is automatically immune from destitution. Hence, what McCarthy

celebrates most of all in the political sphere is unpretentious, silent insubordination. McCarthy's anarchistic spirit is spectacularly distant from the vocal anarchism of the revolutionary. His anarchism is founded more on the idea that disobedience and contingency are the norm rather than a pointless anomaly, residing at the very core of the state of nature. Order is disorder. His characters are especially interesting because of their smallness, precarity and pettiness. McCarthy's anarchism is not grandiose, humourless or solemn, but instead exemplifies innumerable sites of informal resistance and communal aid which undermine sovereign order and regulation, devoted to delivering exemplars of fleeting moments of non-alienated life.

Conclusion

I have argued throughout this book that McCarthy is one of literature's 'great unifiers', amalgamating nature and artifice, spirt and matter and, in this case, order and disorder. Beginning with an account of *The Orchard Keeper* and its representation of the social and political effects of the TVA, I have argued that a conspicuous trend in McCarthy's work is a meld of anti-state sentiment combined with a sense of weird egalitarianism. This chapter has also argued that the best way to understand the political implications of McCarthy's fiction is by situating his work in tandem with Alexis de Tocqueville's *Democracy in America*, which in turn enables me to propose an anarchistic strain in McCarthy's political imaginary. It has been especially necessary to illuminate the Tocquevillian strains of McCarthy. Tocqueville showed American democracy as a mix of equality and liberty, where equality of opportunity engenders a radical freedom for self-invention. In McCarthy, too, we find these contested egalitarian and libertarian impulses. This unique political outlook demonstrates how McCarthy characteristically attempts to paradoxically unite order and disorder as the decisive human impulse. The drive towards equality, solidarity and consensus is mutually enabled and disrupted by an anti-authoritarian pursuit of liberty. As with *Blood Meridian*, McCarthy's metaphysical perspective implies that life is invariably at war with itself. This ontological commitment is isomorphic to his representation of the political sphere. Political organisations are also at war with themselves. Community formation invariably implies the existence of class, lobby, association, faction and special interest. This very agonistic view of politics has distinct literary consequences for McCarthy's fiction.

The effort to form hierarchical regulatory processes for fixing of the body politic generates an equally elaborate and recalcitrant underworld, where community, solidarity and consensus are continually coming to life. McCarthy's political imaginary presents us with communities of a spectral underclass, an underclass inhabited by horror, broken bodies, monsters and ghoulish histories. The most orderly of orders always generates its own anomalies, its own ghosts. And it is here that McCarthy's literature resides in a unique synthesis of spirit and matter, an anarchist spirit; McCarthy's novels enact a haunting of the fictions of state, nation, propriety and institution with a fiction of disorder. This is a fiction where our spirits reside in a common flesh, written in the idiom of skin, bone and blood.

Notes

1. According to David Kushner's *Rolling Stone* profile, McCarthy has never voted. See David Kushner, 'Cormac McCarthy's Apocalypse', *Rolling Stone*, 27 December 2007, <http://www.davidkushner.com/article/cormac-mccarthys-apocalypse>
2. See David Holloway, 'Mapping McCarthy in the Age of Neoconservatism, or the Politics of Affect in *The Road*', *The Cormac McCarthy Journal* 17, no.1 (2019): 4–26. See also Dianne Luce, *Reading the World: Cormac McCarthy's Tennessee Period*, 18–23.
3. Holloway, 'Mapping McCarthy in the Age of Neoconservatism', 17–23.
4. Ibid. 23.
5. Ibid. 20.
6. Ibid.
7. Ibid. 21.
8. Cormac McCarthy, *The Orchard Keeper* (London: Picador, 2010), 233.
9. Aristotle, *Politics*, trans. C. D. C. Reeve (Indianapolis, IN: Hackett, 1998), 1253a29.
10. McCarthy, *The Orchard Keeper*, 3.
11. Luce, *Reading the World*, 37.
12. See Richard B. Woodward's profile of McCarthy in, 'Cormac McCarthy's Venomous Fiction'.
13. The extent to which Tocqueville can be called 'conservative' is certainly contestable. Many scholars suggest that Tocqueville's personal political perspective was classically liberal. However, Tocqueville, in his scepticism of untrammelled progress, his appreciation of values and tradition and his doubts about the ability of governance to jettison uncertainties from efforts to rule, would sit comfortably with many components of the conservative political ethos. Not unlike McCarthy, it is Tocqueville's resistance to glib classification that allows his work to have an enduring

appeal. For a good summary of the way Tocqueville has been appropriated by a variety of political theories – postmodernism, democratic pluralism, liberalism, neo-conservatism – see Cheryl Welch, *De Tocqueville* (Oxford: Oxford University Press, 2001), 217–55.

14. Alexis de Tocqueville, *Democracy in America*, trans. and ed. H. C. Mansfield and D. Winthrop (Chicago: University of Chicago Press, 2000).
15. Ibid. 484.
16. Ibid. 43.
17. Ibid. 67.
18. There is one other significant figure from political philosophy that I do not deal with here: Niccolò Machiavelli. While a study of the Machiavellian elements of the political dimension of McCarthy's writing would surely be an interesting project, it would need more than just an account of scheming, strategy and subterfuge. The least sympathetic characters in McCarthy's *oeuvre* – for example, the Judge, Chigurh and the boy's mother in *The Road* – all exhibit traits of strategic and tactical pragmatism. If one were to do justice to a Machiavellian account of McCarthy, one would have to pay attention to Machiavelli's *Discourse on Livy* as much as *The Prince*.
19. Tocqueville, *Democracy in America*, 665.
20. Ibid. 359.
21. Cf. Mansfield and Winthrop, 'Editors' Introduction' to *Democracy in America*, lxvii.
22. Tocqueville, *Democracy in America*, 409.
23. The kid in *Blood Meridian* is born in 1833. Tocqueville visited America between 1831 and 1832.
24. See John Cant for the definitive account of McCarthy and American exceptionalism in Cant, *The Myth of American Exceptionalism*, 32.
25. Tocqueville, *Democracy in America*, 358.
26. See Alexander Hamilton, *The Appeal of Fascism* (London: Anthony Blond Publishing, 1971), xxii.
27. Tocqueville, *Democracy in America*, 248.
28. McCarthy, *Suttree*, 15.
29. McCarthy, *The Border Trilogy*, 292–3.
30. Katja Laug, *Mementoes of a Broken Body: Cormac McCarthy's Aesthetic Politics* (Ph.D. diss., University of Warwick, 2019), 62.
31. McCarthy, *The Stonemason*, 30.
32. Ibid. 31.
33. McCarthy, *Cormac McCarthy Papers (1964–2007)*, Box 66: Folder 5, 21.
34. McCarthy, *The Stonemason*, 65.
35. Ibid. 133.
36. Ibid. 63, 67.
37. Ibid. 64.
38. Laug, *Mementoes of a Broken Body*, 138. Cf. also 98–104.

Conclusion

Three forces make and mold a human being, heredity, environment and the unknown agent X.

Vladimir Nabokov[1]

Your busiest day might be watching some ants carrying bread crumbs.

Cormac McCarthy[2]

The purpose of this work has been to articulate the guiding themes that constitute Cormac McCarthy's literary-philosophical reflections and consequently, to reveal how to understand McCarthy as a literary philosopher. At the inception of this book I aimed to reveal McCarthy's 'physics of the damned', with 'physics' used in the idiosyncratic sense I outlined in its introduction. My thesis was that McCarthy's literature functions through a synthesis of materialism and metaphysics. Although in a conceptual sense materialism and metaphysics are not naturally aligned collaborators, it is imperative to bring these seemingly contrary positions into dialogue. McCarthy, after all, is in the main a writer of fictional novels, drama and screenplays. Insofar as he is a writer of these texts, I have argued that he is at his most compelling when his work blends the philosophical and the literary. The unholy alliance of philosophy and literature, science and spirit, ethics and transgression, order and disorder, I propose, is wholly necessary for understanding the provocations McCarthy's work presents to us. My overall thesis, in turn, has enabled me to construct and draw out insights into broader philosophical questions posed in McCarthy's writing, allowing me to illuminate how McCarthy treats specific philosophical questions pertaining to human mortality, language, evolution, education, ethics and politics.

Starting in Chapter 1 with an account of how McCarthy explores the linguistic human being in *Whales and Men* and 'The Kekulé Problem', McCarthy, I argued, offers a fusion of unconscious evolutionary and mythic forms, forms which co-exist alongside concrete and historic sense-making human capacities. In addition, this chapter demonstrated how McCarthy writes across styles, in this case science and myth. This analysis of language provided a foundation from which to understand language as literature in Chapter 2. Therein, I argued that Maurice Blanchot's philosophy of literature illuminates the way McCarthy allows literature and philosophy to enter reciprocal dialogue, particularly in *Suttree*. If my first chapter showed how our cognitive sense-making capacity exists against a long backdrop of myth and evolutionary processes, my second chapter showed how McCarthy adopts questions of form and content to push readers' thinking towards broader questions of metaphysics and ethics.

In Chapter 3, in terms of coming to understand McCarthy's unique blend of literature and philosophy, the ethical element of McCarthy's writing came to the fore. In order to argue that McCarthy continually embeds his characters' moral psychology in tandem with a struggle against an implacable and lawless physical universe, it was necessary to tackle his purportedly most nihilistic work, *Blood Meridian*. If McCarthy, as I suggested at the outset of this chapter, operates in the wake of the death of God, then why can we at all say that his work is of any value for ethical discourse? I argued that McCarthy's *Blood Meridian* itself is a torturous reflection on different types of nihilism. Using Nietzsche as my guide, I contended here that although *Blood Meridian* is far from an optimistic book, there are distinct elements in the novel where McCarthy directly confronts and challenges untrammelled nihilism. If there is a specific book that most represents a 'physics of the damned', it is this one. Judge Holden, I argued, manifests the most acute outlet for McCarthy's fatalistic view of the cosmos. The cosmos itself is war and if all is war, humans are necessarily beastly. However, what I attempted to show was that this portrayal was far from the only concern of *Blood Meridian*. I argued that the novel, despite its nihilistic tendencies, through the character of the kid, demonstrates some shreds of dignity which in turn offer alternatives to nihilism. Specifically, examining the epilogue of *Blood Meridian*, I argued that ultimately what defines human beings is our tenacity, persistence and resilience to begin anew, even when inhabiting the worst of all possible worlds. The importance of this chapter to my overall argument is that it allowed me to show the nuance of McCarthy's appreciation of a distinctly mortal ethics in confrontation with the moral vacuum of nihilism.

Chapters 4 and 5 built on the preceding observations to explain how the philosophical elements present in McCarthy's writing placed seemingly disparate discourses together. Therefore, Chapter 4's analysis of *The Sunset Limited* was particularly apposite, as there I showed that although the antagonistic philosophical positions of Black and White – Black's spiritualism and White's rationalism – are seemingly asymmetric, they are in fact underpinned by a deeper symmetry and solidarity. This approach underlined my overall thesis of McCarthy's propensity to unite the material and the metaphysical. Chapter 5 continued this vein of analysis by arguing that *The Road* offers a specific example of how McCarthy's scientific, literary and philosophical thinking combine. I argued that the best way to understand *The Road* is through understanding the novel as an attempt to present a form of material ethics as well as a strange 'anti-metaphysics'. I argued that *The Road* is philosophically interesting in that it rejects narrow scientific and theological discourse. It is imperative not to cast McCarthy as being guilty of the crassest scientism or naïve reductionism, or of dogmatic theological pieties. *The Road* is philosophically interesting because it continues McCarthy's longstanding philosophical reflections, understanding the human being as caught up in broader material processes of the world. Thus, the anti-metaphysics of *The Road* reveals a more radical material metaphysics, where humans are entwined with broader material thermodynamic processes of decay and dissolution. In turn, this allowed me to begin articulating some of McCarthy's ethical concerns where, in his later writings, he depicts humans as essentially stateless, borderless beings who hold a persistent and tenacious desire to construct alternate forms of being-together.

To develop my prior discussion of ethics, it was necessary to show how McCarthy's literary philosophy holds the conceptual sophistication to offer a nuanced account of ethics. Thus, I proceeded to discuss ethical deliberation in Chapter 6 in relation to *No Country for Old Men*. The cosmic contingency of *Blood Meridian* is also relevant to *No Country for Old Men*. Sheriff Bell's agonising confrontation with Chigurh reflects the kid's with Judge Holden. I argued that Sheriff Bell's deepening wisdom stages McCarthy's philosophical concern to show how ethical deliberation, if it is to be ethical deliberation, must be necessarily contingent and transgressive. To prove this, I focused on how the novel showed the central dissolution of Bell's morally conservative shibboleths. If there is a heroic archetype in McCarthy's work, the closest we can come to it is in the character of Sheriff Bell. The profoundly weak, flawed and inauthentic character of Bell provides a clear manifestation of the moral consequences of a physics of the damned. Bell, I argued, contrary to many readings, is a figure of uncertainty and chaos, whereas Chigurh is representative of a nihilistic mechanical rationality. Bell comes to accept the precarious nature of our moral principles and comes to understand, even if only partially so, the place of humans in the wider processes of life and death. As I suggested in the conclusion to this chapter, McCarthy is once again therefore not offering a simplistic material reductionism, but is instead providing both an elemental and metaphysical reflection on ethical deliberation, where humans decide and participate in a deep web of processes of the physical world. This position is diametrically opposed to the hyper-determinism of Chigurh's mechanistic materialism.

In Chapter 7 I turned to the political questions in McCarthy's work. In many ways, I think this chapter presents the most distinctive contribution of this whole book. If McCarthy is a great unifier of seemingly disparate philosophical positions then this strategy continues in the political element of his writing, specifically through the way in which it reflectively unifies the realms of order and disorder. In this chapter I placed McCarthy in dialogue with Alexis de Tocqueville, which enabled me to show how McCarthy, in terms of political philosophy, attempts to think a politics of contingency. The political, for McCarthy, as with all his other philosophical preoccupations, is necessarily embedded in the wider processes and the unfolding of the material world. Tocqueville equipped me with the conceptual resources to explain how McCarthy's writing can be characterised by a unique form of anarchism. McCarthy holds an indefatigable suspicion of states, institutions and governance, as well as their symbolic representatives, such as police officer, lawyer, professor, social worker, priest or taxman. However, I concluded by arguing that, while not recommending forms of anarchist rule or prescriptions for anarchist organisation, McCarthy retains an anarchistic spirit and holds a deep respect for the human capacity to construct precarious and autonomous communities outside mechanisms of governmental and institutional surveillance, even despite such mechanisms' desire to impose control and regulation on the lawlessness of nature itself.

I think McCarthy is unquestionably a philosophical writer. It has been my aim that this work should be essential for helping us to comprehend McCarthy's *oeuvre*. If we do not understand the philosophical dimension of McCarthy's work then, in my view, we do not understand McCarthy's literature or, at the very least, we can only attain a seriously incomplete understanding of his writing. More specifically, I hope that this work will be valuable, whether agreeable or disagreeable, to those who wish to pursue research and scholarship into how McCarthy adopts philosophical questions in his work and, more generally, as an inventive exercise in how to think literary philosophy.

Whether I have been successful in these endeavours, I will leave to readers and infinitely more qualified Cormackians to judge.

By focusing on *The Orchard Keeper*, *Suttree*, *Whales and Men*, *Blood Meridian*, *The Road*, *The Sunset Limited*, *No Country for Old Men* and 'The Kekulé Problem', I have attempted to give as representative an account of McCarthy's work as possible, whilst drawing support from McCarthy's other novels, screenplays and dramatic works. That McCarthy fearlessly tackles and fuses, whether successfully or otherwise, seemingly contradictory positions is necessary for the vocation and significance of literature itself. Elucidating how McCarthy operates as a philosopher, thinker and writer is more broadly important because he directly tackles the questions and contradictions which all humans will eventually confront in their lives. I would go further, in fact: McCarthy presents an exemplary case for any future scholar who is attempting to understand the intersection of philosophy and literature. If what distinguishes McCarthy as a 'literary philosopher' is the unique mix he presents of the archaic and modern, the mythic and scientific, as well as the spiritual and material, then to understand any literary-philosophical work, McCarthy is paradigmatic.

There are two lingering questions worth reflection prior to closing. If, as I have argued, McCarthy's writing offers a unique form of literary philosophy, this proposition does beg the question as to where (or whether) McCarthy fits in the canon of philosophical novelists especially. At the inception of this book, I speculated as to where McCarthy might be placed alongside writers in the canon of great philosophical novelists such as Atwood, Camus, Hesse, Le Guin, Morrison, Pynchon and Sartre. This list is not exhaustive: to it we could add Thomas Mann, Iris Murdoch, Robert Musil, Simone De Beauvoir, Bret Easton Ellis and Chuck Palahniuk, among others. There is no doubt that McCarthy can be considered a philosophical novelist, or that he writes 'novels of ideas' in keeping with how Fyodor Dostoevsky, Mann and Herman Melville did. We need to be cautious, however. It is certainly the case that McCarthy has themes overlapping with those of the aforementioned authors and also themes in the tradition of Existentialist literature, especially in his concern for illuminating the stakes of human mortality. I think, however, that to engage in an act of literary classification of this sort would be counterproductive in the case of McCarthy. These writers have their own unique idioms and discourse and, if my argument herein is defensible, McCarthy stands apart. Elsewhere, if McCarthy's literary-philosophical register operates at the intersection of science, religion and philosophy, then perhaps it might be plausible to argue that the best literary-philosophical tradition in which to place McCarthy might be science fiction. Indeed, *The Road* is often cast as an apocalyptic science fiction novel and all of McCarthy's writing could be said to contain a distinct otherworldliness. However, the assignation of sci-fi to McCarthy, I think, would also be unsatisfactory in the end, if only for the obvious reason that most of McCarthy's writing does not conform to any salient features of science fiction. There is a distinct difference between otherworldliness and the fantastical representation of other worlds. If there are philosophical writers and novelists who could be kindred spirits for McCarthy, it would be those who push the limits of language beyond the mechanics of expression. Here I am thinking specifically of writers like Samuel Beckett, James Joyce, Franz Kafka, Iris Murdoch, Máirtín Ó Cadhain, or Robert Musil: writers who confront the limits of expression as a prerequisite for letting literature allow the cosmos to shine forth, so to speak. I think these writers would be some of the closest literary-philosophical precursors to McCarthy. However, these are not an ideal match for him either, especially given the experimental nature of their prose. For all McCarthy pushes language beyond style and form towards the deepest levels of reflection, he still writes stories – stories which enchant and transport readers out of their world. Thus, while interesting parallels can be drawn with the above authors, ultimately, McCarthy is possessed of a distinct philosophical vision, one which I hope to have outlined in this book. Like Blanchot's, McCarthy's literary philosophy transgresses the limits of style and language in order to express the inexpressible and to reveal how language transcends the function of basic signification, social and economic determinism, as well as natural determinants.

The second lingering question which needs to be addressed is the looming status, at least for my purposes, of *The Passenger*. At the time of writing, *The Passenger* is McCarthy's forthcoming book, one which reportedly might be split into two books. While I do not want to engage in speculation about the nature of this book – it will come if will it come, and it will be what it will be – nonetheless, judging from McCarthy's own comments, it would appear that he will be continuing to touch on themes which I have talked about in this volume, such as death, suicide, madness and the proximity of mathematics, art and science. Thus, at this point, McCarthy seems willing to continue writing novels of ideas, still feeling comfortable in putting disparate disciplines together. According to David Krakeur, the novel will be 'a mathematical-analytical novel' incorporating 'Feynman diagrams, strings' and 'peppered with scientific themes'.[3] If this information accurately reflects the content of the final product of *The Passenger*, then at a minimum, these clues promise to offer further insights into McCarthy's efforts to blend discourses – in this instance, science and art. Additionally, the new book will offer further insight into McCarthy's scientific interests. For my own purposes, at this point, all I can do is look forward to how *The Passenger* may reflect my own thesis and be prepared to make revisions where it contradicts it.

Beyond these lingering questions, the future for evaluating McCarthy's work is exceptionally promising. If, as Chris Eagle suggests, the philosophical thrust of McCarthy's writing requires stepping beyond the finding of a 'pyrrhic question of transcendental meaning in our post-theological, post-industrial, late-capitalist, technocratic world', then this work, I hope, will have contributed in a small way to responding to this challenge by convincing readers that McCarthy is utterly vital as a philosopher, thinker and writer.[4] Beyond the themes I have discussed herein, we can look forward to thinking about how McCarthy's novels help us make sense of a variety of existential challenges which our species is confronting. McCarthy's writing will be relevant for urgent problems we are currently grappling with and will help in turn to do justice to the challenges we find in ecological collapse, technology, automation, gene modification, health elongation, post-nuclear aesthetics, consumption, ageing populations, war and even gender.[5] In a way, the apocalypse may not be now, but it is to hand. Only by adopting the critical and reflective pose of McCarthy's writing can we even begin to think of how we might go about solving these issues.

The most banal appreciation of literature accords with a forcing of the literary text to conform to the habits of our world. Efforts to reduce literature to subjective feelings and opinions, or to prevailing customs and habits, ultimately de-alienate the literary work. The consequence of such attempts makes the literary work safe, defanged, aligning our reading with our existing and preferred convictions, where we absorb the domesticated textual style into the orbit of everyday life, even allowing us to make familiar characters as if they were our very own friends and enemies. If we engage with literature thus, we are engaging in an egregious act of forgetting. It would involve the process of actively forgetting what literature is. Literature requires, as Plato knew of philosophy, a polemical disposition towards common sense. Common sense is the most ubiquitous calculative activity, whether in the guise of banal generalisations, the dull classifications of prejudicial opinion, common conceptions of how things ought to work, appeals to convention, or even in the slick tutelage of the great opinion-making mechanisms of our age, like statistical political polling. Common sense domesticates the strange into the familiar.

Literature, if it is to be at all meaningful, is most powerful when it criss-crosses philosophical depths, accepting the radical strangeness and contingency of the world. This is what makes the most striking literature profound: literature actively resists generic impulses of common sense and classification, and their attempts to impose a relative order on a fundamentally lawless world, the world we fretfully know to be ruled by the gods of havoc. Literature puts us right there. This, it should be made clear, is not to endorse chaos for the sake of chaos, nor is it a romantic affirmation of the illogical, the senseless and the inexplicable. I hope to have shown convincingly that McCarthy does none of these things.

Only where literature performs its most important task, that is, by resisting the general, the commonplace, the tediously obvious, in favour of the luminously particular, the specific, and in creating what is occurring, only then can it be said to be carrying forth its most important purpose, indeed, engaging its own rigorous logic. Rejecting what is taken for granted, the dull matter-of-factness of assumption, reveals literature's singular purpose, and that is to reveal the force, rapidity, originality and sheer presence of the world unfurling. Literary writing is most philosophical when it allows a radiant fusion of past, present and future. This vocation differentiates the literary work from the shopping list, the doodle, or the text message; the profoundness of literary work is most palpable when the mechanical literary work, the physical book itself, dissolves and the whole universe can come close. As I mentioned in the introduction, the philosophical concerns of literature do not preclude the importance of style. The style of the literary work is all, because it is precisely what makes the work fantastic, the literary unique and, most importantly, what gives the work the capacity to respond to the unfolding of historical events and issues of perennial human concern. Insofar as the style of the literary work becomes philosophical, this is when style makes manifest the most significant questions of the day. While a philosophical vocation may not align to the mission of every writer, the taste of every reader, nor indeed be the mission of many canonical writers, it has been my basic contention that McCarthy writes in this literary-philosophical vein and, when at his best, lets the literary and the philosophical coalesce.

Notes

1. Vladimir Nabokov, *Lectures on Literature* (New York: Harvest, 1980), Chapter 1, loc. 2536, Kindle.
2. John Jurgensen, 'Hollywood's Favourite Cowboy', *Wall Street Journal*, 20 November 2009, <https://www.wsj.com/articles/SB1000142405274 8704576204574529703577274572>
3. Ulrike Duhm, 'One reporter's account of SFI's "Genius and Madness" event in August'. Originally published in *Sueddeutsche Zeitung*, 15 September 2015, <https://www.santafe.edu/news-center/news/genius-and-madness-sz-trans-english>. Additionally, there is no reason to doubt Krakeur's description of *The Passenger*. While at the time of writing *The Passenger* material at the Wittliff Collections is restricted, on some rough stray draft pages, we see McCarthy definitively writing in what can only be described as a style approximating what Krakeur calls 'mathematical-analytical' prose. For example, consider this excerpt: 'The Yang-Mills vector bosons. Yes. Glahow had come up with a gauge theory around 1960 for the weak interaction that included both of the W particles and what he called the Z particle his name as massive particles. But there was no real explanation for the mass. They just sort of stuck it in. Then in 64 Higgs proposed his mechanism and Weinberg got the notion that if you used the Higgs mechanism as a way to break the symmetry you could assign a mass to the vector bosons. The W particles would up with masses of forty GeV's and the Z particle eighty. Weinberg published a paper on this in 1967 and nobody read it. But my father read it. The theory still spun off these infinities that nobody could get rid of. There didn't seem to be any way to square renormalisation with Yang-Mills. T'Hooft finally figured it out in 1971 but in the meantime my father already saw his edifice trembling and he sat down and worked on the Higgs approach and he couldn't get it to work but he had good intuition and he thought that it could be made to work only he couldnt do it. And if it could be made to work then his theory was – I'll use his own word – incoherent.' See McCarthy, *Cormac McCarthy Papers (1964–2007)*, Box 68: Folder 4, 115. For a scholarly account of the genesis of *The Passenger* material see Dianne Luce, 'Creativity, Madness, and "the light that dances deep in the Pontchartrain": Glimpses of *The Passenger*, from Cormac McCarthy's 1980 Correspondence', *The Cormac McCarthy Journal* 18, no.2 (2020): 85–99.
4. Chris Eagle, 'Editor's Introduction', in *Philosophical Approaches to Cormac McCarthy: Beyond Reckoning*, ed. Chris Eagle (London: Routledge, 2017), 1.
5. Although McCarthy famously reports a reluctance, even an inability, to write about women, there is clear evidence of at least a willingness to write about themes pertaining to gender and hormonal therapy. In a fascinating unpublished narration McCarthy writes: 'Anyway, she said,

a year later I was working in New York in an upscale restaurant as a waitress and sharing a walk-up flat with a real girl. I was fifteen. Just. I had forged papers and I was making good money and I had started my hormone treatments. This doctor I was going to told me that I was a gracile mesomorph. And I said yes, and you're a nasty bugger. I was just kidding. We were friends by then. So I asked him what it meant and he said it means that you're going to be a goodlooking girl. I said that's not good enough. What about spectacular? And he kind of smiled and he said: We'll see. And we did.' See McCarthy, *Cormac McCarthy Papers (1964–2007)*, Box 68: Folder 4, 96.

Bibliography

All websites last accessed 17 June 2021 unless otherwise specified.

'Actresses pull a gender flip on *The Sunset Limited*'. *Florida Weekly*: Key West Edition, 30 May 2019. <https://keywest.floridaweekly.com/articles/actresses-pull-a-gender-flip-on-the-sunset-limited>

Agamben, Giorgio. *Homo Sacer: Sovereign Power and Bare Life*. Trans. Daniel Heller-Roazen. Stanford: Stanford University Press, 1998.

Allen, Joseph. 'The Quest for God in *The Road*'. In *The Cambridge Companion to Cormac McCarthy*, ed. Steven Frye. Cambridge: Cambridge University Press, 2013, 133–43.

Arendt, Hannah. *On Violence*. New York: HBJ Publishers, 1970.

Aristotle. *Nicomachean Ethics*. Trans. Christopher Rowe. Oxford: Oxford University Press, 2002.

Aristotle. *Politics*. Trans. C. D. C. Reeve. Indianapolis: Hackett, 1998.

Arnold, Edwin T. 'Cormac McCarthy's *Whales and Men*'. In *Cormac McCarthy: Uncharted Territories/Territoires Inconnus*, ed. Christine Chollier. Reims: Presses Universitaires de Reims, 2003, 17–30.

Bell, Vereen. *The Achievement of Cormac McCarthy*. Louisiana: Louisiana State University Press, 1988.

Bell, Vereen. 'The Ambiguous Nihilism of Cormac McCarthy'. *The Southern Literary Journal* 15, no.2 (Spring 1983): 31–41.

Bergson, Henri. *Time and Free Will*. Trans. F. L. Pogson. New York: Dover, 2001.

Blanchot, Maurice. *The Blanchot Reader*. Ed. and trans. Michael Holland. Oxford: Blackwells, 1995.

Blanchot, Maurice. *The Space of Literature: A Translation of 'L'Espace Litteraire*. Trans. Ann Smock. Lincoln: University of Nebraska Press, 1990.

Blanchot, Maurice. *The Unavowable Community*. Trans. Pierre Joris. Barry Town: Station Hill Press, 2000.

Blanchot, Maurice. *The Work of Fire*. Trans. Charlotte Mandell. Stanford: Stanford University Press, 1995.

Blanchot, Maurice, and Jacques Derrida. *The Instant of My Death/Demeure: Fiction and Testimony*. Ed. and trans. Elizabeth Rottenberg. Stanford: Stanford University Press, 2000.

Bloom, Harold. 'Interview: Harold Bloom on *Blood Meridian*'. AV Club, 19 May 2020. <https://bit.ly/3aCAqgF>

Bloom, Harold. 'On Violence, the Sublime, and *Blood Meridian*'s Place in the American Canon', last modified 16 October 2019. <https://lithub. com/harold-bloom-on-cormac-mccarthy-true-heir-to-melville-and-faulkner>

Brewer, Mary. '"The light is all around you, cept you dont see nothin but shadow": Narratives of Religion and Race in *The Stonemason* and *The Sunset Limited*'. *The Cormac McCarthy Journal* 12, no.1 (2014): 39–54.

Broncano, Manuel. *Religion in Cormac McCarthy's Fiction: Apocryphal Borderlands*. New York: Routledge, 2013.

Buckley, F. H. 'Ten Great Conservative Novels'. *National Review*, 21 January 2010, accessed 19 January 2016. <https://www.nationalreview.com/ nrd/articles/339722/ten-great-conservative-novels>_

Canfield, Douglas. 'The Dawning of the Age of Aquarius: Abjection, Identity, and the Carnivalesque in Cormac McCarthy's *Suttree*'. *Contemporary Literature* 44, no.4 (Winter 2003): 664–96.

Cant, John. *Cormac McCarthy and the Myth of American Exceptionalism*. London: Routledge, 2009.

Cant, John. 'The Silent Sheriff: *No Country for Old Men* – A Comparison of Novel and Film'. In *Intertextual and Interdisciplinary Approaches to Cormac McCarthy*, ed. Nicholas Monk. London: Routledge, 2012, 90–9.

Carroll, Joseph. *Evolution and Literary Theory*. Columbia, MO: University of Minnesota Press, 1995.

Cooper, Lydia R. 'Cormac McCarthy's *The Road* as Apocalyptic Grail Narrative'. *Studies in the Novel* 43, no.2 (Summer 2011): 218–36.

Cooper, Lydia R. 'He's a Psychopathic Killer, but So What?': Folklore and Morality in Cormac McCarthy's *No Country for Old Men*'. *Papers on Language and Literature* 45, no.1 (Winter 2009): 37–59.

Cooper, Lydia R. '"A Howling Void": Beckett's Influence in Cormac McCarthy's *The Sunset Limited*'. *The Cormac McCarthy Journal* 10, no.1 (2012): 1–15.

Cooper, Lydia R. *No More Heroes: Narrative Perspective and Morality in Cormac McCarthy*. Baton Rouge: Louisiana State University Press, 2011.

Cremean, David. 'For Whom Bell Tolls: Cormac McCarthy's Sheriff Bell as Spiritual Hero'. In *From Novel to Film: No Country for Old Men*, ed. Lynnea C. King, Rick Wallach and Jim Welsh. Toronto: Scarecrow Press, 2009, 21–31.

Cutchins, Dennis. 'Grace and Moss's End in *No Country for Old Men*'. In *From Novel to Film: No Country for Old Men*, ed. Lynnea C. King, Rick Wallach and Jim Welsh. Toronto: Scarecrow Press, 2009, 155–72.

Daugherty, Leo. 'Gravers False and True: *Blood Meridian* as Gnostic Tragedy'. In *Perspectives in Cormac* McCarthy, ed. Dianne C. Luce and Edwin T. Arnold. Jackson: University Press of Mississippi, 1997, 159–74.

Davenport, Guy. *The Geography of the Imagination: Forty Essays by Guy Davenport*. London: Picador, 1984.

Dennett, Daniel. *Darwin's Dangerous Idea*. London: Penguin, 1995.

Derrida, Jacques. 'Force of Law: The 'Mystical Foundation of Authority'. In *Acts of Religion*. Trans. Mary Quaintance, ed. Gil Anidjar. London: Routledge, 2002, 228–98.

Derrida, Jacques. *The Gift of Death; And, Literature in Secret*. Trans. David Wills. Chicago: University of Chicago Press, 2008.

Derrida, Jacques. *Learning to Live Finally: The Last Interview*. Trans. Pascale-Anne Brault and Michael Naas. Hoboken: Melville House Publishing, 2007.

Derrida, Jacques. *The Politics of Friendship*. Trans. George Collins. London: Verso Books, 2005.

'Donald Trump Nevada Watch Party & Victory Speech'. Streamed Live February 2016. YouTube Video, 5:28. Posted by 'Bright Side Broadcasting Network', February 2016. <https://www.youtube.com/watch?v=kdA4ru5Z1aI>

Donoghue, Denis. 'Reading *Blood Meridian*'. *The Sewanee Review* 105, no.3 (Summer 1997), 401–18.

Duhm, Ulrike. 'One reporter's account of SFI's 'Genius and Madness' event in August'. Originally published in *Sueddeutsche Zeitung*, 15 September 2015. <https://www.santafe.edu/news-center/news/genius-and-madness-sz-trans-english>

Dutton, Dennis. *The Art Instinct: Beauty, Pleasure and Evolution*. Oxford: Oxford University Press, 2009.

Eagle, Chris. 'Editor's Introduction'. In *Philosophical Approaches to Cormac McCarthy: Beyond Reckoning*, ed. Chris Eagle, 1–4. London: Routledge, 2017.

Ellis, Jay. *No Place for Home: Spatial Constraint and Character Flight in the Novels of Cormac McCarthy*. New York: Routledge, 2006.

Farooq, Mohammad. 'Cormac McCarthy Interview on the Oprah Winfrey Show'. 8 June 2014. YouTube video, 8.46. <https://www.youtube.com/watch?v=y3kpzuk1Y8I>

Fernández Labarga, Noemí. '"No gray middle folk did he see": Constructions of Race in *Suttree*'. *The Cormac McCarthy Journal* 18, no.2 (Fall 2020): 128–46.

Feynman, Richard. 'New Textbook for the "New" Mathematics'. *Engineering and Science* 38, no.6 (1965): 9–15.

Frye, Steven. 'Histories, Novels, Ideas: Cormac McCarthy and the Art of Philosophy'. In *The Cambridge Companion to Cormac McCarthy*, ed. Steven Frye. Cambridge: Cambridge University Press, 2013, 3–14.

Frye, Steven. *Understanding Cormac McCarthy*. Columbia, SC: University of South Carolina Press, 2009.

Gallivan, Euan. 'Cold Dimensions, Little Worlds: Self, Death, and Motion in *Suttree* and Beckett's Murphy', in *Intertextual and Interdisciplinary Approaches to Cormac McCarthy*, ed. Nicholas Monk (Albuquerque: University of New Mexico Press, 2002), 145–54.

Gell-Mann, Murray. *The Quark and the Jaguar*. London: Abacus, 1994.

Goldstein, Rebecca. *Plato at the Googleplex*. London: Atlantic Books, 2014.

Greve, Julius. '"Another kind of clay": On *Blood Meridian*'s Okenian Philosophy of Nature'. *The Cormac McCarthy Journal* 13, no.1 (2015): 27–53.

Greve, Julius. *Shreds of Matter: Cormac McCarthy and the Concept of Nature*. Hanover, NH: Dartmouth College Press, 2018.

Hamilton, Alexander. *The Appeal of Fascism*. London: Anthony Blond Publishing, 1971.

Hasse, Ullrich, and William Large. *Blanchot*. London: Routledge, 2001.

Hawkins, Ty. *Cormac McCarthy's Philosophy*. Gewerbestrasse: Palgrave Macmillan, 2017.

Heidegger, Martin. *Poetry, Language, Thought*. Trans. Albert Hofstader. New York: Harper and Row, 2001.

Heidegger, Martin. *The Essence of Truth: On Plato's Cave Allegory and Theaetetus*. Trans. Ted Sadler. New York: Continuum, 2002.

Hillier, Russell. *Morality in Cormac McCarthy's Fiction: Souls at Hazard*. Gewerbestrasse: Palgrave Macmillan, 2017.

Hillier, Russell. 'The Judge's Molar: Infanticide and the Meteorite in *Blood Meridian*'. In *They Rode On:* Blood Meridian *and the Tragedy of the American West*, ed. Rick Wallach. Bakersfield: The Cormac McCarthy Society, 2013, 58–64.

Holloway, David. *The Late Modernism of Cormac McCarthy*. Westport, CT: Greenwood Press, 2002.

Holloway, David. 'Mapping McCarthy in the Age of Neoconservatism, or the Politics of Affect in *The Road*'. *The Cormac McCarthy Journal* 17, no.1 (2019): 4–26.

Iyer, Lars. *Blanchot's Communism: Art, Philosophy and the Political*. Basingstoke: Palgrave-Macmillan, 2004.

Jacob. 'Interview with Cormac McCarthy (2012)'. September 28, 2018. YouTube video, 6.46. <https://goo.gl/p1PnV9>

Jaeger, Werner. *Paideia: The Ideals of Greek Culture*. Vol. 2, *In Search of the Divine Centre*. Trans. Gilbert Highhet. Oxford: Blackwell, 1947.

James, William. 'Dilemma and Determinism'. Uky.Edu, accessed 20 May 2020. <https://www.uky.edu/~eushe2/Pajares/JamesDilemmaOfDeterminism.html>

Josyph, Peter. *Adventures in Reading Cormac McCarthy*. Toronto: Scarecrow Press, 2010.

Jurgensen, John. 'Hollywood's Favourite Cowboy'. *Wall Street Journal*, 20 November 2009. <https://on.wsj.com/36KI7yP>

Kelly, Adam. *American Fiction in Transition: Observer-Hero Narrative, the 1990s, and Postmodernism*. London: Bloomsbury, 2013.

Krauss, Lawrence. *The Quantum Man*. New York: Norton, 2012.

Kunsa, Ashley. 'Maps of the World in Its Becoming': Post-Apocalyptic Naming in Cormac McCarthy's *The Road*'. *Journal of Modern Literature* 33, no.1 (Fall 2009): 57–74.

Kushner, David. 'Cormac McCarthy's Apocalypse'. *Rolling Stone*, 27 December 2007. <http://www.davidkushner.com/article/cormac-mccarthys-apocalypse>

Laug, Katja. *Mementoes of a Broken Body: Cormac McCarthy's Aesthetic Politics*, PhD diss., University of Warwick, 2019.

Leiter, Brian. *Nietzsche on Morality*. London: Routledge, 2002.

Lilley, James D. 'Of Whales and Men: The Dynamics of Cormac McCarthy's Environmental Imagination'. *Southern Quarterly* 38, no.2 (2002): 111–22.

Luce, Dianne C. 'The Bedazzled Eye: Cormac McCarthy, José Y Gasset, and Optical Democracy'. *The Cormac McCarthy Journal* 17, no.1 (Spring 2019): 64–70.

Luce, Dianne C. 'Cormac McCarthy's *The Sunset Limited*: Dialogue of Life and Death (A Review of the Chicago Production)'. *The Cormac McCarthy Journal* 6, no.1 (2008): 13–21.

Luce, Dianne C. 'Creativity, Madness, and "the light that dances deep in the Pontchartrain". Glimpses of *The Passenger*, from Cormac McCarthy's 1980 Correspondence'. *The Cormac McCarthy Journal* 18, no.2 (2020): 85–99.

Luce, Dianne C. *Reading the World: Cormac McCarthy's Tennessee Period*. Columbia, SC: University of South Carolina Press, 2009.

McCaffrey, Enda. 'Crimes of Passion, Freedom and a Clash of Sartrean Moralities in the Coen Brothers' *No Country for Old Men*'. In *Existentialism and Contemporary Cinema: A Sartrean Perspective*, ed. Enda McCaffrey and Jean-Pierre Boulé. Oxford: Berghahn Books, 2014, 25–142.

McCarthy, Cormac. *Blood Meridian*. London: Picador, 1989.

McCarthy, Cormac. *The Border Trilogy: All the Pretty Horses / The Crossing / Cities of the Plain*. London: Picador, 2007.

McCarthy, Cormac. *Child of God*. New York: Random House, 1973.

McCarthy, Cormac. *Cormac McCarthy Papers (1964–2007)*. The Wittliff Collections, Alkek Library, Texas State University in San Marcos.

McCarthy, Cormac. 'Cormac McCarthy Returns to the Kekulé Problem'. *Nautilus*, 30 November 2017. <https://goo.gl/AiFPKM>

McCarthy, Cormac. *The Counsellor*. London: Picador, 2013.

McCarthy, Cormac. *The Gardener's Son*. New York: Harper Collins, 1996.

McCarthy, Cormac. 'The Kekulé Problem'. *Nautilus* 19, March/April, 2017.

McCarthy, Cormac. 'McCarthy's Drafts'. The Wittliff Collections, Alkek Library, Texas State University in San Marcos.

McCarthy, Cormac. *No Country for Old Men*. London: Picador, 2005.

McCarthy, Cormac. 'Oprah's Exclusive Interview with Cormac McCarthy', interview by Oprah Winfrey. *Oprah Winfrey Show*, ABC, 5 June 2006. Online Video. <https://www.oprah.com/oprahsbookclub/oprahs-exclusive-interview-with-cormac-mccarthy-video>

McCarthy, Cormac. *The Orchard Keeper*. London: Picador, 2010.

McCarthy, Cormac. *Outer Dark*. London: Picador, 2010.

McCarthy, Cormac. *The Road*. London: Picador, 2006.

McCarthy, Cormac. *The Stonemason*. New Jersey: The Ecco Press, 1994.

McCarthy, Cormac. *Suttree*. London: Picador, 2010.

Malewitz, Raymond. *The Practice of Misuse: Rugged Consumerism in Contemporary American Culture*. Stanford: Stanford University Press, 2014.

Mangrum, Benjamin. 'Accounting for *The Road*: Tragedy, Courage, and Cavell's Acknowledgement'. *Philosophy and Literature* 37, no.2 (October 2013): 267–90.

Mangrum, Benjamin. 'Democracy, Justice and Tragedy in Cormac McCarthy's *No Country for Old Men*'. *Religion and Literature* 43, no.3 (Autumn 2011): 107–33.

Marr, David. *Vision*. San Francisco: Freeman, 1982.

Merker, Björn. 'The Liabilities of Mobility: A Selection Pressure for the Transition to Consciousness in Animal Evolution'. *Consciousness and Cognition*, 14, no.1 (2005): 89–114.

Miyagawa, Shigeru et al. 'Integration Hypothesis: A Parallel Model of Language Development in Evolution'. In *Evolution of the Brain, Cognition, and Emotion in Vertebrates*, ed. Shigeru Watanabe, Michel A. Hofman and Toru Shimizu. Tokyo: Springer, 2017, 225–47.

Moore, Ian A. 'Heraclitus and the Metaphysics of War'. In *Beyond Reckoning: Philosophical Perspectives on Cormac McCarthy*, ed. Chris Eagle. London: Routledge, 2017, 93–108.

Mundik, Petra. *A Bloody and Barbarous God: The Metaphysics of Cormac McCarthy*. Albuquerque: University of New Mexico Press, 2016.

Nabokov, Vladimir. *Lectures on Literature*. New York: Harvest, 1980.

Nietzsche, Friedrich. *Beyond Good and Evil*. Trans. Marion Faber. Oxford: Oxford University Press, 1998.

Nietzsche, Friedrich. *The Gay Science*. Trans. Walter Kaufman. New York: Vintage, 1974.

Nietzsche, Friedrich. *On the Genealogy of Morals and Ecce Homo*. Trans. Walter Kaufman. New York: Vintage, 1989.

Nietzsche, Friedrich. 'Truth and Falsity in an Ultramoral Sense'. In *The Philosophy of Nietzsche*, ed. Geoffrey Clive, trans. Oscar Levy. New York: Mentor Books, 1965, 503–15.

Nietzsche, Friedrich. *The Will to Power*. Trans. Walter Kauffman. New York: Vintage, 1968.

Oates, Joyce C. *In Rough Country: Essays and Reviews*. New York: HarperCollins Publishers, 2010.

Peebles, Stacey. *Cormac McCarthy and Performance: Page, Stage, Screen*. Austin: University of Texas Press, 2017.

Phillips, Dana. 'History and the Ugly Facts of Cormac McCarthy's *Blood Meridian*'. *American Literature* 68, no.2 (June 1996): 433–60.

Pinker, Steven. *The Language Instinct*. New York: William Morrow and Co., 1994.

Plato. *Gorgias*. Trans. Robin Waterfield. Oxford: Oxford University Press, 2008.

Plato. *Protagoras and Meno*. Trans. W. K. C. Gutherie. Harmondsworth: Penguin, 1956.

Plato. *Republic*. Trans. Desmond Lee. Harmondsworth: Penguin, 2003.

Plato. *Symposium*. Trans. Christopher Gill. London: Penguin, 2003.

Potts, Matthew. *Cormac McCarthy and the Signs of Sacrament: Literature, Theology, and the Moral of Stories*. London: Bloomsbury, 2015.

Pudney, Eric. 'Christianity and Cormac McCarthy's *The Road*'. *English Studies* 96, no.3 (March 2015): 293–309.

Rorty, Richard. 'The Contingency of Language'. *London Review of Books*. 17 April 1986. <https://bit.ly/3nG9b8i>

Runciman, David. 'How the Educational Gap is Tearing Politics Apart'. *The Guardian*, 5 October 2016. <https://bit.ly/2dIYjmz>

Sanborn, Wallis R. *Animals in the Fiction of Cormac McCarthy*. Jefferson, NC: McFarland, 2006.

Sartre, Jean Paul. *Being and Nothingness: An Essay on Phenomenological Ontology*. Trans. Hazel Barnes. London: Routledge, 2003.

Scarry, Elaine. *The Body in Pain: The Making and Unmaking of the World*. Oxford: Oxford University Press, 1985.

Schimpf, Shane. *A Reader's Guide to* Blood Meridian. Seattle: Bon Mot, 2008.

Sdobric. 2014. 'Cormac McCarthy – Subconscious is Older than Language'. 19 October 2014. YouTube video, 5.24. <https://www.youtube.com/watch?v=Qidyx3oXqpY>

Sennett, Richard. *The Corrosion of Character: The Personal Consequences of Work in the New Capitalism*. New York: Norton, W. W. & Company, 1999.

Siani, Alberto. 'Nowhere Between River and Road: A Nagelian Reading of *Suttree* and *The Road*'. In *Philosophical Approaches to Cormac McCarthy: Beyond Reckoning*, ed. Chris Eagle. London: Routledge, 2017, 202–20.

Skrimshire, Stefan. '"There is no God, and we are his Prophets": Deconstructing Redemption in Cormac McCarthy's *The Road*'. *Journal for Cultural Research* 15, no.1 (January 2011): 1–14.

Snyder, Philip A., and Delys W. Snyder. 'Modernism, Postmodernism, and Language: McCarthy's Style'. In *The Cambridge Companion to Cormac McCarthy*, ed. Steven Frye. Cambridge: Cambridge University Press, 2013, 27–38.

Spencer, William C. 'The Seventh Direction, or Suttree's Vision Quest'. In *Myth-Legend-Dust: Critical Responses to Cormac McCarthy*, ed. Rick Wallach. Manchester: Manchester University Press, 2000, 100–7.

Spoden, Erika B. 'Let There Be Blood: The Vein of Vietnam in *No Country for Old Men*'. *The Cormac McCarthy Journal*, 10, no.1 (2012): 76–92.

The Sunset Limited. DVD, directed by Tommy Lee Jones, Burbank, CA: Warner Home Video, 2012.

The Sunset Limited. DVD, directed by Tommy Lee Jones, Burbank, CA: Warner Home Video, 2012.

Tatum, Stephen. '"Mercantile Ethics": *No Country for Old Men* and the Narcocorrido'. In *Cormac McCarthy: All the Pretty Horses, No Country for Old Men, The Road*, ed. Sara Spurgeon. London: Bloomsbury, 2011, 77–93.

Tocqueville, Alexis de. *Democracy in America*. Trans. and ed. H. C. Mansfield and D. Winthrop. Chicago: University of Chicago Press, 2000.

Tsutserova, Yuliya. 'Seeing Nothing'. In *Philosophical Approaches to Cormac McCarthy: Beyond Reckoning*, ed. Chris Eagle. London: Routledge, 2017, 186–201.

Tyson, Alec, and Shiva Maniam. 'Behind Trump's Victory: Divisions by Race, Gender, Education'. Pew Research Center, 9 November 2016. <https://pewrsr.ch/2IrtQex>

Tzu, Lao. *Tao Te Ching: A Book about the Way and the Power of the Way.* Trans. J. P. Seaton and U. K. Le Guin. Boulder: Shambala Publications, 1998.

The Unbelievers, DVD, directed by Gus Holwerda, London. Revelation Films, 2014.

Wallace, Garry. *Meeting Cormac McCarthy Plus 9 Notable Essays of The Year*. Independent: CreateSpace Independent Publishing Platform, 2012.

Wallach, Rick, 'Sam Chamberlain and the Iconology of Science in Mid-19th Century Nation Building'. In *They Rode On: Blood Meridian and the Tragedy of the American West*, ed. Rick Wallach. Bakersfield: The Cormac McCarthy Society, 2013, 38–45.

Walsh, Christopher. *In the Wake of the Sun: Navigating the Southern Works of Cormac McCarthy*. Connecticut: Newfound Press, 2010.

Welch, Cheryl. *De Tocqueville*. Oxford: Oxford University Press, 2001.

Wielenberg, Erik. 'God, Morality and Meaning in Cormac McCarthy's *The Road*'. *The Cormac McCarthy Journal* 8, no.1 (Fall 2010): 1–19.

Wierschem, Markus. 'At a Crossroads of Life and Death: The Apocalyptic Journey(s) of Cormac McCarthy's Fiction'. In *The Journey of Life in American Literature*, ed. Peter Freese. Heidelberg: Winter, 2015, 159–85.

Wierschem, Markus. 'The Other End of *The Road*: Re-Reading McCarthy in Light of Thermodynamics and Information Theory'. *The Cormac McCarthy Journal* 11, no.1 (2013): 1–22.

Williamson, Eric M. '*Blood Meridian* and Nietzsche: The Metaphysics of War'. In *They Rode On:* Blood Meridian *and the Tragedy of the American West*, ed. Rick Wallach. Bakersfield: The Cormac McCarthy Society, 2013, 261–273.

Wittgenstein, Ludwig. *Philosophical Investigations*. Trans. G. E. M. Anscombe. Oxford: Blackwell, 1997.

Woodson, Linda. 'McCarthy's Heroes and the Will to Truth'. In *The Cambridge Companion to Cormac McCarthy*, ed. Steven Frye. Cambridge: Cambridge University Press, 2013, 15–263.

Woodson, Linda. 'Materiality, Moral Responsibility, and Determinism in *No Country for Old Men*'. *From Novel to Film: No Country for Old Men*, ed. Lynnea C. King, Rick Wallach and Jim Welsh. Toronto: Scarecrow Press, 2009, 1–12.

Woodward, Richard B. 'Bernard Madoff and Anton Chigurh: the Con Man as Serial Killer'. *Huffington Post*, 29 December 2015. <https://www.huffpost.com/entry/bernard-madoff-and-anton_b_152860>

Woodward, Richard B. 'Cormac McCarthy's Venomous Fiction'. *New York Times Magazine*, 19 April 1992.

Wyllie, Robert. 'Kierkegaard Talking Down Schopenhauer: *The Sunset Limited* as a Philosophical Dialogue'. *The Cormac McCarthy Journal* 14, no.2 (2016): 186–203.

Young, Thomas D. 'The Imprisonment of Sensibility: *Suttree*'. In *Perspectives on Cormac McCarthy*, ed. Dianne Luce and Edwin T. Arnold. Jackson: University Press of Mississippi, 1999, 97–122.

Index